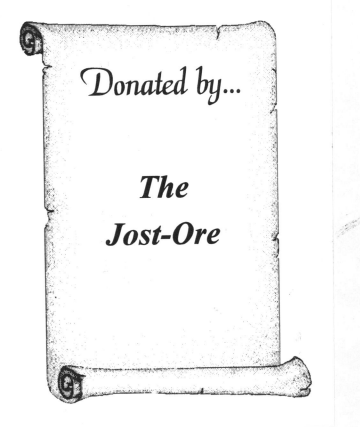

Donated by...

**The
Jost-Ore**

Assignment
America

A Collection of Outstanding
Writing from *The New York Times*

E. F. Jost
Rochester, N.Y

8/24/76

Assignment America

A Collection of Outstanding
Writing from *The New York Times*

edited by
GENE ROBERTS and DAVID R. JONES

QUADRANGLE/THE NEW YORK TIMES BOOK CO.

Library of Congress Catalog Card Number: 73-79930

International Standard Book Number: 0-8129-0384-6

Dedicated to the
memory of
Emanuel R. Freedman

ACKNOWLEDGMENTS

This book would not have been possible without the cooperation of many able hands, including *The New York Times* deskmen who edited the articles that appear on these pages. Special thanks are due to John Storm, who helped select the articles; Gary Haynes, who located and edited the pictures; and Gloria Giannone, our invaluable secretary, who prepared the manuscript and did a thousand other chores. Not the least of our appreciation, however, goes to the families of *The New York Times* reporters whose stories appear in this book—for the sacrifices they have made along the way.

G.R.
D.R.J.

Contents

IV.   TROUBLED AMERICA

Preface

The New York Times, a newspaper that prides itself on its straightforward presentation of the news, has become blessedly deceptive of late. While to many readers it still looks gray, dull, and austere, those who probe beneath appearances find an increasing number of stories that fascinate and delight. They bob up on the front of the second section, snake their way around the Gimbels and Macy's advertisements, and steal onto the bottom of the front page.

The emphasis on fine writing is gaining momentum so fast that on any given day *The Times* may contain more "good reading pieces" than any other publication in the country. What makes these stories important to American journalism is not simply their literary quality. Their significance lies in the definition of news that they embrace. Once *The Times* was almost exclusively preoccupied with the big event (war, exploration, historic discovery) and with developments from Washington, foreign capitals, city halls, state-houses, organizational headquarters, and other conventional news centers.

Today, *Times* reporters are prying themselves away from officials and taking themselves to the people. They have learned that many, and perhaps most, major stories do not break; they trickle, seep, and ooze. *The Times* is covering the ooze. Americans turning to mobile homes by the tens of thousands? Interstate highways loosening the fabric of small-town living? Wild mustangs disappearing? Tourist homes fading? Blacks returning South? No official called a press conference to announce these stories. Yet they were all in *The Times,* and they—along with many others—add up to a running account of a changing America.

The definition of news was not always so fluid. Looking back upon the internal affairs of the country in the first half of this century, one notices few developments seem to have had greater impact on the nation than the movement of blacks from the South to the North and the seep of whites from city to suburb. Neither development received widespread attention from the press until the flow and sweep had turned into a flood. How valuable it would be to historians if they could flip through yellowing newsprint and find vignette after vignette describing the plight of blacks as they wrenched themselves from the earth of cotton and cornfields and then adjusted fitfully to the sidewalks of major cities.

A historian at the turn of the twenty-first century, leafing through the pages of *The Times,* seeking an understanding of the late sixties and early seventies, may find the going easier. He will find, for example, that *The Times* discovered the energy crisis well in advance of the U.S. Congress. He will also find a roundness and fullness to reporting that was not always there. Reporters have added a dimension to their stories that might, for want of a better term, be called "journalistic counterpoint." When women's liberation swept New York, *Times* reporters not only covered it there but sifted through a small Midwestern town to see if the lives of the women were being touched by the new movement. While urban dwellers fretted over nuclear power plants, *The Times* found a small town that was due to serve as a garbage dump for nuclear waste and loved the idea because the dump meant more jobs. While reporting growth of the Eastern megalopolis, *The Times* also found time to describe life in the Midwestern towns that were losing population. And when pollution was becoming the big concern in the cities, *The Times* found a Maine county with an entirely different set of problems. Potato growing had become unprofitable and the county, although pollution free, was plunged into economic depression.

It all adds up to journalistic balance. *The Times* now not only tells what is happening, but what is not—what is changing and what is remaining constant. If any newspaper focused only on city violence in an era of unrest without ever wandering into the countryside, it would distort the state of the nation. And of course the obverse is equally true. A national newspaper has an obligation to report on the festerings and the radiance of health, the beauty spots as well as the blemishes.

The Times is fascinated, too, these days with the vagaries of man, his pastimes, his fads, and his idiosyncracies. Wealthy farmers souping up their tractors? A *Times* reporter is on the case. *Times* reporters also popped up at a Cajun festival in Louisiana, at a campers' haven known as Grandpa's Farm, at a swinging singles' apartment complex, at a Chicago ward on Election Day, at a fiddlers' convention in the Blue Ridge Mountains, at a football weekend in Birmingham, and at a church homecoming in the clay hills of Georgia.

For all the talk of "Eastern elitists," *The Times* is uniquely qualified to tell of the diversity of the nation because its ranks of reporters are diverse. There are reporters who come from some of the wealthiest families in the East and some of the poorest in the South—Jews from Brooklyn and the Bronx, hillbillies, Midwestern farm boys, European immigrants. And the backgrounds add dimension to the stories. The writing of Roy Reed, the son of an Arkansas grocer, for example, meanders like an Ozark stream.

Only a portion of the fine writing in *The Times* appears in this book. It is not intended to be a definitive chronicle of writing or of the history of the nation over the last 5 years. Almost all of the principal news events and major political figures of the period were deliberately excluded, in fact, to make room for the illuminating incidents and workaday people. You will not find a story about Mayor Lindsay in the book, but you will find one about an old woman who lived alone on New York's West Side, and would have died unnoticed had she not been discovered by a reporter on the city staff of *The Times*. Presidents and generals were excluded too, in favor of a Congressional Medal of Honor winner who died in a Detroit holdup and old men whittling away the hours on a bench in a small Missouri town. Presidents, mayors, generals, and congressmen have dominated the top half of the front page. This book belongs to the others, who rounded out the news on the bottom half of the front page and filled up an occasional hole on the inside. *The Times* would have been incomplete without these people. So would any account of recent developments in the nation.

Gene Roberts
David R. Jones

Constant
America

A holiday pilgrimage by rail to the South

ROY REED

Aboard the *City of New Orleans*
December 20, 1970

Chicago could not have been grayer. It was 8 o'clock in the morning and still barely daylight, so thick were the clouds.

The travelers pulled their coats tight as they hurried through the dimness of Michigan Avenue's Central Station to get aboard the black and orange cars. They were nearly all Southerners, black expatriates headed home for the holidays, leaving behind for a little while the toils and pleasures of Chicago, the northernmost of the Southern outposts on the historic Illinois Central line, to refresh themselves in Port Gibson, Memphis, and the hundred others places they and their fathers sprang from.

Like all immigrants who yearn for "the old country," these, too, must return home from time to time. Christmas is a favorite time for returning. Some go by bus and some by automobile, but a great many still choose to go by the way they originally went up—on the aging coaches of the Illinois Central Railroad.

This is the great trunk line that ties together the northern and southern extremities of the nation's middle. When thousands of Negroes began to migrate from the oppressive agriculture of the South after the Civil War, it was largely the Illinois Central that delivered them to the industrial North, out of the bondage of Mississippi into the Promised Land of Illinois.

This year's pilgrims, as always, included those who remembered home and those who had never seen it.

3

In one car rode Dr. John H. Mitchell, 88 years old, a Chicago dentist for 56 years. He sat straight upright in his seat, polishing his ebony cane with his thumb as he talked of going for a visit to his boyhood home, Canton, Miss.

In another car, Theodore Mims, 5 months old, was being carried to Drew, Miss., for the first time to be formally presented for the admiration of grand-parents and uncles and loving aunts.

There were 300 to 400 altogether. That was not so many as might have gone on this particular train the last Saturday before Christmas. The recession had cut the number. But, for the fortunate who were going, the anticipation was as keen as the first throb of a toothache.

Children had been prepared for weeks. Even those too young to know the South firsthand seemed to feel the pull.

A little way down the line, a conductor would come through a car shouting, "This way out to North Cairo," and a dark-eyed, 5-year-old beauty named Marva Crockett, who was making her first trip to Mississippi, would protest to the whole car, "I don't want to go to North Cairo. I want to go down South, right now."

The train pulled out at 8:05 A.M., away from the soot and overcoats of the city, and in less than an hour it was crawling through the flat, black land of Central Illinois, which, except for the red barns and neater houses, is so like the flat, brown land of the Mississippi Delta.

The club car was the first to melt the tensions of leave-taking. When the train crossed the Ohio River into Kentucky, just south of Cairo, an elderly man was so relaxed that he was able to sing for a laughing and appreciative audience. "Take me down to the water to be baptized."

Dewitt Howard, 28 years old, had begun drinking beer as soon as the train left Chicago. By 10 A.M. he was in a very friendly game of cards with a lonely woman traveler.

At the other end of the club car four men also played cards as they drank, and from time to time one would draw a lucky card and purr, "How sweet it is."

Mr. Howard's older sister, Mrs. Laura Gaines, sat two cars forward with Marva Crockett, her stepdaughter. Mrs. Gaines, an ample woman who flashed gold with every smile, talked of the friends and kin she would see in Port Gibson, Miss., and of the Christmas dinner they would eat—ham, undoubtedly, and perhaps collard greens and almost certainly homemade muscadine wine.

The train stopped at Dyersburg and let off Stephanie Morris, 18, one of the few white persons on the trip. Miss Morris is a city person and, unlike the other travelers, she was not happy to be South.

"The South depresses me," she said. The trip was a kind of duty. She felt she ought to visit her friends in Dyersburg, where she once lived briefly.

Among the black passengers, however, the Southern wrongs of the past seemed to be forgotten, at least for the holidays. Not a good word was heard about Chicago. Several spoke strongly of their dislike for the city.

Mrs. Susie Williams said she knew several persons who had moved back South.

"The North used to be the place to go," she said. "But now the South is going to be the North and the North is going to be the South."

When Miss Morris got off, the train seemed to be left entirely to blacks. The laughter became louder and the talk freer as the train approached Memphis.

A large group left at Memphis, and soon the Christmas lights were looming up from the darkness of the Mississippi Delta.

Dewitt Howard, now switched to bourbon, got into a brief unpleasantness with a white conductor and a black porter over a cup of water he had spilled on the floor.

"I ain't never going to ride this train again," he said.

He had already disclosed his plans. He was leaving Chicago after 10 years of working in a sporting-goods factory, putting laces in footballs, and was heading back to take over the family's 40-acre farm south of Port Gibson.

A second young woman had caught his eye in the club car earlier. She was leaving Chicago for another reason. Her recent husband, whom she described as a notorious philanderer, had had the sour luck to catch her in the act when she had indulged in a single indiscretion, and now was searching for her and was, she believed, going to kill her.

Mr. Howard pursued her with great vigor and little success, and finally, half-seriously, he proposed marriage to her just north of Fulton, Ky. She rejected him, but not before he had told her:

"I'll take you huntin' with me. I'll take you *fishin'*. There's a lake down there that's a *mile long*, and I've got a motorboat sittin' on that lake right now. You don't believe me? Come on home with me."

Later, he talked once more of what he was leaving and what he was going home to.

"I didn't like the life up there. You get up in the morning and you go to the factory and you do the same thing every day. Down here, I can get up when I please and do what I want to do."

He said he had been robbed about 15 times in Chicago. "I ain't never been robbed in Mississippi," he said.

"Lot of people out of work in Chicago. You go down by that employment office and there's long lines of people standing there, waiting. I won't have nothing to worry about down here."

He paused. "My mother makes a garden. You can make it on a farm. I won't have nothing to worry about."

By midevening, south of Jackson, Mr. Howard had begun to pay court to another woman, and as the train moved past the low hills his voice talked and sang of how it would be when he reached the green, green grass of home.

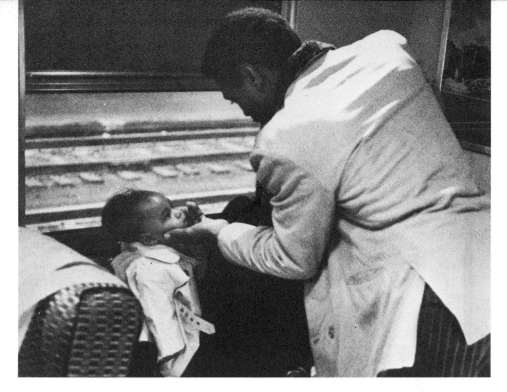

Going home for Christmas: Theodore Mims, 5 months, waits for a train with his family and gets a kiss from his father aboard a coach on the Illinois Central Railroad.

NYT/GARY SETTLE

It was nearly morning now, very early, and the travelers were much diminished. Of those left, a surprising number were awake, nursing their 18-hour weariness in the dark, their heads pitching and rolling with the endless pitch and roll of the railroad track.

The train was moving into New Orleans, past the raised tombs of the first cemeteries, past the first of the raised cottages and gingerbread porches.

The porter who had angered Dewitt Howard had relaxed at last and was sitting on one of the worn seats in a nearly deserted car, sweet-talking a lonely and comely matron—the last evidence of holiday spirit on the City of New Orleans as it went home to Christmas.

Lost glory sought in a "souped-up" tractor

B. DRUMMOND AYRES JR.

Louisville, Ky.
February 10, 1971

The last 12 months have not been good to John Klug.

Somewhere back around planting time, his big 10-wheel utility truck skidded on a turn and messed up a fender.

Then blight hit the corn.

Then some drunk smashed into the side of the truck, messing up the fender again.

But if you farm, as Mr. Klug does, there is always a little optimism left, and this night it is welling up as never before, for he is competing in the Kentucky Derby of the rural set—a national invitational tractor-pulling contest.

Only the best will run this snowy evening.

The bad times are past. The endless hard days back on those 360 acres of black gumbo outside Farmington, Iowa, are forgotten.

Now there is nothing left but 250 feet of dirt track. If John Klug can just make it that much further when his turn comes, he stands a good chance of finding his lost glory.

There are people watching, 12,684 of them, all out better than $3 each for a seat and stacked to the rafters of the Louisville arena. The man at the gate is telling late arrivals: "Sorry, nothing really good left."

The lucky ones grow quiet. This is what they journeyed up from the red Carolina hills and down from the flat Dakota plains to see.

9

They like John Klug. Only a man with an extra supply of heart could angle a woolly old Alpine hat over his eyes like that.

Mr. Klug revs up his engine. Dirty gray smoke spews out of the exhaust, and the huge 12,000-pound, $10,000 machine creeps forward an inch or two, tightening the chain connected to a sled weighing almost 18,000 pounds.

"Okay," he says, nodding to the track boss and thrusting out his solid jaw, weathered a ruddy red by 39 years in the midwestern wind and sun.

Americans seem to have a mania these days for such settings. Wheresoever so many as two or three engines are gathered together, competition of some sort results.

First it was stock cars and dragsters, then motorcycles and dune buggies, then snowmobiles. Now come the big John Deere diesels with oversized tires, the fire-engine-red International Harvesters with propane-driven superchargers, the gaudy Allis Chalmers with nicknames like "Orange Power."

In the last decade, what started out in colonial days as a pickup Saturday afternoon contest between the old gray mare and dobbin has become a national sport, with as many as 3000 or 4000 farmers competing annually in 500 or so "pulls" for pots ranging from $500 to more than $10,000.

As with the stock cars, many of the manufacturers are getting into the game, quietly and without leaving too many fingerprints.

But they are doing it with a headlong determination that springs from the cold fact that more than one good old boy has bought a new tractor on the basis of what he saw at a county fair or Lions Club tractor pull.

After all, it takes only about $1000 and a couple of days' hard work to "soup up" a machine fresh off the assembly line. After that the "beast" can be—and usually is—"desouped" and returned to the field until the next contest.

Meanwhile, any novice can get free advice from company engineers. But John Klug has no patron. Thus far he remains a tractor-pulling purist.

Sitting down on the arena track, straining to go, his tractor looks as though it just came off the farm after long, dusty hours out in the sun.

But closer investigation discloses certain subtleties.

Hidden under the dull-red hood is a supercharger, called a turbo, that speeds the flow of diesel oil and air to the point where an engine officially rated at 105 horsepower is turning up 400 horsepower.

Weights have been carefully distributed over the frame to give exact balance.

The rims of the rear wheels have been widened and the tires now balloon out ominously large.

The treads have been ground to a precise angle—Mr. Klug's secret—and puzzling notches have been cut into the leading edges.

Finally, the fuel mixture has been set "just right," for the humidity and temperature levels that prevail around Louisville in mid-February. Mr. Klug studied weather reports for three weeks to determine them.

And so everything is ready.

Mr. Klug has drawn the 14th starting position in a field of 21 tractors. The 13 previous runs have chopped up the track badly and much skill will be needed to stay out of power-draining ruts.

The flag drops.

Mr. Klug lets out the clutch. The front of his big machine rears up two or three feet as the great engine and huge tires strain to get the load under way.

Within five seconds, he is more than 100 feet down the track, going about eight miles an hour, darting around ruts, clods of dirt flying out from under his wheels, exhaust glowing pink-hot.

Back atop the sled a dolly loaded with several thousand pounds of scrap iron has started inching forward on special rails, driven by a wheel and a differential pulled behind the sled.

Every inch the little dolly travels adds more weight to the front of the sled, which then becomes harder and harder to pull. But Mr. Klug's roaring machine seems equal to the strain.

At 200 feet, the crowd is up cheering: "Go! go! go!"

At 240 feet there is bedlam. The rebel yells drown out the whine of the 400 horses.

And then Mr. Klug is across the finish line.

Pow!

His motor blows a gasket and with it his hopes for glory and the $800 first prize. For several other tractors also made it all the way, and so a "pull off" has been scheduled, with even more weight added. There is no time for repairs.

John Klug is out. Maybe it had to be. But try *that* with the old gray mare.

Autumn in the southland:
You can go home again

JAMES T. WOOTEN

Lithonia, Ga.
November 6, 1970

One Sunday morning, not long ago, O. G. Lee wheeled his car from an asphalt road near here and smiled ever so slightly when he heard the familiar crunch of gravel against the tires.

There, just ahead of him at the end of a narrow, curving drive, stood the Rock Chapel United Methodist Church, the sanctuary of his youth and early manhood, shining bright white in the Sabbath sun.

"I'm 66 now and driving over here ain't so easy any more," he complained as he parked in the shade of a massive, thousand-year oak. "But I always get back for homecoming day and I expect I will till they put me away."

He lives in Atlanta now, a one-hour drive from these rolling, red clay hills where he was born—but like thousands of other Americans who couldn't be kept down on the farm, he still cherishes a chance to touch his rural roots.

Homecoming day, now an autumn tradition in many of the South's country churches, provides the perfect opportunity. There are singing and praying and preaching and handshaking and backslapping, and although the origins of the event are obscure, its meaning is clear:

Thomas Wolfe's opinion notwithstanding, some people certainly can go home again—and, once a year, thousands do, driving miles and hours from their homes in the cities back to the little churches where they began.

Most who return, like Mr. Lee, are middle-aged or older, an indication

12

perhaps that the past may be more precious to those who have more of it. They were part of that sizable segment of America's populace drawn from the farms to the cities. They left years ago and stayed, caught up in mortgages, car payments, insurance premiums, their jobs, their progeny, and the precarious pursuit of urban happiness.

"But you know," Mr. Lee philosophized later in the day as he strolled casually around the church lawn, "it's awful hard to take the country out of a fellow. I reckon a day don't pass but what I think about how good it is out here, and to tell the truth I've always thought some day I'd move back."

But he never did, even though he is now retired from his position as an office manager, and he probably never will. And so he settles for homecoming day, when the memories he has kept of yesterday are superimposed on the realities of today.

As in most of the other rural congregations of the South where homecomings are staged, Rock Chapel's began in midmorning with Sunday school and ended late in the afternoon when the final good-byes had been said and the 250 celebrators were on their way home.

Some of them had driven from such distant points as Raleigh and Louisville and St. Louis—and during the day they had sung the old hymns and songs their parents had taught them years ago, heard two sermons, one in the morning and one in the afternoon, and treated themselves to the kind of food for which the South has long been famous.

The homecoming meal is of vital importance to the success of the day. It is usually prepared in the kitchens of the women who stayed on the farms and still attend the church. In many areas it is served outside.

The ladies of Rock Chapel "really did themselves proud," Mr. Lee said as he glanced down the two long tables in the tiny basement of the church. They sagged beneath the weight of casseroles and cakes and fried chicken and puddings and ham and biscuits. "If there's one thing a country boy don't forget how to do, it's enjoy good country cooking," Mr. Lee said.

"O, Lord, we thank Thee for this bountiful, beautiful meal and for the labors of those who have gone before us," the Rev. Stanley Landrum, the pastor, prayed just before lunch—and his own "Amen" was softly echoed by most of the parishioners and visitors waiting to eat.

In a matter of moments, most of the bowls and dishes were empty and the men, segregating themselves from the women, ate with plastic forks from paper plates.

Mr. Landrum, a 45-year-old native of Mississippi, frankly concedes that the role of rural churches like his own is rapidly diminishing in America's urban-oriented society.

"The bright lights are still very tempting to country people and the young folks really don't like the farming very much, so the rural churches keep getting smaller and smaller," he said, an observation supported by the statistics of the Protestant denominations with churches in the South.

"I think that's why a homecoming day is so important to the life of a country church," he continued. "It means many things to many people, I suppose, but for the church itself and the people who stay behind, it's a glimpse of the better days."

His church's better days began more than a century ago when devout Methodist farmers picked the glade as the site of their first house of worship in this small rural community a few miles from Lithonia.

Theirs was the first church in De Kalb County and it served as a cornerstone for the organization of others. Over the years, informality became a hallmark of the life of the church and it remains so now.

The pastor is called "Stan" by some parishioners or simply "Preacher" by others. The music in the services of worship is basic and simple, and the theology in the sermons and in the discussions in the church school is Fundamentalist.

These are all reflections of the tempo and tenor of rural life and the faith of evangelical denominations that "religion's form is less important than its content," as John Wesley put it.

"That's what wrong with the city churches these days," Mr. Lee said as many of the homecoming guests prepared to leave. "Maybe that's what's wrong with everything these days: It's all too modern—too fast and too formal," he complained, sounding a favorite theme among those who return to their rural origins, and particularly those who attend church homecomings.

For one reason or another they have chosen to live in one world with their heart in another, and the resolution of the two is difficult.

Mr. Lee was ready to head back home. He walked toward the little cemetery on the south side of the church, stopped suddenly, and raised his arm toward the north. "I was born right over there," he said, "and baptized just across the road.

"The preacher used to come to dinner at our house every so often and me and his boys would whale the dickens out of each other about once a month.

"Then we'd come on back over here to the church and listen to their daddy preach that night. I mean he could sure lay it down. It was pure Bible preaching, not like these fellows nowadays, no offense to brother Landrum."

He was at the end of the cemetery now and he pointed down to two weathered markers. "That's my daddy and momma," he said, and the same smile that had slipped across his face when he heard his tires hit the gravel crept over his features again.

"This sounds funny to say, I know," he said "but, in a way, I'm glad they're not living now—not around to see what's happening to the world. It just ain't good what's going on and I'm glad they don't have to live through it."

Then he climbed into his car and headed back to Atlanta.

W. C. Fields honored:
Dog is kicked and child abused

WAYNE KING

Philadelphia
January 30, 1973

On the whole, I'd rather be in Philadelphia.

Epitaph attributed to
W. C. Fields

W. C. Fields, who was known to his scandalized childhood neighbors as Whitey Dukenfield, scourge of the streets and bane of the North Side Philadelphia saloonkeepers, left the city of his birth under something of a cloud sometime in the 1890s.

Last night, a group of the civic-minded Philadelphians, whose Pecksniffian foibles Fields endlessly maligned, gathered together to honor him on what would have been his 93rd birthday. Moreover, they did it with the purpose of promoting civic pride and the fame of Philadelphia, a city Fields sometimes described as difficult to function in, as it was usually closed on Sunday.

A large plaster likeness of Fields, squinty-eyed, bulbous-nosed, majestically suspicious, was set up for the occasion in Burey Hall, a lecture hall at Temple University, and one of those who came to honor Fields noted that it was doubtless as close to a college as Fields ever got.

At different times he put his years of formal schooling in Philadelphia at somewhere between one day and four years, squeezed in between raids on grocery carts, dodging the police, various swindles, and visits to local saloons—where, he said, he never imbibed anything stronger than beer until he was 7 years old.

More in keeping with the Fieldsian image were the festivities of the evening, which included:

· A child-insulting competition, in which entrants were allotted one minute to inflict assorted forms of billingsgate on an 11-year-old child.

· A dog-kicking event, judged on contestants' ability to loft a stuffed canine for maximum yardage.

· A martini-oliving contest, in which entrants were required to pitch over-sized olives at a large martini glass from a distance of 8 feet.

· A Fields monologue competition that drew a half-dozen contestants—including one woman—who attempted to mime the comedian's gestures and capture the undulating, nasal cadences of his delivery.

The master of ceremonies, Robert I. Alotta, a member of the Shackamaxon Society, the Philadelphia civic organization that sponsored the commemoration, announced sadly that the Humane Society had bitterly complained of plans to abuse a dog, and it was thus necessary to substitute a stuffed animal. As compensation, Mr. Alotta gallantly stole a toy from his 6-year-old daughter to accommodate the kickers.

Since the Humane Society applied no restrictions to abuse of humans, Mr. Alotta provided his apple-cheeked son, Peter, to absorb the verbal abuse, albeit with a stipulation that he could not be physically attacked—a caveat that would have vexed Fields no end. It was also deemed unfair to use obscene language, imbibe before the contest, or "expectorate on the child"—all activities that Fields, who delighted in dragging children into saloons, would have regarded as the height of sportsmanship.

(It develops that Fields did not, however, spike the orange juice of the infant actor, Baby LeRoy, as legend and various Fields biographies have it. Actually, according to the best sources, it was a glass of milk he adulterated with a dollop of gin, and the recipient was not Baby LeRoy at all. "There were two children," according to his grandson, William Claude Fields III, who attended the gathering, "named Butch and Buddy, and both got drunk.")

Despite the restrictions on conduct in the child-insulting contest, the victim was made to suffer what Fields would have regarded as satisfying abuse. One insulter began by sizing up the youngster, leaning nose-to-nose, and declaring: "This must be the dog-kicking contest. Where's the kid?"

Others resorted to threats of mayhem. Only one contestant—a Temple coed—lost control at being addressed as "a big turkey," and seized the youngster, an act that brought forth a razzberry from Peter—"Nyaah, you touched me!"—and immediate disqualification of the contestant.

Winners collected bottles of W. C. Fields cologne ("Ah, yes, a veritable banquet to the nose . . . wards off stray animals and obnoxious children . . ."), other Fields memorabilia, and a case of Philadelphia beer.

In Fields's memory, a contestant tries for distance in a dog kicking competition.
NYT/BILL WINGELL

Unfortunately, state law forestalled the awarding of the case of beer to its rightful winner, 10-year-old Pat Patrick, who became the sentimental favorite in the Fields monologue contest when he stepped forward from a self-produced puddle on the stage to provide the best Fields imitation.

Mr. Alotta, who helped provide a Fieldsian touch of his own to the whole affair when he was struck in the face by a pie thrown by his son, said the events were intended to "improve the city's image by commemorating one of her noted citizens."

The choice of heroes was somewhat dubious. Besides his well-known public aversion to his place of nativity ("I was born in Philadelphia, God rest its soul"), his childhood there was less than exemplary.

According to his own later reminiscences—which those who knew him say were probably highly exaggerated—he left the city after holding a fraudulent "benefit" for himself and absconding with the funds donated by the gullible and inflated by gifts from the assorted grocers, bartenders, and policemen who were glad to contribute to ridding the city of a youngster whose larcenous exploits put him in a league with Jesse James and the Artful Dodger.

The one bright spot he found in his childhood in the city, he said after he left the city, was that it was "a great town for breweries." Otherwise, a haze of Puritanism lay over his youth: "Anyone found smiling after the curfew rang was liable to be arrested," he once said. "If a woman dropped her glove on a street, she might be hauled before a judge for stripteasing."

The Fields persona remains swaddled in legend and it is difficult to winnow fact from hyperbole and outright mendacity—mostly perpetrated by the master himself in talking of his Philadelphia boyhood.

Even the famed epitaph, "On the whole, I'd rather be in Philadelphia," is largely fanciful. Fields was cremated and his ashes rest in Forest Lawn Memorial Parks and Mortuaries in Los Angeles, with this simple legend:

W. C. Fields
1880–1946

In Westport, arr. 7:37 is no certainty

JOHN DARNTON

Westport, Conn.
July 9, 1970

On a recent workday morning, the 7:37 did not arrive because, as Frank Bonagiuso, the cheerful ticket-seller, explained, "the engine caught fire."

The announcement unleashed a stream of antirailroad talk that has not been heard here since the lean winter months.

Lately, there had been grudging acknowledgment that things were looking up, in physical appearance if not in on-time performance. The trains still seemed to lose 5, 10, or 15 minutes in the Bronx.

"I kill the time by doing calculations," said a mechanical engineer. "Assume the train carries 1000 passengers. If their salaries average, say, $20,000 a year, and they are late 15 minutes, how much money is being lost?" The answer is $2740.

Doesn't the train ever arrive on schedule? "Let's see," said David Birtwell, puffing on a pipe as his mind traced over 7 years of commuting. "There was one time back in '68. . . ."

For hundreds of executives, the railroad station here is more of a center of town than Main Street.

They descend upon it in ever larger droves, fighting for parking spaces, buying newspapers, scaling staircases with briefcases in one hand and coffee containers in the other, to meet that odd-minute timetable—6:31, 6:58, 7:37 —that lends the illusion of Swiss-watch precision. Then they're gone—old-

19

time commuters and recent suburbanites, all enlisted in the growing ranks of urban emigrants.

The earlier trains carry a younger, racier businessman, with maybe a mustache and sideburns. He is driven to the station by his wife; they part with a kiss. Later comes the older executive, more often alone, who carries *The Wall Street Journal* and walks with measured strides even when his train seems about to depart.

He will be late for work if he misses it. But the railroad—the New Haven division of the Penn Central—is financially strapped, and he is not.

By 8:10, when the next train was due to arrive, the crowd was leaning over the roadbed to stare up the empty tracks. The news that it would be 10 minutes late brought groans—but also some laughter.

The riders of the New Haven accept delays, cancellations, schedule changes, even schedule mistakes, with an attitude of fatalism usually reserved for natural disasters.

Their approach is symbolized by the Abercrombie & Fitch campstools that some of them carry in their briefcases to cope with the seating shortage.

Some attribute it to the we-are-all-in-this-together attitude of the railroad personnel. Conductors are often given doughnuts by women riders, and they answer complaining queries with such lines as: "You know as much as I do," which often seems to be the case.

"These riders are conditioned," said a Briton who has been observing them for 2 years. "They've been completely subdued. It's like Pavlov's dog."

"We even slobber when the train comes in," put in his friend.

At 8:20, the 8:10 arrived, 25 minutes before the 7:37 chugged in.

Someone once commented that the New Haven could be bailed out of the red by the donation of every fourth poker pot on board. But for several years—except for an occasional round of red dog on the 6:08 return train—the great money games are a thing of the past.

"The police put a stop to it," explained a white-haired commuter of 25 years' standing. "It happened after two fellows lost everything they owned, their houses and cars included. The wives complained."

Now the cards handed out by the brakemen, who charge 25 cents per player, go into the more discreet games of bridge and gin rummy. But the games are still compelling enough to continue after the train has come to a stop in Grand Central.

Nobody sets his watch by the 7:37
NYT/DONAL HOLWAY

"There was this fellow named Morgan," recalled George Danneman, a bridge-playing regular. "He got so used to playing that he still took the train every morning after he retired. He would get out, have a drink at the Commodore, and take the next one back."

Six months ago, the commuters' sleepy eyebrows were raised by a transformation in their day's starting point: the coffeehouse across the street from the station.

For 22 years it had been run by Charles and Helen Palmer, who dispensed coffee containers quickly but were not overly fastidious about grease spots on the wall.

Then the shop was bought by a young couple. Its name was changed to Love and Serve, and the changes began. A new floor was laid, the walls paneled, the front shingled. Exotic spices were displayed in the window. Indian tapestries were hung. Then came the smell of incense and deep-fried bread. And the recorded sounds of the sitar.

The couple had been told to go into the restaurant business by their guru, Sri Chinmoy Kumar Ghose, who holds meditations in Queens and in Wilton, Conn.

"I think guru wanted us to manifest ourselves in a harsher reality," observed 21-year-old Kimberly Gilbert, a former New York receptionist who now goes by the name of Pujarini (adoration for the Supreme). Her husband, Premananda (divine bliss), was a carpenter named Eversley Childs, whom she met through their practice of bhakti yoga.

The guru, whose picture in cross-legged position hangs near the coffee urn and is displayed on buttons worn by the help, chose the name Love and Serve from the lines of one of his poems.

The restaurant is doing so well that it is taking over a laundry next door. Everyone is happy, especially the commuters, who start their day by reading quotations on the cash register such as: "I am never happy except when I am crying—crying to the Supreme for the Supreme."

For the row of little shops next to the station, the early business hours are like having a gold rush every 45 minutes.

At 10 o'clock the pace slackens, but it picks up again at noon for lunch at Mario's, a favored drinking spot that includes among its customers a number of suburban housewives.

In the deep afternoon, the streets could belong to a Mexican village. Only a handful of people are waiting on the platform—visitors who overstayed, black domestics returning home, and one or two early arrivals from the dwindling crowd that still goes to the city for nighttime entertainment.

Fourteen-year-old long-haired Stacy Sheehan was among them, carrying a knapsack and a guitar case painted in red, white, and blue. She was going to Greenwich Village to visit her uncle, Robert Downey, the director of *Putney Swope*.

"Don't forget to tell him to do *One Flew Over the Cuckoo's Nest,*" said her companion before she boarded the train.

"Somehow the ride home always seems longer," remarked one executive, looking up at a sign that asked him what he knew about mutual funds.

On the way back, the passengers read, sleep, spend their time in the bar car ("because it's air-conditioned," said one), or try to strike up conversation with the one or two young women.

Sometimes these talks turn on revolution or the youth cult, or, if the executive has the upper hand, on the necessity of working within the system.

At the station, the train is met by a fleet of taxi drivers, scurrying around as if they were in Naples, and by an assembly line of cars. These contain wives, dogs in the back seat, and children, sometimes in pajamas.

Some men perch on the train steps, to swing out like parachutists before it has come to a stop and run to their cars. Others dash through an underpass to meet their wives at a strategically placed rendezvous across the tracks. The aim is to beat the mammoth traffic jam and gain more time before tomorrow morning's 7:37.

The Quarter, an enchantress who always keeps secrets

ROY REED

New Orleans
July 10, 1972

The Old City never fully reveals itself.

It is called the French Quarter, but its name, like all else, stops short of describing its fullness and, in fact, is little more than a hint of its origins.

Its dominant architecture is Spanish; its French population has virtually all moved away; its rowdiest bars are likely to be Greek. These are small mysteries that any tourist can solve in a day.

But the serious student of the Quarter is fascinated by a harder question. Does anything interesting occur any more in those lush, vine-shaded courtyards behind the crumbling old blank walls that the public sees from the narrow streets?

One person reports having seen, through an uncovered window on Chartres Street, the same couple making love every night for a week. That is diverting, but for lasting interest that bedroom is hardly in a class with the house up the street where a band of Creole gentlemen reportedly plotted to rescue Napoleon from Elba, or the cottage on Dauphine Street where John James Audubon is believed to have painted, or the house on Ursulines Street where Stephen F. Austin is supposed to have planned the Texas war of independence, or the house (now gone) on St. Ann Street where Marie Laveau practiced voodoo, or the apartment on Pirate's Alley where William Faulkner lived, or any of the dozen or so taverns and houses where Andrew Jackson

24

In The Quarter, a group stops in the street to unburden itself of some jazz.
NYT

and Jean Lafitte are reliably reported to have planned the Battle of New Orleans.

Nor can it be compared to that old ballroom on Orleans Street where young Creole men came to choose their octaroon mistresses.

There is a suspicion among professional cynics such as journalists that the French Quarter of the twentieth century is becoming much like any other American place. That is hard to prove because the Quarter still hides more than it reveals.

A few things are obvious. The population is changing drastically. Preservationists got hold of the Quarter several years ago when it had almost rotted to the ground, and in the wake of the restorers came adventurous young business and professional people who discovered, as others discovered in Georgetown, that a fading old house with character could be turned into a charming place to live if enough money was spent on it.

So many of the deteriorating old cottages and mansions and even stables with hidden patios and courtyards have now been converted to high-rent houses and apartments that the former population of poor Italians and Negroes has largely been pushed out. Only a small pocket of Negroes remains.

With the restorers also came the entrepreneurs who perceived that a place as beautiful and decadent as the Quarter was bound to be attractive to tourists. Whole streets are now given over to clever gift shops, expensive antique stores, and purveyors of lore.

Some are convinced that the place has become a permanent live-in, look-in museum. Even the music on Bourbon Street is mainly archival Dixieland. Modern jazz can be heard in New Orleans, but rarely in the Quarter, where the form was invented. It is played mainly in black clubs in other parts of town.

The old city is not easy to destroy, however, the cynics notwithstanding. The assault of the American middleclass might finally be no more effective than the two great fires during the Spanish rule of the late eighteenth century, which burned nearly all the French buildings but could not displace the essential Frenchness of the place.

The Quarter is no longer very French, except for the menu at Antoine's and a few other vestiges. But there is evidence that it may remain a different, a not fully Americanized, place for a long time.

For one thing, it is rich for those who like the small private discoveries that are increasingly rare in many American cities, like twilight on the river observed from the roof of a certain small hotel.

Some discover private joys merely walking down the middle of Bourbon Street, which the city has closed to automobiles after dark, as they carry drinks in their hands and literally rub shoulders with fellow keepers of the spirit while the bands blare from the open cafes and sidewalk barkers urge one and all to come inside and watch the girls take off their clothes.

For another thing, those who live in the old city and become its true citizens develop tastes that would be considered bizarre by most Americans.

A woman resident was heard recently to say that she cherishes the smells of the Quarter, not just those of the jasmine and the roasting coffee beans carried on the lazy summer wind, but also those of the decaying fish and rotting fruit from the French Market and the fermenting from the Jax Brewery settling like slow rain in the humid streets.

The more devoted residents develop a similar appreciation of the people with whom they share the Quarter, the Greek and Spanish sailors who drink and dance in the bars on Decatur Street, the numerous young long-haired transients called "undesirables" by the police, even the tourists from Texas and Iowa.

Some have quietly adopted the ways of the counterculture. Go behind one of those blank brick walls to the upstairs apartment of a successful young businessman and you might see a lid of marijuana on the coffee table and a picture of Mao Tse-tung on the wall.

Or observe an influential black lawyer who keeps an office in the Quarter. During the week, he is a model of middle-class respectability, well-connected at City Hall, a friend of the Mayor. On weekends he puts on a dashiki and lolls on the ground in Jackson Square with the long-haired young, listening to music.

One persuasive bit of evidence that the Quarter remains different is the difficulty the residents have in moving away. Perhaps the reason is the same promise of mystery not yet solved that brings thoughtful visitors back. Perhaps it is simple languor. A woman who writes for a living tried once to leave. Like so many of the true citizens here, she had migrated to New Orleans from up the Mississippi River. Then she surrendered to a restlessness that she misconstrued as ambition and went to work in New York.

She suffered there a full season and fled home to Chartres Street, where she now breathes the secret fragance of night-blooming jasmine as it flowers illegitimately, overlooked by an imperious and insensitive landlady, from low-lying branches in a heavily planted courtyard. The Quarter is that kind of place. Its appeal is not readily uncovered, and less readily uprooted.

A small town in summer—Nightly ritual

ANDREW H. MALCOLM

Sacred Heart, Minn.
July 20, 1973

Carla Harried came for an ice cream cone. Val Jacobson came to show off Chuck Johnson. Palmer Eliason came to talk about crops. Paul McKenzie bought a root beer. But Debbie Reiten didn't come by at all, so Jerry Agre went to see why.

Like the residents of thousands of small towns scattered about the country, Sacred Heart's 696 people have a regular summer evening hangout for socializing once the long day's chores are done.

Some of the old folk prefer to play cards at Helen's Pool Hall, where 'there hasn't been a pool table for two decades. It is air-conditioned at Helen's and you can buy 3.2 beer.

But at some time on these muggy July evenings nearly everyone drops by at least briefly at Earl's Drive-In on Main Street, about 120 miles west of Minneapolis.

Here, the regulars stand under the bare light bulbs out front or sit on the two picnic tables, chat about things in general or nothing in particular and offer themselves as living sacrifices to starving swarms of mosquitoes.

It is by and large a pleasing pastime, a relaxing change of pace from the long, lonely days in the corn, soybean, and pea fields or from eight hours at some noisy machine in one of the slowly increasing number of small factories around Sacred Heart.

The town is a small, tidy collection of white homes with china lightning rods that was named by a sick priest who recovered on a heart-shaped river island nearby.

"If you get lost here," said one resident, "you better not leave."

Downtown at Earl's there is gossip to be passed, impressions to be made, Cokes to be drunk, and dates to be set. So, especially for the younger residents of Sacred Heart, an evening at Earl's has become something of a tradition with the accompanying ritual.

There is dinner around 6 P.M. That's when the fire siren blows every night. No one knows what the 6 o'clock siren means, but no one is about to change it, either.

"It's blown as long as I can remember," says Rusty Rustad, the town's police force.

There is another siren at 9 P.M. It used to blow at 10 P.M. to mark the actual start of a curfew for young people. However, too many sleepers were awakened then, so it becomes a 9 o'clock warning instead. But, Mr. Rustad notes, "As long as things are quiet, no one pays any attention to the curfew anyway."

Around 7 P.M., with dinner completed, a few children take to the streets on their bicycles for some ice cream at Earl's. Harlan Sundquist, the new owner who hasn't gotten around to changing the Earl's sign, says he sells 10 to 12 gallons of ice cream a day, depending on the temperature.

There is, however, an occasional chase and Mr. Rustad boasts that he can get his 9-year-old police car up to 100 miles an hour in second gear, a trick he eagerly shows to visitors.

Whenever Mr. Rustad cruises by the drive-in, the kids all wave.

"He's a good guy," says 18-year-old Paul McKenzie.

By 9 P.M., as if by some coincidence, the girls and boys have gathered at Earl's and the crowd is substantial by Sacred Heart standards. The jukebox is playing, the pinball machine is pinging. And gallons of Coke are flowing.

Jerry Agre arrives on his motorbike to report shyly that Debbie Reiten, his girl friend who stayed home tonight, wasn't mad at him after all. And Mark Erickson takes Marcia Gunter for a ride on his Suzuki motorbike. The helmet musses her hair. By 10, things are slowing down.

It wasn't always this sedate in Sacred Heart, where the 12-page telephone book contains seven pages of instructions. In the 1860s the village's first family, the Enesvedts, had a misunderstanding with the Indians that resulted in several deaths.

The railroad came in 1878, but soon after James McIntyre, the depot agent, died violently. His guns discharged as he climbed over a fence on a rabbit hunt.

In 1882 Ole Fjugleskjel, who, it is surmised, was Norwegian, opened a lumberyard here and Andrew Anderson erected Sacred Heart's first saloon. Two days later, however, the town's women tore it down.

By 8 o'clock when Mr. Rustad goes on duty, the bikes are giving way to motorbikes and specially prepared cars. These are driven by boys.

The cars' rear ends are jacked up high. The tires are oversized. The win-

Young people pass a summer evening at Earl's Drive-In on Main Street in Sacred Heart, Minnesota.

NYT/GARY SETTLE

dows are open. The radios or tape decks are on full blast. And the muffler seems to have broken. To avoid any mixups some cars have their name painted in foot-high white letters on the rear fender.

The cars rumble up and down the shady streets, back and forth, around and around, almost like a chase scene in a Peter Sellers movie or a mating dance by some exotic bird.

The girls, meanwhile, have dressed in cutoff jeans with halter tops or slacks with pullover jerseys. In pairs they walk up and down the sidewalks, acting surprised and giggling when some boys honk their car horn or "peel" their tires when the stop light changes.

This is actually one of the more serious problems for Mr. Rustad, who each evening gets several complaints about young people spinning their tires on some of the town's unpaved streets. The other night, though, a youth was caught riding his bicycle in the graveyard at midnight.

Mr. Rustad's other nightly problems are confined to an occasional drunk and some quiet cars out on Parkers' Prairie, the local lovers' lane.

"It don't take me long to make my rounds," he says. "Anyone needs me, they just sit down on the curb and I'll be by presently."

Nowadays, by 11 P.M. the crowd at Earl's has dwindled to a hardy few wearing insect repellent. And the talk centers on the perennial problems of the Sacred Heart Vikings, the football team.

As midnight nears, Earl's is closed. The crickets are chirping. A lone paper cup rattles across the cement. And Rusty Rustad is checking the doors on Sacred Heart's one block of stores.

Every few minutes another heavily laden grain truck blasts through town, sometimes grinding up through four gears in one block. It makes the only breeze in town.

Then Mr. Rustad walks to the southwest corner of Main and another street nobody has bothered to name. He opens a metal box. He flicks a switch. The town's sole stoplight becomes a yellow blinker.

And one more night has officially come to Sacred Heart.

An occasion for sadness in a New York school

JOSEPH LELYVELD

New York
January 22, 1971

For three months after she received a curt notice that the tenement building in which her family had its small railroad flat was about to be demolished, Mrs. Felicita Romero searched for an apartment nearby that would make it possible for her to keep her two sons at Public School 198.

It was a hopeless search, for there is more demolition than construction taking place in the East 90s these days.

Housing officials told her there was no point in adding her name to one of the long lists of those waiting for places in city projects. And the private relocating agency whose signboard was nailed to the front of her building on Second Avenue offered only one apartment—in a building eight miles away in Queens, which was, for Mrs. Romero, another world.

By last week there were only three families left in her building, and addicts, winos, or other displaced persons had twice broken into vacant apartments and started fires.

Mrs. Romero still had not found a place to live but decided she had no choice but to squeeze her sons, husband, and herself into her mother's apartment on East 27th Street. While she continued her search, the boys—Javier, who is 9 years old, and Aurelio, 6—could enroll at Public School 116 on East 33d Street.

In Class 4–4 at P.S. 198, word that the Romeros were moving aroused feelings of loss and injury, especially in the teacher, Dorothy Boroughs, who had once called grave, solicitous Javier "the best monitor I ever had."

Nearly every afternoon Miss Boroughs leaves school burdened with more papers and books than two hands can carry; Javier always stayed by her side until she reached her car, providing the extra hands.

"As a teacher, you have to try to harden yourself to this," she remarked. "Children come and go all the time."

In P.S. 198's office, such comings and goings are called "transactions." Last Monday there were 11 of them; nine out and two in. Since school began in September, moving and demolition have caused the enrollment to drop from about 1000 to 930. Class 4–4 is now down to 26 children—a net loss of eight.

The average turnover in the school runs to about 30 percent a year, according to its acting principal, Mrs. Charlotte Schiff, who said there were other schools in which it was even higher. The constant flux, Mrs. Schiff said, raises questions about the significance of the average reading scores published each year by the Board of Education on a school-by-school basis.

On a child-by-child basis, the flux simply adds to the discontinuity in education that a student usually experiences inside a single school as he is passed from teacher to teacher and grade to grade.

Miss Boroughs could speak of the need for a teacher to harden herself to the loss of a favorite child, but on Javier's next-to-last afternoon in her class she impulsively kissed him and said, "I'm going to miss you very much."

On the last afternoon she gathered the class around his desk and presented him with a book she had bought and a note, on her stationery with her name in lavender art-nouveau lettering, addressed to "Master Javier Romero."

The note said: "Thanks for being such a cooperative and interesting member of our class. Please do not forget us."

Javier seemed astonished by all the attention, almost dazed.

The look had not quite worn off by the time he put in his appearance at his new school. Both Javier and his brother were wearing neckties and black shoes Mrs. Romero had carefully shined for the occasion. As they waited in the office to be placed in classes, Aurelio worked away at his notebook, doing examples in addition he made up for himself in order to demonstrate his prowess; Javier drummed his fingers on the arm of his chair.

"The boys are raring to go, they're ambitious," a secretary in the office noted approvingly.

Miss Veola Harper, an assistant principal, called Javier into a side office and tested his reading ability by asking him to read a story about a raccoon. Then she asked him to count by fours. When he got to 28, Javier stumbled and had to count on his fingers.

His reading was good enough to convince Miss Harper that he belonged in the top class in the grade—known by the teachers at P.S. 116 as 4–1 but called 4–320 whenever students are around, in a hopeless effort to hide from them the fact that the classes are grouped according to skills.

Class 4–320 was just leaving for gym when Javier and Miss Harper reached the room. Once again Javier had drawn a poised and attractive teacher. Her name was Susan Jaffe, and as introductions were made, she extended her hand to shake that of her new student. In response, Javier stuck out his left hand.

"How about the other one?" the teacher asked, laughing.

Holding him close to her as she spoke, Miss Jaffe announced to the class: "This is Javier. He'll be in our class. Go up to him in gym and say 'hello.' When we get back to the room, we'll welcome him formally."

Javier had a wary, alert look when he took the last seat in the last row after Miss Jaffe assigned it to him.

"I don't want you to get scared when you see all of these," the teacher said as she piled 10 textbooks and workbooks on his desk, not one of which had been in use in his old school.

Then she informed him that loose-leaf notebooks, like the one he was carrying, were banned from the school. The principal, Miss Hazel R. Mittelman, considers them messy.

Next, Javier was told that 20 spelling words were handed out every Monday, leading to regular tests; also, that he would be expected to learn the multiplication tables. Finally, the new student heard that the class had nearly finished its study of the explorers in social studies and was about to move on to the founding of the American colonies.

Almost immediately it became clear also that two students speaking at once invited trouble in 4–320. The girl sitting next to Javier spoke out of turn and was quickly rebuked. "Will you wait, young lady?" Miss Jaffe said. "That's being extremely rude to your classmate."

In 4–4, talking when another student had the floor was much less likely to irritate the teacher than failure to pay attention; the explorers had been almost totally ignored; math concepts were stressed rather than memorizing times tables; formal tests came irregularly, usually without much fanfare; textbooks were rarely used, and desks were arrayed in clusters, not in orderly rows all facing front.

Knowing there are bound to be differences between any two classrooms, Miss Boroughs had assumed that Javier would have considerable adjusting to do in his new school. Specifically, she had a premonition that his new teacher would already have started long division, a subject she had yet to touch. So last week she hastily gave him a cram course.

Luckily, 4–320, like 4–4, still had that frontier to cross. As for the differences that were apparent, Javier hardly seemed to notice them. He was too busy trying to fit in.

Fraternal clubs thrive in U.S. towns

DOUGLAS E. KNEELAND

Kearney, Neb.
November 15, 1970

Jim Anderson sat hunched over a tall scotch and water and searched for the words to explain—the Elks, Kearney, a way of life.

Sipping his drink, the close-cropped, blond insurance man, a past exalted ruler of Kearney Lodge No. 984 of the Benevolent and Protective Order of Elks, gazed thoughtfully around the darkened 450-seat clubroom, taking in the five o'clock crowd at the 40-stool circular bar with its red-lighted fountain playing in the center. Suddenly he seized on the deep red carpet streaked with other hues of red and orange.

"Take this carpet," he said. "When we built this place, we had a long debate about the carpet. This stuff goes for $22 a yard. We could have gotten some cheaper stuff, but in a place like this, a lot of us thought we should go first class all the way. It's all wool and just look at it."

A lot of other lodges—Elks, Moose, Eagles—in hundreds of small and middle-sized cities across the land are going "first class all the way." For their members—even after the new homes have been built, the new cars bought, the freezers installed, the power mowers purchased—there is money left to spend at "The Club." As modern clubs have been built, many with swimming pools, golf courses, and bowling alleys, their membership has grown faster than prairie corn.

36

In this sprawling city of almost 19,000 in the flat, fertile valley of the Platte River in south-central Nebraska, the Elks Club has more than 2200 members and—like those in countless other small cities—is the center of the community's social life.

The long, low brick building across from the old Fort Kearney Hotel was completed in 1956. As it attracted more and more of those with a few extra dollars and a little extra time to spend, the club had to build an addition last year. It is now valued, including land and furnishings, at about $725,000.

"People in the East and in California and places like that," Mr. Anderson said, "they just don't know how we live out here.

"I had a friend in the service and he and his family are living in California now. Well, they came out here to visit us a while back, and after a couple of weeks he really didn't want to leave. He kept saying, 'I just didn't know how you folks lived here.' You know, you live about three minutes from the office, and you have all this."

Then, lest the good works of the lodge be lost in his account of its good life, Mr. Anderson began to catalogue the Kearney Elks' civic projects. The Boy Scout troop and Pony League team they sponsor. The crippled children they assist. The playground equipment they contribute to parks.

"The fraternal aspect of this organization so far as the good you do in the community can't be measured," he said. "It makes you proud to be an Elk, really."

Leaning back and glancing again around the plush club, he concluded: "We like to think we're doing a good job Elkwise."

At a time when much of urban America may not know the B.P.O.E. from the L.I.R.R., a lot of other lodges apparently like to think the same.

From the days of its founding in February, 1868, in New York City by 15 actors, entertainers, and others associated with the theater, the Benevolent and Protective Order of Elks grew rather steadily to a membership of 839,429 in 1924. At that point, it started a decline that left it with only 466,520 members in the Depression year of 1936.

However, with the new affluence after World War II, the order expanded rapidly through the 1950s and 1960s to 1,508,050 members this year. Its 2146 lodges represented a gain of more than 800 over the total of 50 years ago.

The Elks are not alone. As millions of middle Americans have flocked to fraternal organizations during the years of postwar affluence, the Loyal Order of Moose, for instance, has seen its membership rise from a 1935 low of 306,955 to 1,137,948 this year. The Independent Order of Odd Fellows, while reluctant to give out any other information, reports a membership of 1,250,000. And the Fraternal Order of Eagles said it had about 850,000 members, which a spokesman conceded was a decline from the more than a million who belonged in the late 1940s.

Where do these holdovers from a simpler age take root and flourish? And why?

An elk head on the wall and $22-a-yard carpeting on the floor is the pride of the Kearney, Nebraska, Elk's Lodge.

NYT/JOHN NOLLENDORFS

The Elks, perhaps the largest and fastest growing, seem to be representative. Spokesmen in Chicago at the Elks National Memorial Headquarters, whose ornate rotunda overlooks Lincoln Park and Lake Michigan and is a stop on guided bus tours of the city, offer some explanations.

While the old No. 1 Lodge in New York City still has 1270 members and the Queens Lodge is the largest in the state with 4093, they say, the greatest growth has come in the small and medium-sized cities across the nation.

Frequently, but not always, the spokesmen say, the Elks have thrived in areas where there was a dearth of social and recreational facilities; where law or custom made it impossible or embarrassing for a local businessman to drop into a public bar for a drink on his way home from work.

They are quick to argue, however, that the attraction is not all social, that the Order of Elks spends about $14 million a year in helping physically handicapped children, in assisting servicemen and veterans, and in promoting patriotic programs.

And while the real strength of the organization may be among the silent majority in such places as Tacoma, Wash., Fargo, N.D., Long Beach, Calif., Salina, Kan., and Kearney, they note with pride the four presidents who have been members: Warren G. Harding, Franklin D. Roosevelt, Harry S. Truman, and John F. Kennedy.

Being a member of the Elks or other fraternal organizations has long been considered a must by politicians in many areas, but there have been times in recent years when their refusal to admit blacks has been a sensitive issue for members who were candidates. And the Elks have shown no enthusiasm for changing their restrictions. Last summer at their convention in San Francisco, they voted overwhelmingly for the second time against a proposal that the racial bar be dropped.

Although the Elks maintain a nonpolitical position, they are aggressive in their Americanism. Among other patriotic programs that they have pursued with enthusiasm in the last few years, they have distributed hundreds of thousands of flag decals, bearing the Elks' emblem and the words "Our Flag, Love It or Leave."

Here in Kearney, that decal decorates the plate-glass doors and the club's entrance, along with another that proclaims the Elks Club to be a member of the Kearney Chamber of Commerce.

Set amid some of the best farmland in the country, a prosperous corn-, alfalfa-, and cattle-producing region, Kearney also has almost a dozen small but busy manufacturing plants. The low-slung downtown business district is healthy. Unemployment is low. Kearney State College, which has never had a serious demonstration, has grown from about 1500 students in 1960 to 5800 now.

Flags fly along the streets of Kearney under the somber November skies. Flags are important to the people here. And the Kearney Elks Club makes them available free to almost any group or institution that wants them. Last year the Elks gave away about six dozen, according to Chester Marshall, secretary of the local club and of the state association. The Elks Club has grown with Kearney. In 1955 it had an old wooden house and 600 members. It also has $300,000 in the bank, saved from World War II days, when Kearney had an Air Force base and slot machines (long since gone) enriched the club.

The new club has no golf course, as do more than 100 Elks Clubs, no swimming pool, no bowling alley, as do many more. But it is the place to go in Kearney. Its membership outnumbers the local country club by more than 10 to 1. It costs about $250 annually to belong to the country club, while an Elk pays a $45 initiation fee and $25 a year in dues.

For his money and pledge of fraternal loyalty, the Elk joins a broad cross-section of Kearney society—lawyers, bankers, insurance men, store owners, plant managers, mechanics, farmers, teachers, morticians.

And he buys the right to enjoy 50-cent drinks in the big downstairs stag bar while he plays a few hands of poker, shoots some pool, or cheers Nebraska's touchdowns during televised football games. Or to dress up and treat his wife to a $3.50 steak dinner in the tastefully decorated, 150-seat dining room. Or to take the whole family out to a $1.75 Sunday buffet. Or go to the monthly free stag dinners. Or play Bingo every Thursday. Or dance to a big band each Saturday in the oversized lodge room used as a dance hall, hearing the old favorites like "Stardust," "Goody Goody," or "Woodchoppers Ball."

On Saturdays, Elks and their ladies sit and sip martinis and stingers and grasshoppers and Golden Cadillacs, while the dancers whirl around the crowded floor in almost-forgotten fox trots, and muse about why it's good to be alive and an Elk, in Kearney, Neb.

"The thing that makes me so sad in San Francisco," Jean Freese, wife of Harold Freese, the 43-year-old exalted ruler of the Kearney lodge, said the other night, "is the kids. All those sad-eyed children, hippies. When I get home to Nebraska, I'm so glad to see these clean-cut kids. Of course, some of them aren't so clean-cut, but they look pretty clean-cut compared with those others out there."

And Gale Leitner, the esteemed leading knight, watching the dancers and the drinkers, most of them laughing, joking, calling to friends, added:

"When we were in Chicago, on that tour, the bus driver said, 'Look at all those smiling faces.' You know, there weren't any smiling faces in that crowd."

Pausing and looking around him again, he shook his head sadly.

"You know how it is in the cities," he said.

The Senior Prom: Some still find it's a night to remember

JUDY KLEMESRUD

New York
June 11, 1972

It all began to happen around 6 P.M. Friday: He fastened a tiny corsage of red roses around her right wrist. She pinned a white carnation on the lapel of his rented dinner jacket. They toasted each other with Cold Duck. They kissed.

It was prom night.

And unlike many other young people today, Louis Battagliola, 18 years old, and his red-haired steady girlfriend, Roberta Bryce, 17, both of the Bronx, were getting ready to "live it up" on what they regarded as the most exciting night of their high-school careers.

Yes, the prom is still alive, although it is not nearly as well as it used to be. Because many teen-agers today dismiss the traditional prom as irrelevant, Establishment, and overly expensive, many high schools have canceled their proms altogether—or instituted cheaper substitutes such as Flushing High School's three-hour "Senior Float" yacht cruise.

"We used to get big groups of about 100 after proms," said Eugene R. Scanlan, director of food and beverage at the Waldorf-Astoria Hotel, where prom business this spring is down 20 percent from five years ago. "But now we mostly get smaller groups of six to eight. I guess the kids just don't dig wearing white jackets and long gowns any more."

Many still do, of course, especially those from parochial and suburban

41

high schools, and anyone who has been near midtown Manhattan on a recent weekend night has probably run into "prom kids" in their one-night finery near such traditional prom stops as the Copacabana, the Plaza Hotel, and the hansom cabs in Central Park.

"The only kids I know who don't go to proms are the girls who don't have boyfriends," said Roberta, shortly before she and Louis left her home for her senior prom, "Starry, Starry Night," at the Fountainhead restaurant in New Rochelle, N.Y.

Roberta is a senior at St. Raymond's Academy, and Louis is a senior at St. Raymond's High School. They described themselves as "very average students" at the Roman Catholic schools, which are a block apart in the Bronx.

To earn the $200 he thought would be necessary to give them a night to remember, Louis went to work as a delivery boy for a Manhattan messenger service for two months. Roberta, in turn, paid the cost of the prom—$30 per couple—with money she earned working weekends at a Woolworth's store in the Bronx. (Her parents are both dead, and she lives with an older sister and younger brother.)

"I've wanted to go to the prom ever since I was a little kid," Roberta said dreamily. "I watched my sister get ready for her prom, and I used to watch the girls on the block leave their houses in their prom dresses. They all seemed so excited."

Friday had been a long and exciting day for the couple. Both had exams in the morning, Louis in psychology and Roberta in philosophy ("I can never remember that word.") They spent the rest of the day getting ready. Roberta paid $7 to have her hair done in "Grecian curls" at a beauty parlor, and then went home and put on the $34 lilac chiffon gown with a lacy white top that she had bought at Alexander's.

Louis washed the green station wagon he had borrowed for the evening, then donned his rented ($30-a-night) ensemble that would make him one of the more colorful males at the prom: a cranberry ruffled shirt and a burgundy crushed velvet dinner jacket, over black pants with black satin stripes running up the sides.

"I'm really glad the prom is not in the high-school gym this year," Roberta said as Louis guided the car towards New Rochelle. "It's kind of hard to be romantic in a gym with those basketball nets hanging down."

As of 6 p.m. Friday, Louis and Roberta had been going steady for exactly "five months, 17 days, and 18 hours," according to Roberta's calculations. They live a block away from each other, and have somewhat similar backgrounds: Her father was a truck driver, and so was his. They both live in eight-room apartments on the second floors of two-family houses. They are both passionate New York Yankee fans.

"I just love Fritz Peterson [the Yankee pitcher]," said Roberta, whose tiny bedroom is festooned with pictures of Yankee heroes. "Once a girlfriend and

Louis Battagliola, 18, and his steady girl, Roberta Bryce, 17, both of the Bronx, N.Y., on prom night.

NYT/DONAL HOLWAY

I waited outside of Yankee Stadium for him, and kissed him on the cheek as he was signing autographs. We cried all the way home on the subway."

Neither Roberta nor Louis is very interested in politics or protest movements. Roberta, however, has registered to vote, and said she would probably vote for President Nixon.

"I just can't get too interested," said Louis, who is 6 feet 2 inches tall, rail thin, and bespectacled. "The other day when I was walking down Fifth Avenue and didn't stop to register at a voter registration booth, a middle-aged guy came running after me. He said, 'You're a phony just like the rest of your generation, because you could have a lot of power if you'd use it.'"

Huge bottles of Royal Crown Cola graced the tables at the Fountainhead, where the couples mockingly toasted each other and whispered they'd be sipping "the hard stuff" later on. The prom drew 53 of the 87 girls in Roberta's class and their dates—"a typical turn-out," she said.

Louis didn't have to lift his fork very often during the meal (fruit cup, soup, prime rib, green beans, potato, chocolate tart), because Roberta was feeding him— a custom of today's steady-dating couples.

"When we go to the Steak and Brew she feeds me the whole thing," said Louis, who fed Roberta a bite now and then, too. "The whole thing!"

At 11 P.M., the couple said goodbye to their friends and drove to the Waldorf-Astoria Hotel where they saw one of Roberta's favorite singers, Melba Moore, do the midnight show. Afterward, the couple had planned to join some friends at Orchard Beach in the Bronx, but chilly weather and a light drizzle made them change their plans to a ride on the Staten Island ferry.

While waiting for the 2 A.M. ferry to arrive, Roberta and Louis talked about the widely held belief that sex and the senior prom were practically synonymous.

"Sure everybody talks about it," said Louis, "but that doesn't mean you just automatically go to bed with someone on prom night. It depends on how meaningful your relationship is."

Roberta agreed, and added: "I trust him and I trust me. I'm a virgin and I intend to be after the prom. I don't have to go to a motel to have fun; I can have just as much fun riding the Staten Island ferry or burying someone in the sand at Orchard Beach."

After the ferry ride, they headed back to the Bronx to await graduation and the next big moment of their lives: their first full-time jobs. Roberta begins work later this month as a clerk for a Manhattan insurance company; Louis as a trainee in a bank ("I hope to be a teller").

The night to remember was over.

If Middle America needs a capital, there's always Dubuque

CHARLOTTE CURTIS

Dubuque, Iowa
April 5, 1970

When the late Harold Ross rejected the little old lady in Dubuque as lacking the sophistication to read *The New Yorker*, he inadvertently made her into a lasting symbol of American provincialism. She and her friends fought back by subscribing to *The Reader's Digest*.

Forty-five years have elasped since that somewhat tentative feud begun. Since then, Dubuque, a picturesque town with the best of the gabled frame houses on the bluff overlooking the Mississippi River, has nestled even further into its hills.

The population, nearly 80 percent Irish or German Catholic, has reached 63,000, including perhaps 40 blacks. A new generation of little old ladies has cropped up. And although these women are still something less than intellectually, culturally, and politically with it—or hep, as they say in Iowa—their fight for what they consider the good life continues.

In the fifties, they decided Titian nudes and John Steinbeck's *The Wayward Bus* were obscene. In the sixties, they were reasonably successful in getting Christ back into Christmas. And in the seventies, they are after the producers of what they call "sex-ridden" movies.

"Why, it's a disgrace what the movies are today," Mrs. Delbert Hayford said. "There's entirely too much nudity. The stories don't do anything for

45

you. Does the movie of today encourage you to marriage and a family? No, it doesn't. I don't approve."

Mrs. Hayford and her husband, a retired postal clerk, heard about "the new movies" and decided to see one for themselves. They went to *John and Mary*, which concerns a young couple who meet in a bar and then go to bed without knowing each other's names. The Hayfords were shocked.

"We didn't like it at all," the 66-year-old grandmother said, shaking her head.

Miss Emma Trenk had a similar reaction to *Gaily, Gaily*, the story of a youth who goes to a big city to live in what 68-year-old Miss Trenk correctly identified as "a house of ill repute." And at 70, Mrs. Anthony Eberhardt is so upset she's boycotting the movies altogether.

"We're being deprived of one of the great arts," Mrs. Eberhardt moaned. "I think my individual rights are being trampled. I believe in family movies— things like *The Shoes of the Fisherman*."

What Mrs. Hayford, Miss Trenk, and Mrs. Eberhardt say may not coincide with *The New Yorker*'s movie reviews, but their opinions matter in this comfortably isolated Middle Western town.

Dubuquers, or Dubuquelanders as some natives also call themselves, respect and admire these women not just because they are senior citizens but because they, and such others as Mrs. Louise H. Halliburton, are to Dubuque what the Astors and the Vanderbilts are to New York.

What Mrs. Hayford says is particularly significant, however, for she is something of a celebrity—the only official Little Old Lady of Dubuque.

The Chamber of Commerce selected her in a contest 6 years ago, sent her to New York (which she didn't much like although she did meet television's Ed McMahon), and boosted her as representative of what Dubuque likes to think is wholesome about its community. Mrs. Hayford believes she's fairly typical.

"I was born and raised in Dubuque, and I expect to die here," she said. "My ties are very strong. I like living where I know everybody and everybody knows me. I'd be nobody in a big city."

Mrs. Hayford was wearing a lime-green knitted dress and jacket with a pink-and-white crocheted collar and cuffs. Her long white hair was up in a bun at the back of her head. Her forehead was obscured by wavy bangs. She had little curls over her ears.

With the ensemble, she wore thin-heeled lime suede pumps, glasses with the mother-of-pearl plastic frames edged with rhinestones, silver earrings set with aquamarines, pink lipstick, and pearlized nail polish. She was as chic as anyone in Dubuque.

"I was a flapper when I was a girl," she said. "I shocked my mother when I had my hair shingled. I wore boots with the buckles open. They went flap, flap."

Mrs. Hayford went to a Catholic girls school and on to Clark College for two years.

"In my day, if you weren't married by the time you were 21 or 22, you were dead," she said. "I went back later to study interior design."

The Hayfords' living room is their special joy. Gold satin draperies are bunched down the sides of the windows. The ornate Victorian love seat is brocaded in scarlet. The grand piano has been antiqued or maybe modernized with cream paint. The chandelier is baroque. The candles are wood with flame-shaped electric lights. Mrs. Hayford decorated the room herself.

"We're the little Heidelberg of America," she explained. "We have art and symphonies. Everybody's very culture-minded."

Aside from a Salvador Dali print or two, religious paintings including portraits of Jesus Christ, and family photographs, the art in homes is mostly native to Iowa. There is no art museum, although exhibitions of local works are held now and then.

But Dubuque does have an orchestra, three colleges, three theological seminaries, and a Young Women's Christian Association that gave a short course in Negro history.

"If we wanted to see a play, we'd go into Chicago," Mrs. Hayford said, adding that Clark College has a lively dramatics department. "We see lots of television."

The Hayfords' 27-inch color television is on regularly between 7 and 10 P.M. They rarely miss "Family Affair," about a rich bachelor, his butler, and how they're raising three orphaned children; and "The Carol Burnett Show," because Mrs. Hayford met and liked Miss Burnett.

Miss Trenk has a TV set, too, but she rarely turns it on. Instead, she reads travel books, the Audubon Society's magazine, the *National Geographic*, *Life*, and *The Reader's Digest*.

"The people in Dubuque are racist," the retired schoolteacher said flatly. "They don't want to know what a Negro is like. If one gets to the city, he has a hard time."

For 40 years, Miss Trenk taught economics, American history, and "a little bit of everything in social studies" at the senior high school. She figures she taught 10,000 children, only six or eight of whom were black.

"The racial issue was always a hard one for me," she said. "So many parents were prejudiced."

When she wanted to show what discrimination was about, she divided a class into two groups. One blackened their faces. The others didn't. They then played out the stereotyped roles.

"I think I did a pretty good job," she said, adding that her students had joined Vista and the Peace Corps. "I can hear my mother saying, 'Self-praise stinks,' but I did do a good job."

Like the other women, none of whom have ever confronted a thoroughly alienated young radical, Miss Trenk sees no real generation gap.

"About revolution," she said, "I always say if you want revolution, you'd better build something, produce something better—not just destroy. If laws are bad, you work to change them."

Miss Trenk doesn't like long hair on boys because "it's so effeminate," but concedes that "Thomas Jefferson had a long wig, so I suppose it's all right." Her definition of a hippie is a drug addict.

While an increasing number of local homemakers look to prepackaged convenience foods, Miss Trenk grows her own fruits and vegetables and makes everything from soups to grape juice. She is famous for her strawberry shortcake and for clothes she bought on a trip around the world.

On a typical day, she's likely to wear a brightly flowered silk from Hawaii ("I wasn't sure I dared in Dubuque"), pearl earrings from Japan, and a carved ivory necklace from India.

"Mrs. Halliburton and I made the trip together," Miss Trenk said. "We loved everything. We cried when we saw the Taj Mahal."

Mrs. Halliburton is a widowed artist. At noon on Wednesdays during Lent, she and perhaps 30 other residents could be found in a solemn line on the Washington Park sidewalk facing the Federal Building. Each wore a sign reading "Silent Vigil for Peace."

"We've been coming here on Sunday mornings since 1966," she said. "One Sunday it was 14 below zero."

A pacifist since she saw the first draft numbers drawn out of a fish bowl in Washington before World War I, Mrs. Halliburton has fasted for peace, picketed for civil rights and against the Vietnam war, leafleted at the Pentagon, and consistently befriended Iowa's conscientious objectors.

"I'm a native of Dubuque," she said proudly, "but I feel very privileged that I've had an opportunity to live in other communities."

She went to the Corcoran Art School in Washington, married a Quaker economics professor, and lived in Indiana and New Jersey. In recent years, she refused to pay the Federal telephone tax because it helps finance the war and urged her friends to boycott grapes on behalf of the Mexican grape-pickers in California.

"I don't get into arguments," she said. "Nobody talks about what I do. The conversations are usually very uninteresting. People avoid discussing the real issues."

Mrs. Halliburton doesn't own a television, will not be drawn into the movie fight, reads *The Progressive*, exhibits her sketches of nudes, entertains black friends, and defends Dubuque.

"So many people have lacked exposure to other viewpoints," she said. "They're turned inward to their families. But they're changing a little. I think maybe we're moving into the 20th century."

While Mrs. Halliburton speaks hopefully of the future, Mrs. Eberhardt, a grandmother who spearheaded Christ in Christmas and the obscenity raids, plays "Love Me Tender, Love Me True" on her guitar, reads detective stories, and talks about her European trip.

She and her husband, a retired post-office supervisor, took pictures of castles along the Rhine, admired St. Peter's in Rome, toured the Alps, and were photographed in Paris at the base of the Eiffel Tower.

"After it was all over," she said, "it was wonderful to get back to the Old World charm of Dubuque. You know the hills here are very reminiscent of Switzerland. And, oh, our river! Now I've never seen anything, neither the Danube or the Seine, that's as beautiful as the Mississippi."

For an imaginative young adventurer, New York still is Fun City

MICHAEL T. KAUFMAN

New York
December 3, 1971

Michael Edmonds, who is 11 years old, has rescued a runaway spider monkey from the upper branches of a maple tree in Riverside Park.

He has climbed to the top of every lamppost in his neighborhood. Last summer, he was arrested for scaling the outer wall of Belvedere Castle in Central Park to the bell tower, where he was looking for pigeon eggs.

Michael has camped out overnight with a sleeping bag in the rubble heap behind the deserted building at Columbus Avenue and 91st Street where his family lives. He has gone to City Hall alone to see where the Mayor works.

He thinks the best thing in the world is the roller coaster at Palisades Amusement Park, and he once spent a week building a working likeness of it from found objects.

Michael has lived in three welfare hotels in the last 4 years. He has been at dozens of demonstrations and court hearings.

Yet, through it all, his life has been a celebration of boyhood, a joyful mastery of a city that so many of his elders find menacing.

Michael knows Manhattan as Huckleberry Finn knew Hannibal, Mo. Each day after school he seeks out adventure, and recently he consented to have an older, note-taking friend accompany him on his impromptu rounds. "You can come if you can climb," Michael said.

50

The big project in Michael's life at the moment is transforming the vacant apartment next door to his family's into a clubhouse.

He and his 14-year-old brother Mark, a Bronx High School of Science sophomore, have swept out the front room and hung pictures of Muhammad Ali on the walls. They have also hung up a mechanical timer they found, which rings after three-minute rounds in boxing bouts with their friends.

An adjoining room has been turned into a steam bath by the brothers. A defective valve on a radiator pours vapor into the room and Michael, who is fast, shifty, and undersized at 65 pounds, says the steam keeps him loose.

The other day he was in the boxing room tidying up when he looked out the window and saw three men approaching the building at 636 Columbus Avenue. "It's the junkies," he said, and darted off.

The front door of the vacant apartment has been barricaded with tin, and the only way out is through a window, out the fire escape, and into Michael's apartment, the only one that is occupied in the building.

The Edmonds family is the last of a group of 215 squatters that took over a group of buildings slated for demolition. They have been there since August, 1970.

Once inside his own fifth-floor apartment, he raced down the long hallway, grabbed a jacket, and got to the third-floor landing just as the suspected addicts had entered the vestibule. There he stopped, and in a loud voice began talking to no one. "Honestly, officer, I was just looking around for some old wood. No, there's no one with me. O.K., officer, I won't come back."

Then he raced down. As he passed the three men, he said, "Watch it, there's a cop up there." They turned and left. Five minutes later Michael returned to his apartment.

"That usually works," he said.

His brother and his friends, who were expected, had not shown up. So Michael decided to take a walk, or rather, a scamper. First he went up to the roof to hurdle the stiles that separate the row of tenements. Then he showed off the coop in which he keeps his pigeons.

"I let them go when it got cold—it's bad enough keeping them penned up when it's warm," said Michael, who also has gerbils and tropical fish in his house.

"Let's go to the tree-stump house," he said. And without waiting for an answer, Michael swung, slid, and vaulted on and over banisters, the six flights to the street.

The "tree-stump house" is a building on 89th Street that is being wrecked. "It's no bigger than a tree stump," explained Michael, who often goes off on his own after school, covering a territory of friends and acquaintances that runs from 145th Street to Washington Square Park.

At the house he climbed a staircase to nowhere and said: "Why are they beating the hell out of this place. This house never did nothing to nobody." Michael found some wire and bent it. Then he smashed some light bulbs.

Michael Edmonds, 11, on an adventure on New York rooftops.
NYT/LEE ROMERO

Michael decided to visit his mother, who was in St. Luke's Hospital, at Amsterdam Avenue and 113th Street, with torn ligaments in her back. While Mrs. Edmonds was ill, her friends—Donna Peacock, Cathy Jara, and Christine Patterson, whom everyone calls C.R.—took care of the apartment. Mrs. Jara's 8-year-old daughter, Marisa, is also living there.

Walking up Amsterdam Avenue, Michael spoke of the Children's Workshop School, which he and Marisa attend.

"It's great. You don't have to sit in a hard chair, you can sit on pillows. You can paint or read or play with the rabbits. We go everywhere. Next week we're going to the trial of the Harlem Six."

The school, which is in a brownstone and is free, held a benefit concert at Carnegie Hall recently, with Pete Seeger. Michael, who did not go, explained:

"I told Marisa that we shouldn't go. I mean, we're revolutionaries, what do we want to go and sing peace songs for?" Marisa went and performed at the concert.

Two minutes later he was talking about the books he likes. "You know," he said smiling sheepishly, "I still like Dr. Seuss."

On 95th Street, a boy slightly bigger than Michael ran up to him and started shoving him. "Mess with me now, why don't you? Mess with me now," he said.

Michael did not do anything and took the other boy's curses in silence. The other boy withdrew to a group of his friends and no blows were struck.

"I beat up his cousin in school," Michael explained. Why didn't he fight now? he was asked. "Well, I think he's got a razor knife. And anyway there's a time to fight and a time to run, and this is not a time to fight."

At the hospital, a guard gave Michael a quizzical look. "I'm 12 years old," Michael told him before he could ask anything. "You have to be 12 to visit," he explained in an aside.

Mrs. Edmonds was glad to see Michael. In the few minutes he had to wait for his mother, who was on the phone, Michael cast his eyes over the cigarette stubs to see who had been up to see her. "Now, who smokes Trues? Oh yes, it must have been John," he said mostly to himself.

In the conversation with her, he eventually told her of the wood carving he had made in school and of the boxing ring. Mrs. Edmonds, who has been a dancer, a songwriter, an actress and a community organizer, started telling another visitor about Michael's boundless energy.

"He loves street life and takes in everything. He has a need for freedom and a difficulty in sitting still. Some people love that and some can't understand it. There are problems."

Michael was getting restless. He was sitting by the side of the bed examining the electric controls. "Michael," said his mother softly from the strapped and weighted bed where she was in traction, "don't move me up and down."

"Ooops, sorry," said Michael.

He went home to C.R.'s dinner, read a book called *Yellow, Yellow*, sorted his brother's mineralogy collection, and did not clean out the fish tank as he was supposed to.

A small Ozark town is winning poverty battle

JAMES P. STERBA

Ava, Mo.
April 10, 1969

The checker games in the county courthouse boiler room begin here shortly after the roosters at the edge of town have croaked the sun up to a mid-morning brilliance.

Old and young men, many in ankle-top workshoes and bib overalls, amble inside past a sign that reads, "Do Not Spit on Floor $5 Fine," and down steps to basement checkerboards and to coffee cans that save the floor from tobacco juice stains.

"I don't know that there's been a day in years when there ain't been checker games down there," said Marcus Holman, the Douglas County extension agent, who has an office on the first floor and occasionally joins a game.

In another part of town, Willie Bristol, 74 years old, is hard at work these days on his twenty-second handmade fiddle. And when lawlessness isn't too rampant, and it usually isn't, Deputy Sheriff Edmond Riley can be found picking a tune on one of the banjos he stores in the county jail.

Thus, in an age when pollution and riots are crippling the nation's major cities, little Ava is unusually quiet.

Progress is seeking an accommodation with history in this town of about 2100 people snuggled in the Ozark hills.

54

Ava is the county seat of Douglas County, population about 10,000. It was supposed to be located in the center of the county. But according to a historical marker in the town square, Ava is "12 miles off center."

Grinding poverty, for decades a way of rural life here, is beginning to disappear. In 1960, Douglas County's median family income was $2050, with 538 families making less than $1000. The national average then was about $6000.

During the Eisenhower Administration, however, Douglas became one of 54 pilot counties in rural development, and the results of Federal, state, and local dollars and help are beginning to be seen.

New houses dot the town, many of them adjacent to older structures with split logs stacked high out front to feed wood-burning stoves.

At least 20 small businesses have opened in town in the last five years, and development and promotion of the gentle Ozark hills, with their limestone ridges and caves, streams and lakes, have lured tourist dollars.

There is a new radio station and nine-hole golf course, and a county airport is under construction. Land prices are rising as young men, who deserted Douglas County in droves for city jobs in the past, are beginning to stay. For the first time in 40 years, the county is gaining population.

The top dog in Douglas County is still the hound. From beagles and coonhounds to blue ticks, they can be seen in all shapes and sizes.

Hounds are so popular in this part of the country that an old folk song about them once threatened to become the Missouri State Song, according to J. E. Curry, a former State Senator and retired publisher of *The Douglas County Herald*, the weekly newspaper.

In 1911, Frank Reece, a fiddling genius who "could play any tune he ever heard and play it right now," popularized it in Douglas County. The first verse goes:

> *Every time I come to town,*
> *The boys keep kicking my dog around;*
> *Makes no difference if he is a hound,*
> *They gotta quit kickin' my dog around.*

It was one of the more sinister signs of progress for some old-timers when a few poodles were spotted around town recently. "I betcha a good-sized coon could tree one of those buggers," one whittler remarked.

Country fiddlers, native to the Ozarks and Appalachia, are rapidly becoming an endangered species here. Five-string banjo and mandolin pickers are also declining.

"Oh, we still got some real fiddlers here," said Clarence Singleton, the county treasurer. "There's a few younger boys that's plumb good on the banjo. They sorta inherit it from the family. But now, a lot of kids, I figure, are livin' too fast to learn."

Ava seems to have more spry 70-year-olds than New York has spry 30-year-olds. All are charter members of the town's informal Department of Philosophy—the "spit and whittle" club—and they gather daily on the curb in front of the old Ava Dry Goods Store to sit, whittle, chew, toss pebbles, and chatter for hours.

"Yep," mumbled Roy Cox to no one in particular as he sauntered up, struck a wooden match on a snap of his bib overalls, lit a cigarette, and sat down.

"Springs in this seat plumb near broke down, hey Arthur," said Roy Thompson, a former cabdriver. He plopped down on the cement next to Arthur Bishop, who mows lawns and plows gardens around town.

"That make your oil heat up?" another man asked Mr. Bishop as four girls in bare feet walked by.

"Women don't bother me no more'n a suck-egg dog, no more'n a copperhead snake," he replied. The subject was then women, especially "women gone bad."

"Why they ain't nothing worse than a woman that's gone bad. Why, they're worse than a mean dog."

They stared for a while at several carloads of teen-agers circling the square.

"Sometimes they is three deep," Mr. Bishop told a visitor. "I was born here when they wasn't no cars. Then everybody sold their plow horses and bought tractors. Now the young folks says gas costs too much for the tractors, but it's just right for the cars. So they is no farming going on like they used to be. They is just cars going in all directions."

Softball is big in Sheboygan

J. ANTHONY LUKAS

Sheboygan, Wis.
September 7, 1969

The sweat on Gino Petramele's bald head glistened and he was breathing heavily under his bright yellow shirt, but he sucked in his gut and poked the mushball far enough into center field for both Lou Lusignan and Bob Fiadaca to advance after the catch.

When Ed Zolna and Bob Warnack followed with singles, the Dr. Carlucci Boosters (named after the paunchy dentist from Fox Lake, Ill., who sponsors them) took the lead over Sobie's Tap (named after the Cicero, Ill., bar owned by the former basketball All-American Ron Sobieszyczyk where the team drinks beer).

Despite the urgent pleadings of Eddie (The Champ) Surma—"C'man, c'man, c'man, let's go, c'man, c'man, c'man"—the Sobies couldn't score in the bottom of the inning. After three years as world champions, the pride of Cicero had lost to their archrivals in the World Series of 16-inch softball.

There were some dark mutterings on the Sobie bench after the game. "Big John" Straley, a 250-pounder who can mash the mushball farther than almost anybody in the sport, pounded his big fist into the ground. And when Ed Zolna was named the Series' most valuable player, one of Sobie's rooters couldn't take it any longer. Charging across the first-base line, the tendons in his neck straining in outrage, he bellowed, "Why don't you name a nigger? Why don't you just do it up right and name a nigger?"

57

But there was no cause for alarm. The fan—like most players in the game—was over 30, with a beer belly straining under his shirt and a wife and children in the stands. For 16-inch softball—known as mushball or pillow-ball to distinguish it from the more common 12-inch variety—is a middle-aged, Midwestern sport like nothing played elsewhere in the country.

And, frankly, that was just fine with this spanking-clean green city of 50,000 on the sandy shore of Lake Michigan. For Sheboygan has had more than its share of disorder and dissension in the last decade and it could use a little middle-aged peace and quiet.

From 1954 through 1960, the city went through the marathon Kohler Company strike. One of the longest and bitterest in American history, it was marked by stoning, tire slashing, window breaking and other acts of violence. People here still talk of "Black Tuesday" (July 5, 1955) when rioting broke out over strikers' efforts to prevent the unloading of a shipload of clay for the plumbing ware company.

Then Sheboygan was hit by quite a different form of disorder. The annual Bratwurst Day, honoring the tiny spiced sausage for which this town is famed, was transformed from a purely local festival to a vast young people's brawl. College students from all over the country swarmed into town each August to down sausages and beer, sleep on beaches, and raise hell. Each year there were dozens of arrests for drunken and disorderly behavior and vandalism. Finally, in 1966, the city discontinued the festival.

Since then, Sheboygan has sorely needed some more controlled gaiety—and softball seemed to fit the bill nicely. This has always been an enthusiastic sports town. In the late 40s, it had a National Basketball League team. Until 1952 it had a Dodger farm club in the Class B Tri-State League; although it has never had a professional football team, the locals are fanatic rooters for the Green Bay Packers, only 60 miles to the north.

But softball is Sheboygan's big sport. There is a tradition here called the Sunday morning "Beer Game" in which teams play to see who will buy a half barrel of brew, which both then consume on the spot.

In a variation, a beer keg is placed on second base and each runner who gets that far must have a stein before moving on. "Kinda evens things out when the big sluggers start staggering up to the plate," explains Bob Keitel, a veteran of the game.

The main emphasis given softball in Sheboygan has been provided by the SNAFU Club, a group formed by six sports-conscious men after they returned from the war in 1945 (the club gets its name from the old World War II term for Army inefficiencies). Since then the club has grown to 35 men. It sponsors five softball teams in the city's four leagues, has won five state championships, and has been to six national tournaments.

Two years ago, SNAFU pulled off something of a coup in the softball world when it brought the National Women's Slow Pitch 12-inch tournament to Sheboygan. It is no secret that the club now has eyes set on the men's tournament—and many here feel a 16-inch series was a big step in that direction.

Sixteen-inch softball is not really a Wisconsin game. It developed in Chicago around the turn of the century, partly because the bigger, softer ball does not travel as far as the 12-inch and is well suited to the cramped lots and indoor halls where city kids play.

During the Depression, the game became big time in Chicago. A Windy City League was formed. It played some tournaments in Soldiers Field and boasted such legendary figures as Ted (Skeets) Skadell and Eggs Bromley.

But then the mobsters and gamblers moved in. Huge sums were bet on games, players were bribed to throw them. It is said that the sport got so crooked that at one game there were six of the country's 10 "most-wanted" men in the stands.

Since World War II, 16-inch has gone relatively straight. The sport is now regulated by the Amateur Softball Association, and 18 teams from eight Midwest states showed up here for the tournament that ended today.

The three-day tournament attracted about 2500 fans at two parks—fewer than would have showed up for a 12-inch tournament but not bad considering that the two pickup Sheboygan teams were eliminated the first day.

Some of Sheboygan's stars in 12-inch softball were openly contemptuous of mushball. "It's an old man's game," snorted Gene Ehlers, a 26-year-old outfielder for the SNAFU team.

Others laughed at the ethnic flavor of the visiting teams—overwhelmingly Polish, Italian, and Irish. "A big bunch of Polacks," said one beer salesman. Sheboygan is about 80 percent German (a recent SNAFU team boasted a "murderers' row" of Sauer, Ranniker, Schneider, Luecke and Erzen).

But old Middle European rivalries did not seem too important this afternoon with the sun shining brightly, the bratwurst sizzling over charcoal braziers behind homeplate, and plenty of foamy draft beer to wash it all down.

For residents of Johnson City, the loss is deeply personal

B. DRUMMOND AYRES JR.

Johnson City, Tex.
January 24, 1973

The people of Lyndon Johnson's hill country are taking his death as a personal loss.

He was their friend, neighbor, and comrade in the endless struggle against the tough, unyielding land that stretches across this part of central Texas. No matter how high he rose or how far he roamed, he always came back to the hill country, called its ranchers, housewives, and kids by their first names, then asked how he could help or invited them to a barbecue.

Just last Saturday night he dropped by the cafe in the nearby crossroads of Stonewall to pay Kermit Hahne for helping transplant some trees. He could have sent a check by mail or dispatched a Secret Service agent, but Lyndon Johnson never worked that way down here.

Two nights later he was dead. Mr. Hahne wept.

Late one afternoon a few weeks ago, Mrs. Howard Cravens turned from the soda fountain in the store at Burgs Corner to find the former President towering over her. He wanted an ice-cream cone.

"He was one of us, never forget it," she said.

She referred to him as "Lyndon." The word came out with all due respect, without a trace of glibness.

How will she remember him?

60

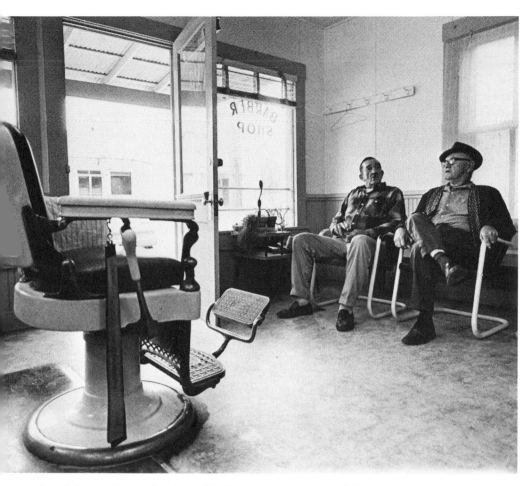

In a Johnson City barbershop, old friends reminisce about L.B.J.
NYT/MIKE LIEN

As an upthrust, waving arm, speeding past her flower garden in a sleek white Lincoln convertible, headed for the LBJ Ranch just down the road.

Mr. Johnson's mark is everywhere.

At the edge of Johnson City—it was named for his forebears—there is a huge sign, adorned by a bigger-than-life Stetson. It proclaims proudly:

"Home of Lyndon B. Johnson."

In the center of town is his boyhood home, a white frame structure with gingerbread trim that draws a steady stream of tourists.

Then there is the new post office. Everybody knows why Johnson City has a new post office.

Finally there is that road to the ranch, 15 rolling miles away—smooth, carefully landscaped, dotted with pleasant waysides—and, inevitably, the LBJ State Park across from the rambling white ranch house.

An outsider might wonder why a man of Mr. Johnson's stature ever came back to the Texas hill country, with its rocky ledges, dusty ravines, twisted mesquite, and gnarled live oaks locked in combat with the wind, sun, and a sterile yellow clay.

But the people who live here know why. They have been through it, and when Mr. Johnson left the easy, sophisticated comforts of the world beyond and returned to it, he won their hearts forever.

"It gets in your blood," said Stella Gliddon, editor of the *Record-Courier* of Johnson City.

"It was always in Lyndon's blood. He once told me that the happiest moments in his life were when he would start to reenter the hills en route back from Washington or wherever."

In *LBJ Country*, a guidebook about this part of Texas, Mr. Johnson himself wrote, "It is impossible to live on this land without being a part of it, without being shaped by its qualities."

Then, touching more precisely on the point, he continued:

"So this is our home. We take what we can from it—as our ancestors did. But like our ancestors, we always seem to have to give more than we take. And after a while, the act of giving becomes an act of respect and, finally, an act of love."

The LBJ Ranch testifies to that act of love. Mr. Johnson turned it into a showplace, fought with the soil until it would feed cattle, bent the Pedernales River to his will, beat the hill country at its own game.

In so doing, he could have inspired envy and covetousness. But in this part of Texas that kind of victory demands respect, nothing less.

Hunched over a gravy-smothered steak in the Danz Cafe, Jerome Liseman, an ice company operator, weighed that victory this afternoon and said:

"He showed us what could be done. We've lost a mighty good man."

To James Ealy Johnson, a first cousin of the former President, the worst thing about the loss was the fact that Mr. Johnson died only a day before a cease-fire in Vietnam was announced. A lanky man with Johnsonian crinkles and an angular Johnsonian nose, James Johnson sat in Johnson City's tiny barber shop this morning and reflected on his cousin, saying:

"Sometimes—though not very often—he would mention the war when we'd be driving around on the ranch. He wanted so badly to see it over, and he just missed.

"But those who go to sea have to go, and some never come back."

James Johnson said the war, the most controversial entry on the former President's long ledger of public life, was "an awfully difficult war." He added: "Hardly anybody understood it."

History will have to decide whether Lyndon Johnson did.

But some clue to what he thought in his own mind can be found in his 1968 State of the Union address, in which he spoke still again of "the land." He said:

"A President's hardest task is not to do what is right, but to know what is right. Yet the Presidency brings no special gift of prophecy or foresight. You take an oath, step into an office, and must help guide a great democracy. The answer was waiting for me in the land where I was born."

Tomorrow afternoon, in a little ranch cemetery hard by the banks of the Pedernales, under the spread of half a dozen gnarled live oaks, Lyndon Johnson will find eternal rest in that land.

Fading
America

Pearl Hutchinson and her tourist home

ANDREW H. MALCOLM

Geneseo, Ill.
August 10, 1972

Pearl Hutchinson's tourist home here has no computerized reservations service, no green glowing message lights, no ice machines, no plastic glasses, no chemically treated shoeshine rags, no vibrating beds, and no souvenir shop selling plastic ice cubes that entomb fake spiders.

Her guest house also has no air-conditioning, no carpeting, no telephones, no swimming pool, no television, and no food services.

In fact, nowadays Mrs. Hutchinson's tourist home has no tourists either.

"Everybody's so rich," said the 74-year-old widow, "who would want to stay at a crummy old house like mine?"

The answer, of course, is very few. Faced with modern competition and tastes, Mrs. Hutchinson's plain, two-story white house at 718 South Oakwood Avenue, and hundreds of other guest homes that sprang up along the nation's highways in the 1930s and 1940s, are steadily dying off, along with their aged proprietors.

Overlooked by speeding sightseers, neglected by comfort-conscious, affluent automobilists, the tourist home is going the way of other old American roadside institutions like the Burma Shave signs or the two-lane intercity highway.

With the exception of some homes in established resort areas, the ranks of the nation's guest homes are dwindling so fast no one even keeps track of them any more.

Mrs. Pearl Hutchinson and her tourist home. The main highway—and time—has passed them by.
NYT/GARY SETTLE

"Motel" is the name of the game today for America's highly mobile population, a population especially on the move in this peak vacation month.

To serve such travelers, there are now more than 52,000 motels in the country with about 2.29 million rooms, an increase of about 500,000 in 10 years. Holiday Inns alone opens a new motel every 72 hours.

The tourists still pass by Geneseo—right by. And if they do stop, it's not in town on old U.S. 6. It's out at the 10-year-old Interstate 80 interchange where they can choose from three modern motels, their giant neon signs drawing travelers like Mrs. Hutchinson's porch lights draw moths.

But in town, just a mile beyond the nearest motel between East Chestnut and East Locust Streets, there's a little lighted lawn sign lovingly taped together by shaking hands.

Mrs. Hutchinson opened her comfortable, immaculate home to weary travelers back in 1939 when the idea of a $9-billion motel industry and a nationwide system of four-lane highways would have made a good Flash Gordon serial.

They were good years then. Almost every night Mrs. Hutchinson's home was full—both rooms upstairs and another one downstairs. And down the street three other ladies rented tourist rooms, and Oscar Drayman next door did, too.

Even after World War II, when the motels started to blossom, business was good. Of course, more people went to motels then, but the overflow always filled the tourist rooms.

However, now the local motels have added restaurants and bars and buffets and dozens of new rooms. One motel here even boards travelers' horses and another offers free breakfasts. So business is very bad at Pearl Hutchinson's tourist home.

It's been more than three weeks since anyone stayed at Mrs. Hutchinson's, now the only tourist home in this town of 5800 and the first one on Route 6 west of Chicago, 160 miles away. In fact, so far this year only six persons have stayed at Mrs. Hutchinson's.

It is a quiet house, one Mrs. Hutchinson's grandfather bought more than 80 years ago. The floors are covered with flowered linoleum. The narrow stairway is solid. Each of the two upstairs bedrooms is furnished with a bed, a chair, and a bare light bulb in a wall socket. The white lace curtains move slowly in an occasional August breeze.

A 1969 calendar hangs on the wall next to a faded poem that says:

> Our Home is just a stopping place
> For Friends who come this way.
> We're glad to see each smiling face,
> And wish they ALL might STAY.

The bathtub down the hall, the one with giant knobs that still say "Hot" and "Cold," may be the biggest tub this side of Moline.

A crib and folded cot stand ready, but unused, in the hall while the soft twin beds are the kind that absorb a sleeper between their crisp white sheets.

"The ceiling may be cracked," says Mrs. Hutchinson, "but, by golly, my house is clean."

Mrs. Hutchinson says the older she gets the bigger her backyard seems. These days it is almost overflowing with bright orange tiger lilies, but those two giant elm trees, the ones Mrs. Hutchinson planted as twigs when she was a girl, are slowly dying. "I can't afford to get them trimmed, not on Social Security," she says.

She also cannot afford a daily or weekly newspaper, so in her abundant spare time Mrs. Hutchinson sits on the front porch and sews clothing for the dolls she makes or watches the traffic move slowly by.

"Time was," she recalls, "when the cars were just packed out there. You know old Route 6 was the main east-west highway in these parts."

Now it's just a bumpy two-lane local road that links Geneseo with such towns as Atkinson, Annawan, and Sheffield in this corn-producing area. Route 6 is used regularly only by farmers or overloaded trucks dodging the state scales.

"Look at all those campers," Mrs. Hutchinson says. "They don't do my business any good. But I can't blame them. Who can afford to pay $20 a night to lodge a family? I charge $8 for a family, and I don't think that's out of line."

Mrs. Hutchinson awakens about 5 A.M. each day to tidy her home and work on her dolls and wait for customers. About 5 P.M. she turns on her sign, "Tourist Rooms," and sits on the porch.

She stays close to home every day. "Maybe someone will stop," she says. There used to be a few regular customers, but they were elderly and have not been here in over a year. "I supposed they've passed on, too," Mrs. Hutchinson says.

Even when someone does stop, Mrs. Hutchinson seems startled and somewhat afraid. "These days you never know about people," she says. So she not so casually tells each guest she· is expecting her "companion" home any minute. There is no "companion."

As the evening wears on, the traffic on Route 6 dwindles even more. Occasionally a teen-ager guns his father's car past and Mrs. Hutchinson smiles. But no one stops.

At 10:20 the eastbound freight train rumbles through. Mrs. Hutchinson is still sewing. No one has stopped.

By 11 the "No Vacancy" signs are on at the motels down the road where the only sounds are the crickets and the whine of truck tires on the interstate.

Every so often Mrs. Hutchinson gets fed up with waiting. "I know one thing," she says, "this is the last summer I'm doing this. That's for sure!"

A few minutes later she muses, "You know if you haven't got something to look forward to, there's no point in living, is there?"

Then around 1 A.M. Mrs. Hutchinson closes up her old Singer sewing machine and prepares for bed. The last thing she does is turn off her sign, "Tourist Rooms." No one has stopped.

"Maybe tomorrow," she says, "maybe tomorrow."

Miles City mourns end of passenger trains

ROY REED

Miles City, Mont.
May 2, 1971

Casey Barthelmess, 80 years old, once a bronc buster and a cowpoke, shifted on his crutches outside the depot. He tried to sound uninterested in what had happened.

"I thought there might be a little excitement," he said, "but it was pretty quiet." His voice had betrayed him by going hoarse in mid-sentence.

He had just watched the coming and the going of the last passenger train through Miles City. As he spoke, the train could still be heard in the distance as it sped toward the end of the line at St. Paul.

It had been a quiet event, as Mr. Barthelmess said. But there was drama in it for the 10 or 12 who had come to the old brick station to say good-bye to 90 years of history.

The eastbound Mainstreeter from Seattle pulled into the dim Miles City station at 10:58 P.M., one hour and three minutes late. It came in like a funeral train, moving about five miles an hour, its bell seeming to toll rather than ring in the night chill.

The engineer stopped the train beside the worn brick platform, and one passenger, a middle-aged man, got off and walked quickly away.

Then two other men, a Montana editor and a companion, got on. Like hundreds of others they were taking a last ride to record, or just to feel, how

72

Casey Barthelmess, 80, watches the last train leave Miles City, Montana.
NYT/GARY SETTLE

it was the day the passenger trains stopped running in southern Montana and in many other places across the United States.

Miles City, a ranching center with a population of about 10,000 on the Burlington Northern line, is one of hundreds of towns and cities that are without passenger trains since the National Railroad Passenger Corporation, or Amtrak, took over all railroad passenger trains this weekend.

In theory, service will improve in the towns that are left with service because of the savings from not having to serve the unprofitable places that have been cut off.

Such places as Harper's Ferry, W.Va., Barnesville, Ga., and Dothan, Ala., are in the same predicament as Miles City, Glendive, Missoula, Forsyth, Billings and Bozeman, Mont. They are all without passenger trains, most of them for the first time since the beginning of the railroads.

The people of Miles City are not simply saddened by the loss of passenger service. They are angered.

Many regard it as another doubtful step in the march of civilization, on a par with the slaughter of the buffaloes and the pollution of the Yellowstone River, which runs past Miles City.

Some even compare it to the passing of open prostitution. A zealous county attorney closed the bawdyhouses here four years ago.

The loss of passenger trains is especially painful to those old enough to remember how good the service once was.

Carter Snell, an 86-year-old retired rancher and wool buyer, said he and his family used to ride the train from Miles City to their ranch 20 miles away and the train would let them off there.

"The trains stopped anywhere you wanted them to, by God, in those days," he said.

Miles City has had only two daily passenger trains east and two west for several years. Many here admit that they have not used the trains much since the coming of good highways and easy automobile travel. But they still resent having the trains taken off.

Part of the resentment is peculiar to the western states. The Federal Government gave the railroads large tracts of land in the 19th century to induce them to extend their lines into the undeveloped areas of the West.

The Burlington Northern still owns 1,439,137 acres in Montana, most of it valuable for ranching, oil, and coal. These holdings stir deep animosity among many people.

Half a dozen men sat drinking at the bar of the Golden Spur yesterday afternoon. "Damn it," said an automobile dealer wearing a Stetson and cowboy boots, "if the railroad is not going to run passenger trains, then I say let's make them give back the land and oil and coal we gave them."

Many who have continued to ride the trains here are older people or those with illnesses that require attention in Minneapolis or Seattle. They either fear flying or find it too expensive. And they are uncomfortable on buses.

Mrs. Emily Robinson, 78, has to go to Minneapolis at least once a year for medical attention. She has always gone on the train and she thinks it is a "crime" that the trains have stopped.

"I'll use the plane now," she said. "I don't think I could sit on a bus for 24 hours."

Some will not be able to afford airplanes. Frontier Airlines charges $22 to fly from here to Billings, 145 miles away. The train fare was $6. It costs $5.65 on the bus.

A coach seat on the train from Miles City to Minneapolis cost only $25.75.

Despite the emotional wrench of losing the trains, not many people here went to the station last night to mourn the Mainstreeter's last trip.

It was a Saturday night, much like any other here; 200 or 300 went to the Elks Club for the annual fiddler's contest, and several hundred other men and women crowded the bars and cafes on Main Street and ate, drank, and danced.

But memory or sentiment edged aside the frolic here and there.

Casey Barthelmess left the fiddler's contest early to pay his respects to the trains. Bill Dunn, the postmaster, whose father was an engineer, came and looked on unsmiling with his hands in his pockets. Mrs. Patricia Birdwell and her son Brian rode double on a bicycle to come to the station.

The mourners drifted away as the rumble of the Mainstreeter died in the east. All except Casey Barthelmess. He stayed awhile, slumped on his crutches, and talked of playing on the railroad tracks when he was a boy, and of riding free on the freight cars, and of the day a man was run over by a train.

Finally, the old man tired of talking and the railroad station became the quietest place in town.

Once-booming potato farms die in Maine

BILL KOVACH

Presque Isle, Me.
July 29, 1971

The road to Ralph Smith's farm cuts across rolling hills that his great-grand-father cleared for farming after the Civil War.

At each bend in the gravel road there is some mark of the four generations of Smiths who have farmed the red loam of Aroostook County: "There's where Great-Grampy built the first frame house around here." "Grampy built that pond there using rocks culled from the fields."

At the end the road makes a little fishhook into the yard in front of Ralph Smith's comfortable frame house. Behind the house there are 150 acres of weeds.

"One day," he says quietly, waving toward the fields, "there comes a spring when you can't go any further. You wake up and you're not a farmer any-more."

That spring came this year for Ralph Smith, after 32 years of growing Katahdins, Russet Burbanks, and Kennebecs, the Maine potatoes that once dominated the American potato market. Five straight years of bad weather, poor yields, and low prices have left him and many others here smothered in debt.

When he was unable to make the minimum payments required on Government mortgages, Mr. Smith's equipment was taken by the Farmers' Home

Ralph Smith's farm implements, because he could not run his operations at a deficit, are sold at auction to pay his debts.
NYT/BILL KOVACH

Administration and sold at public auction. When taxes and insurance came due on his house in the fall, he says, he will leave that too.

In the same way all across Aroostook County, Maine's largest and northernmost, families who have dug potatoes from the earth for generations are being squeezed out by changing patterns in agriculture. So far this year there have been five major auctions, the end of an estimated 200 farming families.

Aroostook County, never wealthy except in the days when self-contained farms were the dream of young families, has plunged deep into a depression in the last decade.

The county has lost almost 2500 farm units over 30 years. Most experts agree that many of the remaining 1300 will not remain long on the land. There are 17,000 people—20 percent of the total population—receiving surplus food. Unemployment is set at 12 percent and the young are leaving the county rapidly.

Aroostook's story is one of a traditional single-product economy being swept away by an ever-changing national economy. Aroostook, which produces 95 percent of the Maine potatoes, is now only one small piece in that section of agriculture it once dominated.

"We get the blame for all this, but that just isn't right," complains Cluny McPherson, a local official of the F.H.A. Mr. McPherson approaches discussions of potato farmers' troubles with the caution of a man building houses of cards. As failures mount and F.H.A. foreclosures generate frequent auctions, the confused and frustrated anger of the farmers focuses more and more on Federal programs.

"We get the blame," says Mr. McPherson again, "but the problem is basically one of supply and demand. Prices are down because reclaimed land in the West is going more and more into potatoes. A farmer needs a good year every year and they've had a terrible run of luck here for the past five years."

To bad weather and prices, other students of the economic blight of the Maine potato farmer add several other factors: the land has been worn out and production has dropped from 150 barrels per acre to 135; Idaho, which now overwhelms the market, has a better growing season and a more aggressive sales and promotion program; the growth of large chain stores has created marketing problems.

There may be dozens of other factors, but they all move toward the same result, one manifested by Ralph Smith.

Mr. Smith began growing potatoes in high school as part of a Future Farmers of America project. In 1946, discharge from the Army in hand, he settled with his bride on 150 acres of the Smith homeplace and began raising potatoes and a family.

"It was 1965 that I had my last good year," he recalled recently. "Then everything began to fall apart."

With the reluctance of an independent man who, late in life, has begun to question his own ability and worth, Mr. Smith traces his plunge toward failure this way:

In 1966 prices were so low he held his crop until January, hoping for a better price. The gamble failed and he lost money. For the first time in his life he had to borrow money from the Government to plant a crop in 1967.

Nineteen-sixty-seven "was a bitch from the start." Rain during the fall harvest season kept machinery and hourly paid labor idle for three crucial days, and he sold his crop under an emergency Federal program for a price that did not even cover the harvest.

Nineteen-sixty-eight, 1969, and 1970 were much the same—borrowing to put out a crop and losing money at each harvest. By the end he was essentially sharecropping his land under a "crop and chattel mortgage" that put everything he once owned up against the chance of success.

"I've worked 16 to 18 hours a day on this farm since 1946," Mr. Smith said. "And now I'm 52. I've had three heart attacks. I've still got two children at home and two in college and I'm finished. I'm going to lose it all."

There is confusion in his voice and no little bitterness as he looks around the weed-grown field of his farm and asks: "Wouldn't it be better if they let me keep my equipment and keep farming—at least I could feed my family. It seems if the Government can vote money to help Lockheed, if they can bail out the Penn Central Railroad, they could let me go on farming."

At the auction the next day, Ralph Smith was joined by other farmers who have been forced out in recent years. In each case the story was the same—years of independence ended suddenly by changes they only vaguely understood.

"Look there," Mr. Smith called to a neighbor, "they just sold that truck for $1200. The body alone would cost more than that."

Then they fell to talking about what is going on—about auctions to sell their equipment at less than its worth just to "change some figures on a piece of paper" and to force them off the farms and into an uncertain and glutted labor market.

"It just seems like it would be better if they let me keep farming," Mr. Smith said to no one in particular. "It just doesn't make any sense."

Amid the sand of Nevada, a woman lives alone

EARL CALDWELL

Belmont,Nev.
August 27, 1969

She stood there in the dim kitchen light with a scowl on her face and peered out through the dusty screen door. "You know I just ran two fellows out of here," she said sharply. "That's right, I ran 'em outta here. They come nosing around here, digging into things and not asking anybody. I ran 'em off. These damn tourists."

Rose Walters was in a foul mood. "They go around calling this a ghost town," she continued. "They get that stuff out of those Western magazines. Well this is no ghost town. This was never a ghost town."

The old mining town sits there at the top of the canyon in the shadow of the Toquima Range, and it appears abandoned: The old red-brick courthouse, hollow and empty. The saloon, the old Auger-Hole Saloon, decayed and crumbling. And the dance hall across the street, almost gone.

Down the side of the canyon the jagged shells of the old buildings stick out in the twilight.

The old hotel and livery stable. The blacksmith's shop. The church and the hotel. And the old schoolhouse, now only a crumbling foundation.

Out on Main Street, the wind moves the sand and bounces the tumbleweed off the beaten buildings.

There are only two sounds: Up close, from the emptiness of the court-

80

house, the faint hoot of an owl. And from off in the distance, the rapid putt of a generator.

There is a splash of light down at the saloon. And another across Main Street in a gully, and there also is the light from Mrs. Walters's kitchen.

There are no telephones. No policemen. No firemen. Nothing.

Only Rose Walters. She is the only permanent resident of Belmont, the dirty little mining town tucked away in a quiet valley past miles of desert in central Nevada.

Mrs. Walters is a tall, tough woman with keen blue eyes and perfect white hair, neatly curled and covered with a thin net.

She likes to be abrupt.

"Now I don't like this asking my age," she snaps, acting offended. But she quickly adds: "I'm 76."

Over in Tonopah, about 50 miles away, they call Belmont "Rose Walters's town." She was born and raised out here. She will never leave.

"I'm happy here and happiness is what we're searching for. Isn't it?"

In the summer there are 10—sometimes as many as 20—people living here. The town has an elevation of 7500 feet, and they come here for the summer because it is cool.

But in the winter, Rose Walters is here alone.

Last winter she fell off a stool and broke her arm and had to drive more than 100 miles to get to a doctor. She fell early in the morning. It was dark before she got the arm set.

"Look at it. It's still not right," she said, dangling her right arm.

There is no television in Belmont, only radio. But Mrs. Walters keeps busy with her chores and reading, and she likes to go through what she has collected through the years: pictures, Indian arrowheads, pottery, glass. "My junk," she calls it.

Sometimes she drives to Tonopah for food and other supplies. And she has a son who looks in on her regularly. But mostly, friends drop things off that they think Mrs. Walters might need.

"We always drop in on her," Andrew Eason, one of the county officials from Tonopah said. In the winter they even send a snowplow out the 50 miles to keep the road to Belmont open.

Local papers in Nevada have written stories about her and the town, and tourists now are stopping in Belmont.

"Anymore we don't have much peace and quiet," Mrs. Walters says. "These damn tourists."

The town of Belmont came into being back in 1865 on a rich silver strike. So many people flocked to the town that in two years it was made the county seat of Nye County.

According to historians, the Belmont mining district, once known as Silver Bend, is credited with the production of more than $15 million from 1865 until 1885.

The deepest shaft in the district was reported at 500 feet, and some of the ore mined in Belmont ran $400 a ton.

The most prosperous periods were 1866–67 and 1873–74, at which time the population was about 1500.

But when the ore was gone, the people moved on. Now, there are only the buildings and the memories and the stories and Mrs. Walters.

There is the story of the lynching that took place in the basement of the Auger-Hole Saloon. The basement was used as the jail and, according to legend, two men suspected of being "Mollie Maguires"—members of an organization causing labor trouble by protesting the hiring of Cornish and Welsh miners in numbers exceeding the Irish workers—were to be hanged. But somehow, the rope was not set right and the hanging failed. In anger, the mob that came for the hanging reportedly beat and then shot the two men.

"You can still see the blood and the bullet holes down there," a visitor to Belmont who inspected the saloon said.

The old mining office still stands too. It was built by the mining company and sits at the top of Main Street. Today, it is Mrs. Walters's home. The building has never gone unoccupied, either as an office or residence.

And then there are the stories about the Cosmopolitan saloon and dance hall. "Oh that was the place," Mrs. Walters says with a twinkle in her eyes. "They had the dance hall out back, and they kept the girls upstairs. I hear they had some wild times around there."

On cool summer nights, Belmont is usually quiet. But not always. Since May, the saloon has been open.

"That's Billie Locke's place," as visitors call it. But the sign out front says: "Belmont Saloon." And a smaller sign in the window says, "Open."

Miss Locke came to Belmont a few weeks ago from Sacramento, Calif. "I had to get out of that rat race," she explained. Now, she says that she will stay on the year around, too. "Someone to keep Mrs. Walters company." She hopes to make ends meet with the saloon.

"I have beer, booze, soda, and snacks," she says. "I have mixed drinks and a gas pump too."

Why the gas?

"For the hunters. This will give them that much more range."

Inside the saloon, Miss Locke fingered the long bar. "It's the original bar from the Cosmopolitan up the street," she said.

It was getting late, and the bar was still empty. How long do you figure on staying open, Billie Locke was asked. "Until I run out of customers or get ready for bed," she said. "Whichever comes first."

Mysterious hill folk vanishing in the South

JON NORDHEIMER

Sneedville, Tenn.
August 10, 1971

It has been nearly a century since the first Melungeons walked out of the hills around Sneedville and mingled with the white farm families of the Clinch River Valley in East Tennessee.

Now only a few descendants of the swarthy mountaineers continue to live high up on the brow of Newman's Ridge or in the shadowy pocket of Snake Hollow. And they, like the others before them, are making plans to leave the security of the hills for other places.

"Most's gone now or dead," said one of the mountaineers, Monroe Collins, as he paused the other day at the edge of a hemlock grove that shades a crude Melungeon graveyard on the south slope of Newman's Ridge. Off in the distance, beyond the razorback ridges of Hancock County, were the taller peaks of North Carolina and Georgia, milky islands in the mid-summer haze.

The old man stood over a grave marker and scratched flakes of age from the peeling stone. Wild huckleberry tendrils curled around the marker and a half dozen others that were discernible in the rough field.

"The farmland's growing wild, just like the graveyard," Mr. Collins observed. "Young men'd rather work in a factory in Morristown than tend a patch of corn. To tell the dyin' truth, there's few of the old ridge people left."

Newman's Ridge overlooks Sneedville, a poor community of about 700

83

persons near the Virginia border. In the early nineteenth century nearly 350 Melungeons settled on the ridge, coming down into the valley only on rare occasions to forage for wild vegetables and sell moonshine whiskey. They lived apart from the whites for generations. The ridge was a hilltop sanctuary against the outside world and its prejudice.

The prejudice eventually vanished. And, to a degree, so have the Melungeons. Only 100 or so still live in the Clinch Valley, and many of them, like Mr. Collins, who is 65, are old and fretful about the future.

The South abounds with ethnic subgroups of dark-skinned people whose racial history is cloaked in mystery and sensitivity. Tradition usually ascribes an exotic beginning to the groups other than the simple cross-breedings of white pioneers with Indians and Negro slaves. Typically, members of the subgroups have feared that local whites would regard them as half-breeds or blacks. Traditionally, the white communities have not disappointed them.

Where the Melungeons differ from other subgroups like the Brassankles and Buckheads and Red Bones is the wealth of theories about their origin, none of which has been supplied by the Melungeons themselves. Years of isolation and illiteracy dulled their history, and today men like Monroe Collins are more concerned with the problems of the future than with the mysteries of the past, although the subject continues to excite scholars and romantics.

The recent assertion that a stone found in East Tennessee contained Hebraic lettering led to excited speculation that the Melungeons were a lost tribe of Israel. Other researchers believe that the Melungeons are descended from Phoenician sailors who fled the Roman sacking of Carthage.

The most popular theory is that the original Melungeons were survivors of the destruction of a Portuguese fleet dispatched in 1665 to capture Cuba from the Spanish. Two facts support this contention. The Afro-Portuguese word *melungo* means shipmate, and John Siever, the Tennessee explorer, wrote in 1784 that he found a dark-skinned people in Hancock County who were neither Indian nor Negro and who told him they were of Portuguese descent.

Yet there are no traces of the Portuguese language or of Portuguese social or religious traits among today's Melungeons or among those interviewed by John Siever nearly 200 years ago.

Another theory is that the first Melungeons were deserters from Ponce de Leon's exploration party that cut through the region in 1540 in search of gold. Still another is that they were the remnants of Sir Walter Raleigh's lost colony of Roanoke.

"A considerably less romantic theory," noted Henry R. Price, a Tennessee lawyer who has assembled research on the subject, "runs to the effect that the Melungeons are simply the result of miscegenation among the French, Spanish, and English outcasts who hung around the fringes of the early Virginia and North Carolina settlements, runaway Negro slaves, the Cherokee and Croatan Indians."

*High up on the brow of Newman's Ridge, Susy nestles against her grandfather,
Monroe Collins.*
NYT/KENNETH MURRAY

The French word for mixture, Mr. Price pointed out, is *mélange*.

Except for their dark skin, the Melungeons closely resemble their white neighbors in appearance and customs. Facial features, with some exceptions, are European-Caucasian. Eyes are brown, blue, or gray. Hair is usually straight and black, but there are Melungeons with sandy, blond, or brown hair.

For years Melungeons with fair skin have entered the white community and found social acceptance and success—as much success as was available to anyone in Hancock County, which is, by Government standards, the eighth poorest county in the nation.

Miss Martha Collins, whose father was a Melungeon (Collins is one of the principal family names in the colony), is the president of the only bank in Hancock County (total deposits stand at $3.5 million in a county of 7800 persons). At 76, she is gray-haired, fair-skinned, and blue-eyed. She said in an interview that nothing "hateful" had ever happened to her in Hancock County because of her background, but she was disappointed that she was unable to join the Daughters of the American Revolution 50 years ago despite her contention that her Melungeon forebears fought in the Revolutionary War.

For many years before the Civil War, Melungeons held an uncertain social status in Hancock County, somewhere between the whites and the 3000 black slaves. They were considered "free men of color" when they settled on Newman's Ridge in the early decades of the nineteenth century, and they enjoyed certain civil rights, but there was little social contact with the whites down in the valley.

After the Civil War, however, intermarriage became acceptable, usually the son of a white farmer taking a hill girl for his bride, and there were reports of Melungeon males abducting white girls from distant farms to take into the hills with them. Also, after the freed slaves left the county—only two or three black families live in the Sneedville area today—the local whites grew less anxious about skin pigmentation.

Intermarriage and the mobility of modern times have thinned the ranks of the Melungeons.

Taylor Collins, a man in his late 70s, is one of those who still lives in a tin-roofed house on Newman's Ridge. But at the end of this summer he and his wife are moving to Fort Wayne, Ind.

"Sold out to the doctor in town," Mr. Collins said as he greeted a visitor at the fence outside his house, which has an iron bedstead as a gate. He leaned on a crude sourwood cane that has a handle worn smooth with dependence and spat tobacco juice into the dust at his feet. "Can't go on living up here with no car and no way to get to town," he said in a voice quivering with age.

His wife appeared on the planked porch, next to an old abandoned washing machine. She was a tall woman, with flaxen hair, and she was very thin and looked terribly fragile.

"We were going to stay here and buy another farm," she said, "but I couldn't get the old man to agree. He worked in Indiana during the war, and it's the only place outside of here that he knows."

Later, Monroe Collins sat on the floorboards of his own porch and said he was sad to learn that Taylor Collins was leaving Hancock County. As he talked, he played with his 2-year-old granddaughter, Susy, who was busy chewing a huge plug of tobacco.

"It's a bad mistake," reflected Monroe Collins, stretching out the word "bad" for a full second to show the depth of his disapproval. "Folks can't live up on the ridge all their lives and then pick up and go to the city like that. They won't know what to do. There's no one to look after them. I wish they'd stay."

He stopped to let the little girl scamper outside to play with a scruffy pony that grazed next to a junked car.

"All the ridge people," he said, "have gone up from here and left, or else they're sleeping in their graves, and the ones that leave don't ever find their way back home no more."

At Warm Springs, happy days are gone

JAMES T. WOOTEN

Warm Springs, Ga.
April 12, 1970

A quarter-century ago today, Mrs. Ruth Stevens awoke long before dawn and began the long process of cooking an old-fashioned Southern dinner for the President of the United States.

But Franklin Delano Roosevelt died after lunch, and the glitter he had brought to the little village he had chosen as a retreat faded almost as fast as the succulent aroma of the barbecued pork and lamb he never got to eat.

"He went away and things were never the same," Mrs. Stevens, now 64 years old, said the other day as she reminisced about that 12th of April twenty-five years ago when, for the last time, Warm Springs was an international dateline.

Now a skeleton of its old self, the town is struggling for survival. Like so many small towns in America, its older citizens are dying, its young people are leaving, and tomorrows are not as bright as those promised by Mr. Roosevelt.

Mrs. Stevens, the curator of a museum at the Roosevelt Memorial, joined today with many of her 900 fellow citizens in Warm Springs in commemorative services at the modest white cottage where the President was stricken by a cerebral hemorrhage.

Although Mrs. Stevens saw many old friends in the course of the day, it was not a happy occasion for her. Mr. Roosevelt called her "the Duchess," and she does not like to talk about those days.

"People die and things go down," she said simply and sadly, and visitors here are quickly inclined to agree.

The President was attracted to Warm Springs because of its warm mineral waters, which he found helpful in his struggle with polio. He built a cottage on a hilltop here while he was Governor of New York and returned many times after he became President.

His biographers agree that friendships with Warm Springs citizens and the polio patients who followed him here, along with his observations of rural poverty in the area, were touchstones for many of the social-reform programs of the New Deal.

"This was really a buzzing place back then," Frank Allcorn, a 70-year-old widower who was mayor when Mr. Roosevelt died, recalled this week. "When he was here, things were always happening, business was good, and nobody worried about what came next."

But now, up and down the single main street, vacant stores are boarded up, few cars are seen, the restaurant at the old hotel has closed (leaving only one other in town), and freight trains roar through but rarely if ever stop.

The thousands of tourists who visit the Little White House and the Roosevelt Museum each year find little reason to linger in Warm Springs.

The strength of the town has always been its link with the past. Its tiny airport is named for Mr. Roosevelt. A beauty salon and a florist's shop bear the titles "White House," and a curio shop is filled with mementos of the years when the President would arrive in town with a host of Secret Service agents, reporters, Government officials and the greats and near-greats of that era.

There are ashtrays and plates and postcards and small framed portraits. But they are not enough, and Warm Springs, imitating dozens of other communities, is reaching even further into the past to attract people and dollars.

"I believe all that hammering and sawing down there is going to put us back on the map," Mrs. W. B. Persons predicted in her dark, musty antique shop, pointing toward workmen who are transforming her side of the main street into a nineteenth-century shopping district.

"They're going to call it Old Bullochsville after my stepfather," the 82-year-old widow said proudly. "They're going to have shoot-outs in the street and things like that, and then you can bet those people who come in to see the Little White House will hang around for a while."

"The main thing is money," said Dana R. Burt, the $60-a-year mayor, who runs a grocery across the street from Mrs. Persons's shop and offers his clientele a variety of merchandise including fox traps, fan belts, stick candy in large glass jars, and Barlow knives.

"This new thing ought to help us," he continued, glancing toward the nineteenth-century restoration. "I sure hope it does because we could use some help."

The cost of municipal living has caught up with Warm Springs. The year

Mr. Roosevelt died, the city budget was less than $7000. Now it is slightly more than $35,000, and each year's operation creates a larger deficit.

"If it wasn't for state money coming in, we'd be in worse shape than we are," said Mrs. Randolph Jones, the part-time city clerk.

The municipal water operation, built under Mr. Roosevelt's Work Projects Administration in the 1930s, provides some funds for the city. Business licenses, fines, and taxes produce a bit more. But the budget is tight and there are only two policemen, a single patrol car, and a fire truck operated by volunteers.

The Georgia Warm Springs Foundation, which Mr. Roosevelt helped organize, and the Georgia Rehabilitation Center are treatment centers for dozens of physically handicapped children and adults and they employ about 650 local residents. A fish hatchery, a county hospital, and the Roosevelt Memorial employ 100 more.

For all its international fame, Warm Springs has remained an essentially Southern community.

"We don't have any problems with our Negroes because we've never had any outside agitators," said Mrs. Persons, referring to the 400 Negroes who live in the outskirts of the town.

"Mrs. Roosevelt? Well, she was what you'd call a Negro lover, wasn't she?" Mrs. Persons said, raising an eyebrow. "Martin Luther King? He was a wolf in sheep's clothing. I can't understand how so many white people were duped by him."

Mrs. Persons, a college graduate, believes in white supremacy and is confident that other white people here agree. She thinks that Negroes are intellectually inferior to whites, that their morals are unquestionably low, and that they lack ambition and drive.

"That's just the way they are," she said, smiling benevolently. "But we love them as long as they keep their place."

An example of "their place" in Warm Springs is Mrs. Roosevelt Mullins's house. It is a crumbling shack with a loose-board porch and a spiggot in the front yard. She pays one-fifth of her monthly income to Joe Butts, a white grocer who owns her house and others in the area.

The running water available in the front yard, he believes, shows that "Negroes have come a long way."

Mrs. Allcorn, Mrs. Stevens, Mrs. Persons, and many other local residents have watched their village grow old and they all agree that with just a little effort, one can reach into the past for comfort and assurance.

"Seems like we just get out of one hole into another these days," Mrs. Stevens said. "No doubt in my mind that Warm Springs and the whole country would be better off if Mr. Roosevelt were still around."

Veterans of '98 War savor the old days

EARL CALDWELL

San Diego
September 11, 1969

"Showoffs," the thin little man at the end of the bar argued. "They're nothing but damn showoffs and professional patriots. They keep waving the flag. I hate 'em."

The bartender listened, frowned, and moved away.

"They're living in the past," the man continued. "Christ, this one guy was out there talking about charging up San Juan Hill. They lie so damn much. That's it, they're nothing but a bunch of liars."

It was near dinnertime and the bar, just off the lobby in the U.S. Grant Hotel, was almost empty. But that didn't make any difference. In his harsh voice, the little man kept on cussing the old men—the veterans—the Spanish-American War veterans who were out in the lobby in the midst of their seventy-first annual convention.

They are very old now. Most of them are hunched over, and when they come into the lobby, they lean heavily on their canes.

They come to the lobby wearing their baggy suits that are too long or too short, and they sit for hours. They sit wearing old veterans caps and they keep dozing. They sleep because there is nothing else for them to do.

But they are always eager to talk. "What do you want to ask me," they say. But even before the questions they reach into their pockets and pull out neatly folded newspaper clippings—proof that they are, in fact, veterans of the Spanish-American War.

Most of them are past 90 now but they still talk with enthusiasm in their voices. They talk of many things, but mostly it is of the old days: the war, training, Teddy Roosevelt, and San Juan Hill.

"Nope," said John F. Ebbe, "I'm not in favor of this. These young men afraid to join the Army. Afraid to face the bullet. That's what's wrong with these men now, they are afraid to face the bullet."

Mr. Ebbe, from Milwaukee, is 93 years old, but there is still a huskiness about him. It shows in his tough talk when he makes it clear that he cannot sympathize with the young men who now refuse to accept the draft.

Mr. Ebbe volunteered for service in 1898. "I spent 2 years and six months in the Philippines," he recalled. "I was in six different campaigns. Even had my horse shot out from under me."

He leaned against the wall and pulled a heavy wallet from his jacket. He was careful about unfolding a clipping. It was a picture of him and his wife. The article, "Mr. and Mrs. Old Milwaukee," listed his long war record. "You know I still belong to seven different veterans' organizations," he said.

Eighty-three of these old men came to San Diego from across the country to participate in the convention. A few have put on their old service uniforms. They all wear veterans' caps, and they have badges and buttons on their lapels that identify their old outfits.

All of them were volunteers and they are proud, even those of them who saw no service.

"The President called for us," some of them said in explaining their enlistments. "He asked for 100,000 volunteers and he had them in less than 30 days. And the best men you could pick."

There were other reasons. "The *Maine*. You know we lost 262 men when the *Maine* went down. There was a saying: 'Remember the *Maine*, the hell with Spain.' "

A few others remember it differently.

"Adventure. It wasn't patriotism. It didn't have a damn thing to do with patriotism. It was the excitement and the adventure."

William B. Heald sat off in a corner. His head kept dropping and, finally, he dozed off. When he woke up, the women who had sat watching teased him. "Sleepyhead," they called him and the old man blushed.

Mr. Heald, from Hartford, is 92, but he clearly recalls his enlistment in 1898.

"I lived in Jersey at the time," he said, "and went out in May with the first New Jersey regiment. We came back on Labor Day but we didn't get our discharges until February. You know the war only lasted four months."

It irks Mr. Heald that so few people remember the war. "I stopped some high-school kids and asked them about it," he said. "They told me that they had never even heard of it."

"What do I think about the draft-dodgers?" he asked. "About the same as I think about the hippies. I suppose that in my younger days we had some funny ideas but when you come up to this hippie stuff. . . . You know I was arrested in Hartford for belting one of 'em. He took a swing at me. I blocked it with a left and then drove a right into his belly. He went down."

William L. George leaned off his chair and talked in a whisper. "You know I wouldn't be here if it wasn't for Roosevelt," he said. "He gave me a full pardon. It's very seldom that I tell that," he said. "Very seldom."

He is a small, very thin man who said that he grew up on a horse ranch in Texas. "About 15 miles from Johnson's place," he said. He now lives in Pomona, Calif.

He is one of the three members of Pomona's Spanish-American War veterans' organization.

"Yep, ain't but three of us left," Mr. George said. "One died two weeks ago but we're going to keep on till the last man. Now, there's just Sherman Nash, myself, and John T. Evans."

He pulled out of a sheaf of clippings. One said that he had sailed with the Great White fleet, which it described as a convoy of 16 battleships sent around the world in 1907 by President Theodore Roosevelt to demonstrate United States strength.

"Not many people know about the White fleet now," Mr. George said.

He was asked about the pardon. "I had run off to Mexico with this girl," he began, "but when I couldn't find no work, she broke off from me. I came up to Kansas City and they picked me up . . . for being a hobo, I guess. They took me to Leavenworth. They gave me 18 months for desertion. They was taking me to the depot one day. . . ." He stopped and looked away. "Now what was I saying?" he asked. "You know my mind wanders sometimes now."

In the lobby the women sit together on the big couches. They sit all around the men. There are many more women.

"Oh yes," said Philip Steinman, "there are a lot more women. I guess they just live longer. Well, you know the men are older when they marry."

Mr. Steinman wore an old infantry hat that was too large. It was well down on his forehead. He is 93 and lives in a hotel in downtown San Diego.

"It's the same way down there, too," he continued. "I'd say that the women outnumber the men at least eight to one. And they got all these big bottoms and wiggle all over," he said with a wide grin.

A small group of Negro veterans sat alone in a hallway outside the lobby. John H. Allen, 92, who is a retired Boston postal employe, said that he was a regimental commissary sergeant in the Spanish-American War.

He said he had enlisted at the urging of his grammar-school teacher and that he had served in the Philippines. But the Negroes he sat with talked only of Cuba, San Juan Hill, and Teddy Roosevelt.

"When the other troops failed," said John T. Harris of Chicago, a descendant of the war veterans, "he [Roosevelt] rallied his black troops. He got his black boys and those boys went up the hill with Teddy Roosevelt and they took it.

"That was the Ninth and 10th Cavalry. Yes, sir, those were all colored troops, and most of these kids running around here today don't even know nothing about it. All they know is Vietnam. Shoot, colored troops have been fighting a long time. My grandfather fought on San Juan Hill. In fact, when Roosevelt fell off his horse, my grandfather helped him back on."

Anthony A. Kopke of Dundee, Mich., joked about his age. "I'm 39," he said, "but that's 39 in reverse. I'm the last living member of M Company. I've been pallbearer to most of the boys.

"We were in Cuba two and a half months and never fired a gun. The colonel told us that maybe we thought he had a yellow streak. 'But the truth of it is,' he said, 'is that there wasn't enough Spaniards to go around.'"

Wabash Cannon Ball to rumble no more

B. DRUMMOND AYRES JR.

St. Louis
April 27, 1971

Nothing went right from the start.

First, there was the cabdriver who said:

"To the where?"

"To the train station."

"The train station? Didn't know any of them still ran."

A few do—the Wabash Cannon Ball, for instance. But no longer can one listen to "the rumble and the roar," as the once popular song goes, "from the great Atlantic Ocean to the wild Pacific shore."

These days it squeaks and creaks between St. Louis and Detroit, a 10-hour, 490-mile, $24.25 journey across flat Illinois cornfields, around rolling Indiana hills, and through a dozen heartland towns with names like Litchfield and Williamsport and Delphi and, yes, Wabash.

And even this run, which a jet plane covers in 72 minutes for $39, is about to end. For the National Railroad Passenger Corporation is taking over the 300 or so passenger trains still operating in the United States, canceling a third of them—including the Cannon Ball—and trying to recapture the old pleasures of American rail transportation by injecting Federal funds and the latest operating, scheduling, and passenger-service techniques.

No porters wait in front of Union Station, a granite cathedral with stained-glass windows and marble floors, vestibules and corridors, public rooms, private rooms, an upstairs, a downstairs, a restaurant, even a hotel, all hung with fading yellow signs that read: "Closed."

95

The Wabash Cannon Ball, glorious now in name only, makes one of its final runs, clicking and clacking into oblivion.
NYT/GARY SETTLE

And so down, down, bags punishing knees, to the grimy hollowness where the journey begins and ends, to Track 14 and Norfolk & Western Train No. 304—the Wabash Cannon Ball.

She sits there, a gently hissing relic from the past in a place with a dubious future, one dirt-streaked diesel, one battered baggage car, two fading coaches. The engineer wears a baseball cap.

> *From the great Atlantic Ocean*
> *to the Wild Pacific shore,*
> *From sunny California*
> *to ice-bound Labrador*
>
> *She's mighty tall and handsome,*
> *She's known quite well by all,*
> *She's the 'boes accommodation*
> *On the Wabash Cannon Ball.*

It is 9:30 A.M., time to go.

"All aboaaarrrd!"

The conductor holds up his arm and urges latecomers to hurry, hurry. In the last 2 years, the Cannon Ball has arrived in Detroit on schedule only about a dozen times.

But this morning she gets off on schedule and the passengers—a dozen or so bound for Detroit, 30 or 40 more headed for intermediate stops—settle into the worn seats.

The scenery starts to slide past, slowly, very slowly; first the jumbled St. Louis freight yards, then the languid Mississippi, then the poverty of East St. Louis, then the checkerboard fields of mid-America, the new crops pushing up to greet the spring.

Now the Cannon Ball begins to pick up speed. Its wheels click and clack, and the ties and springs bump and thump, and the rhythm begins to rise, as if from deep within the old stone roadbed itself.

> *Listen to the jingle, the rumble*
> *and the roar*
> *As she glides along the woodlands,*
> *through hills and by the shore,*
> *Hear the mighty rush of the engine,*
> *hear those lonesome hoboes squall,*
> *While traveling through the jungle*
> *on the Wabash Cannon Ball.*

No one knows who first put the rhythm of the Cannon Ball to song, just as no one can remember and no record shows when or where the first Cannon Ball ran. It is not important. There have been as many versions of the song as there have been Cannon Balls.

What is important is that all the songs have the rhythm. And now, somewhere near Decatur, it is broken by a red signal light.

A grinding stop. Freight on the tracks ahead.

"A freight!" cries out Robert Broome, the brakeman, his mouth contorting in disgust. Then, loud enough for all to hear, he observes:

"I can remember when this train didn't stop for anything except passengers—and they had to be quick. Now we take second place to a freight. That tells you something about railroading today, doesn't it?"

> *This train, she runs to Memphis,*
>   *Mattoon and Mexico,*
> *She rolls through East St. Louis*
>   *and she never does it slow,*
> *As she flies through Colorado,*
>   *she gives an awful squall,*
> *They tell her by her whistle—*
>   *the Wabash Cannon Ball.*

The whistle blows, an inelegant diesel honk. The Cannon Ball begins to roll again, some 25 minutes behind schedule.

Start. Stop. Start. Stop.

Babies bawl. Passengers pace, seeking relief in the noise and rush between coaches.

And the towns, the towns, they come and go without end—Tolono, where several students get on, wondering how they will travel once the Cannon Ball is gone; Danville, where a train buff from California gets off, having beaten the April 30 deadline and lived a dream; Lafayette, where a father standing on the station platform holds up his son for a peek into one of the drab coaches.

Now Delphi, where Bob Broome orders the "special" from the tiny buffet— a $1.15 cheeseburger—and recalls the old days when the Cannon Ball pulled four baggage cars, four coaches, and a diner, and the special was a $5.25 Kansas City strip; Logansport, where the air-conditioning breaks down; Peru, where the buffet runs out of cold soft drinks; Wabash, where everybody takes to beer; Adrian, where the battery dies and the lights go out; Milan, where another freight takes precedence.

> *Listen to the jingle, the rumble*
>   *and the roar,*
> *As she glides along the woodlands,*
>   *through hills and by the shore,*
> *Hear the mighty rush of the engine,*
>   *hear those lonesome hoboes squall,*
> *While traveling through the jungle*
>   *on the Wabash Cannon Ball.*

The Wabash Cannon Ball, Norfolk & Western train No. 304, out of St. Louis and nearing the end of her run, finally arrived in Detroit at 9:18 P.M. Eastern time, 43 minutes late.

There were not enough taxis.

Federal aid rebuffed by Missouri town

DOUGLAS E. KNEELAND

Stoutsville, Mo.
May 2, 1973

If anyone went out hunting for towns that looked as if they could use a little help, Stoutsville would surely have to wind up pretty high on the list. This hamlet, tucked among the hardwood ridges and scrubby bottomland along Buck Creek, is about as down as a town can get. Situated in Mark Twain country, just off Highway 24 some 35 miles southwest of Hannibal and the Mississippi, it has watched more in resignation than in anger over most of the last 50 or so years as its population dwindled from over 600 to about 30.

At the end of March, Charles Dennison and his wife, Thelma, closed their small grocery store, the last remaining store on what was once a thriving Main Street, leaving only the tiny village post office open in a sad row of derelict buildings. In May or June, that, too, will move to new quarters near the highway, where Mr. Dennison, who has been postmaster since 1955, says, "I'm kind of looking forward to getting where the cars whiz by."

But despite its kicked-hound-dog appearance, Stoutsville has won some attention by becoming one of the few communities in the country to send back to Washington the revenue-sharing funds that had been passed on to it by the Federal Government.

Not only that, in a letter accompanying the $222 check that was returned, Mayor William A. Moutray and the Town Board snapped back hard at their would-be benefactors in the nation's capital.

99

"The Federal money has strings attached," they wrote. "Strings are for puppets, and we are not puppets, nor do we have any freedom for sale. Thanks a lot, but no thanks."

That wasn't all the letter said. More than just rural pride and a mistrust of big government were eating away at Stoutsville's angry town fathers.

"We have had the United States Government in our town for the past three years, trying to abolish it," they wrote in cryptic explanation of their refusal to participate in revenue sharing.

Actually, while Stoutsville's long decline is reminiscent of the fate of hundreds of small towns in the backwaters of America that have been largely by-passed by the onrushing twentieth-century, the people here have a special gripe.

They may have accepted with country stoicism the decades of deterioration of their way of life that carried them to the edge of the precipice, but in the last few years most of those who have clung to their shrinking village have become convinced that no one less than the Federal Government was trying to push them over the edge.

At his home on a hill, about a mile by a meandering, rutted dirt road from the center of town, Mayor Moutray, a graying 48-year-old farmer with eight children and a yard full of bantam roosters and dogs of uncertain ancestry, is quick to point the finger of blame.

"The Army Corps of Engineers is building a lake here, and it's in farming country and I don't think it helps," he complained, "but they're trying to do away with the town."

When the lake is finished, he charged, the town will be divided into three parts, and the engineers refuse to put in roads that would provide easy access from one to the other.

"Us and the people who live up the road in this part of the town, we're going to have to drive five to seven miles to get to the other part of town," said the Mayor, who has been fighting the project since 1964. "They're doing it for spite. We're so fed up, we don't want any more Federal money. We've seen how they come in here and tell you what to do."

The Corps of Engineers has begun the stages of construction of the Clarence Cannon Dam about 15 miles southeast of Stoutsville on the North Fork of the Salt River. At its scheduled completion in 1978, the dam's 21-mile-long reservoir would at the "top of flood control pool"—as the engineers put it—leave much of the town under water.

Since they began acquiring land for the project in 1966, the engineers have taken over by negotiation or condemnation about three-fourths of the 40 or so homes that remained in Stoutsville. The rest are on high ground that will not be affected by the reservoir.

Most of the small frame houses purchased by the Government have already been vacated, lending a ghostly mood to the whole town that matches that of its abandoned Main Street.

The people of Stoutsville didn't always have to go up to Highway 24 to watch the traffic. Until the 1930s, old Highway 10 was the main road, and it ran right through the business district. Besides, in the old days, when it was known as the biggest livestock-loading center between Hannibal and Moberly, there were plently of trains huffing and puffing through the draws into town.

Stoutsville was founded 102 years ago, and until the 1920s, at least, it was an up-and-coming place. Any old-timer around will recall when it was bigger than its neighbor 13 miles to the northeast, Monroe City, which now has a population of about 2500.

Otto Loutenschlager, 63, a former Mayor and current member of the Town Board, who was born in the house where he still lives, next door to Mayor Moutray, remembers better times.

"It was a busy place," said Mr. Loutenschlager, a short, gray, paunchy man in striped overalls who describes himself as "more or less retired," but who does some electrical and television repair work.

"We had rock quarry," he recollected, "an ax-handle factory, and a pottery factory at one time. And two banks and three blacksmith shops, here in town.

"You take from about 1910 to about 1920, there were two rows of buildings right there in town, and on the south side they were mostly two-story buildings."

Once there were four churches in town, he remembered, and lodges such as the Odd Fellows and Woodmen and a two-story hotel, the Valley House.

"They had moving picture shows over here for years," he went on, eagerly. "We like to say that they had anything you could think of at one time, like any other town."

Fires from the early 1900s on down to the late 1940s destroyed many of the business buildings, even some of those made of locally quarried stone to replace the old frame ones. The Depression closed the banks in the 1930s.

About the same time trucks replaced the railroad as the principal haulers of livestock.

Now, not much is left. Stone hulks on most of the north side of the old main street, which, like all the other streets in town, except for a 300-foot road up to the cemetery, is still unpaved. Nothing on the south side, where the Norfolk & Western tracks were raised years ago to a higher embankment. A rusted-out windmill at one end of the street towering over the stagnant rainwater still collected by the old cement trough where farmers once watered their horses.

"It makes you sick to go to town and see it," Mr. Loutenschlager said sadly, "knowing what it was before and what it is now."

Evolving America

NYT/Gary Settle

New life for young in old mining town

JOHN KIFNER

Ward, Colo.
August 18, 1971

The showy fleabane is purple along the edges of the road and the dirt lanes, and harebells add patches of blue, but it is time to get ready for the long Rocky Mountain winter now, to chop wood, lay in coal for the cast-iron stoves, and fill the chinks in walls of the cabins and houses of this once-bustling mining camp.

The other day the Doc was up on the roof of his log cabin, built in the 1880s, stripping off the old rusty tin sheeting and discovering among the rotting eaves the dry bodies of two perfectly preserved pack rats and parts of their hoard—three corncob pipes, a safety razor, and one-half of a large plastic set of dice.

When scraps of board and plywood were nailed in place, and asphalt shingling and cedar shakes were tacked over them, one of the neighbors dropped by, and it was generally agreed that the repaired roof was "far out."

The Doc is a 32-year-old Harvard graduate who did his medical training at New York University and now prefers to prescribe teas and herbs from a health-food store and would like to deliver a baby in the meadow outside his house.

He is one of a group of young people who now make up most of the permanent population of about 50 in this old mining town perched 9450 feet up on the front range of the Rockies northwest of Boulder; a town that

105

a few years ago turned out its nine qualified voters to elect the seven town officials necessary to retain incorporated status.

They are in their twenties and early thirties, many of them veterans of some form of radical politics or alternative culture, and they are trying to build themselves a new life-style and return to the sense of community of small pioneer towns.

Young people like them have also moved into the canyons and abandoned mining towns in the mountains around here, and others farm in the Connecticut River Valley of Massachusetts and the mountains of Vermont and California in similar experiments of escape from contemporary America.

But in the last few weeks, this little town has become the object of controversy. Some of the tension seems to spring from the fears of older people who own vacation homes in the mountains; some from the actions of some of the bands of young people wandering through or setting up camps in the forest.

The Boulder County sheriff's office has been carrying out a series of raids on the mountain communities, in one four-day period arresting 104 people, many of them youthful hitchhikers.

Some observers, noting that the new sheriff, Brad Leach, a Democrat in a Republican area, has spent 72.1 percent of his annual budget in his first six months, suggest that the raids are a political move to gain support and increased funds.

Because of the sheriff's actions, the town has suddenly become a media attraction, with reporters from Los Angeles, Washington, and New York papers and from two television networks and an independent film company from New York prowling the streets and asking questions.

The rapid influx has left the residents somewhat bemused. They are reluctant to talk to strangers, fearful that any publicity will merely increase the flow of wandering young people—already heavy this summer—and ruin their attempts to build a community.

"We don't want to become Stop No. 5 on the hippie tour," one young woman said, and another resident added, "I guess we've become actually sort of conservative. We want to protect what we have."

The town takes its name from Calvin Ward, who made the first strike of sulphide gold at his "miser's dream" claim in 1858. The Columbia vein, which produced $5 million, was discovered that same year by Sy Deardoff, and the area became the greatest gold-producing camp in northern Colorado.

In its heyday, the town housed 2000 men, women, and children, had three "first-class hotels," several saloons, churches, a brass band, and fraternal societies.

The Colorado and Northwestern Railroad ran a twisting, narrow-gauge line into Ward in 1897, and the event was marked by great celebration, including, *The Rocky Mountain News* noted, "more flags than would be required by an ordinary navy."

A fire in Mrs. McCloskey's two-story boarding house in 1900 spread rapidly through the city and destroyed 54 buildings.

The boomtown had other tempests. The local newspaper, *The Ward Miner*, appeared late in the week of July 20, 1900, "minus local news, etc.," because the editor, a Mr. Burgess, left Ward "in an intoxicated condition," bounced several checks in Boulder, and "was last seen in Denver in the company of a lewd woman," according to the paper.

"Said Burgess has proved himself a cheapskate," the paper continued. "He was well recommended to us, but his downfall comes from his love of whiskey and bad women."

Now the town stretches down a hillside, terraced by dirt roads. There are a few varnished log cabins owned by summer residents, the boarded-up Columbian Hotel and the Odd Fellows Hall, and small frame or log houses of the new and old permanent residents.

Dogs, small children, and occasionally horses wander about, and old cars and trucks rust by the sides of the road. There are four showers in town, two of which are generally available.

Most of the young people get by on part-time or short-term jobs, some receive welfare payments or food stamps, and they help each other work on their cars and houses. They man the volunteer fire department, hold town meetings, rehearse their band, and try to learn the skills that will help them survive in the mountains. The Women's Group has been working on plans for a day-care center, and there has been talk of starting a school.

The old railroad depot is now a cafe that serves as a social center for much of Ward. It is almost always crowded, with a table or two of tourists in clean white tennis shoes and vacation hats at this time of year among the bearded young men wearing hunting knives.

"When you lay in pipe," one of the bearded young men asked another, "is it gravel, pipe gravel? Where does the plastic sheet go?"

Beaufort, S.C., loves Frazier . . . now

DAVE ANDERSON

Beaufort, S.C.
April 10, 1971

Eleven years ago, with perhaps $200 in his pocket, Joe Frazier got on a Greyhound bus here for New York and moved to Philadelphia soon after that. He returned last week as the world heavyweight champion and as a millionaire, arriving with his wife and five children in two Cadillacs, a maroon 1971 limousine and a bronze 1970 coupe.

He was honored today at the city hall, with a church bell pealing on the hour through the magnolias and palmettos surrounding the old white antebellum homes.

Settled in 1562 by French Huguenots, this city of about 12,000 has worked at retaining its look of a century ago after the War Between the States, as it's described here. Inside those old homes, there is old money. Elsewhere, inside the shacks, there is poverty.

"But times have changed," a prosperous white resident acknowledged. "Our schools and hospitals are integrated."

In almost the same breath, the prosperous white snapped that "we just don't want any nigger leaders in here." And in an ironic loyalty to Beaufort's conqueror of Muhammad Ali, an elderly white man was overheard saying:

"Joe must've given that nigger some beating."

But to some, the 27-year-old champion's achievement in winning the title on March 8 was incidental to his fee of $2.5 million.

108

"Joe made two million and a half dollars," a white man said in wonderment. "For only 45 minutes' work."

As a youngster here, he earned 15 cents a crate picking vegetables, but he had returned to select a home site for his mother and to plan an integrated recreation center.

"I got Momma down here," he was saying a few days ago. "That's why I come back."

Two of his three sisters live here and one of his six brothers. The others have scattered.

"But if I didn't have a reason like Momma down here, I might not come back. You got some damn people ain't ever gonna change. Those that don't want to change won't ever change. Tryin' to keep each other down, worryin' about who lives next door. That's out, man. That shouldn't ever been. But let them do what they want to do. I'm going to do what I want to do as long as I don't hurt anybody. But don't hurt me."

Now, from the back of his maroon Cadillac limousine, he told Tom Payne, his bodyguard and driver, to turn off Route 21 toward a dirty white cement building among the drooping Spanish moss trees.

On the building was a sign, "Trask and Sons, Fancy Vegetables," and as the big car rolled to a stop in the dirt yard, Harold (Beanie) Trask, appeared. Whitehaired, with a leathery neck and brown boots, he owns several thousand acres of vegetable farmland here in South Carolina's lower coastal corner. He also owns other acreage for real estate development.

"He owns the land where Momma wants her new house," Frazier said. "We're gonna look at it."

When the champion, in his beige suit and striped turtleneck shirt, emerged from the big car, Trask smiled.

"Nice to see you, Joe, congratulations," he said. "Your brother Bozo was the fastest radish packer we ever had."

The champion smiled. As a youngster here, he had worked in the vegetable fields with his father.

"But you never got me," he said. "Daddy and myself worked for the Bellamys, but Momma worked for you. Momma worked all over the place. Hey, here she is now."

Tall and erect, with a firm step and a firm voice, the champion's mother had arrived with his sister Julia.

"Dolly Frazier," his 62-year-old mother said, announcing herself. "The mother of the champ, how sweet it is."

Trask had been calling over his help, white and black, inside his vegetable-packing plant to shake hands with the champion, but now he turned to Mrs. Frazier.

"You once worked for me on the island, didn't you?"

"I used to go over on a boat," she said. "You can't hide me. I remember all those turnip fields. Dolly helped make those turnips and then Dolly helped eat 'em as well."

"That's what made Joe champion, eating all those good Trask vegetables," the owner said.

"I can't hardly eat no cooked vegetables," the champion said. "Eat 'em raw, man, that's good energy."

"Well, let's get going," his mother said. "Let's take a look at that land, let's see it."

They rode in Trask's white Cadillac sedan to a paved road between uncleared pine woods. The champion has promised to pay for a new home for his mother, and she has selected this site.

"Four lots right here," Trask explained, "at $1500 a lot, that's a good price."

"I didn't think it was that expensive down here," Frazier said. "That's high."

"It's not high, there's no more land around here," Trask said. "But because you're Joe Frazier, I'll give you four lots for the price of three. Or if you want more than twice as much property, from the corner down to that bend there, it's $3000 an acre, and I'll sell you four acres for $9000. I'll sell you three acres and give you an extra one for free. That's a good deal."

The champion peered at Trask, his thrusted jaw snapping from side to side as it always does when he's tense.

"It's up to Mom," he said, glancing at his mother, who was silent. "If she wants the land, she can have it, but it seems expensive for out here."

"It's not," Trask said. "That land on the highway is worth $100,000 a lot now. Where the Burger King is cost $50,000."

"Let my Momma sleep on this thing," Frazier said. "If she wants it, she can have it, but let her sleep on it for awhile."

"You ought to buy the whole tract here, both sides of the road," Trask said. "I guarantee you'll double your money in a year and a half with it. That's what you ought to do with all your money, Joe, put it in land or blue-chip stocks."

The discussion over, the champion escorted his mother toward his maroon limousine for the short ride to her home.

"It's nice high land," his mother said in the car. "No swamps. And we owe him first choice for showing it to us."

"You say give him first choice, Momma," the champion said, "but he can't be first choice if he don't give the right price. He ain't giving you nothing, he's selling it to you. He ain't giving you nothing at all."

Soon the big car turned into the gray sandy yard in front of his mother's shingled home between drooping moss trees. Two junked cars sprawled near a tree to which a goat was tied. About 100 chickens roamed freely.

"Walk into this palace," his mother beckoned, hurrying up the old steps, "said the spider to the fly."

Inside, a framed color photo of John F. Kennedy hung prominently across from a copy of the Lord's Prayer inscribed on a small plate. On another wall was a bronze plaque from the Bright Hope Baptist Church in Philadelphia, honoring the 1964 Olympic heavyweight gold-medal winner. And there was a framed enlarged snapshot of a powerful looking man in a mackinaw jacket, with an empty left sleeve.

"Daddy lost his arm in a car accident, I think, before I was born," the champion explained. "I was his left arm."

As a youngster, he had helped steady a saw for his father. Or if his father was using a hammer, he'd hold the nail.

"He built this house for us, with only one arm he built this house," the champion said. "But he died in 1965 of cancer."

But as he slumped in a blue stuffed chair across from an old piano, Joe Frazier reflected on the land negotiations.

"He's talking that white talk," the champion said, alluding to Trask's conversation. "He was saying that he wouldn't mind if I came over to his house for a cup of coffee. And tell me that I could come back down and live. I'll forgive, but I'll never forget."

In one of the five small bedrooms, there was a TV set, but when he was growing up, his family didn't have one.

"Some of the neighbors did," he said. "I used to watch 'Fights of the Century' on it—Joe Louis, he was great. And sometimes I'd watch live fights—Sugar Ray, Hurricane Jackson, Floyd Patterson, I remember them. I listened to fights on the radio, too. And outside I made a punching bag out of canvas and stuffed it with moss from the trees. I'd stay out there hours at a time."

"Had a little trouble getting him to work when he was punching that bag," his mother said.

"Joe Louis was my idol," the champion said. "Down in the South, the black goes for the black."

But he was working at the age of seven, when he learned to drive a car and later a tractor.

"I quit school after ninth grade, I wasn't learning anything, I was just there taking space. I had a mind of a man early. You name it—outlook, girls, bread. I was chasing girls when I was 13, I was married at 16. When I was in school, I'd go into class and look at the teacher's legs."

Shortly after settling in Philadelphia, he married his childhood sweetheart, Florence, now the mother of their five children.

"Money was the thing, man," he said. "How the hell you gonna live without money? How the hell you gonna do anything?"

Suddenly, as if he were a small boy, he slapped his hand over his mouth, wondering if his strict Baptist mother had heard.

"But money was the thing," he resumed. "I always wanted a new car and pretty clothes. Now I got five cars, the two Cadillacs and three Chevies, including a '34, and I got a lot of pretty clothes. When you get the first car you want another new car, so you work just a little harder. Then you want a bigger house, so you work for that. I live on a challenge basis, life is a challenge.

"My next challenge is getting a hit record out," he said, referring to his career as a rock singer. "I'm just hoping it don't take too long, but maybe it's good if it do because then I won't have another challenge right away. When I got the challenge, I got something to occupy me. The challenge, you got to have that. But fighting to me is no longer a challenge like it was."

It sounded as if he had decided to retire as a boxer, unbeaten in 27 bouts with 23 knockouts.

"No, I didn't say that," he said, rising and glancing out the window. "And you ain't gonna make me say that. You got guys out there, guys been going so long without having a title shot, you got to give him a chance to have a taste of the dollar. The thing about the world today is that the big people look out for the big people, but the big people got to start looking out for the small man."

After a lunch of sausages and fried steak, the champion was outside with his children when two white men drove up.

Paul Taylor, in a brown suit, and Karl Sutker, in a green sweater, had been acquaintances of his for several years and they shook hands with him. They described themselves as investors.

"We heard about your plans for a recreation center," Taylor said. "We want to help you."

"We need it here for the kids," Sutker said. "If you want to do something for the kids, we'll help you do it. The community owes it to you, Joe, you've done a lot for this community. We're proud of you, Joe. You told me to bet on you, that you were going to win. I bet $1000 on you and I won."

"The kids need a place to play baseball, football, basketball," the champion said. "The black kids and the white kids. You let all the good athletes go away and they never come back."

Florida, '69: Generations in collision

JAMES T. WOOTEN

Fort Lauderdale, Fla.
April 1, 1969

Louis, the waiter, cleared his throat with a flourish before offering his luncheon pronouncement.

"The sun also rises," he said with a slight French accent. "By which it is to say that nothing changes, if you know what I mean, mon ami."

His customer wasn't sure.

"Ah, monsieur," Louis explained condescendingly. "It is simple, oui? Each year, the children from the schools of the North come here to spend the day drinking beer on the beach."

His customer nodded knowingly. Fort Lauderdale's fame as a spring vacation mecca for thousands of American college students is no small thing, and this year is no exception. This resort community on the eastern coast of the Florida peninsula is expecting nearly 40,000 collegians this week.

"And the older people come here at the same time because it has always been their custom to do so, and they are no different," Louis sighed. "They stay beside the pool all day sipping the liquors—and they all do not understand one another at all."

It was nearly noon at the Yankee Clipper Hotel, and down at the pool the over-30, Bloody Mary set was into its second round of the day. A pudgy, baldish doctor from Ohio dropped the morning paper into a poolside puddle, reached for his drink, and glared at his wife.

113

"My God, Emma," he said incredulously. "These kids are talking about going naked Easter Sunday."

She yawned and lowered the straps of her orange swim suit. "Just so they don't do it here in the hotel, Marvin," she replied. "I don't want to take you home in an oxygen tent."

As she adjusted the back of her chaise longue and returned to her Harold Robbins novel, a small plane swept low over the hotel patio and zoomed down the beach, trailing an undulating banner that read: "Welcome Collegians! John Reynolds Bail Bonding."

"Hey, that's clever," said Tad, a junior in pre-law at Southern Illinois University.

"I've only seen that a few dozen times before," he said, popping a can of beer and offering it to the coed he had met the night before.

"Oh, wow," she moaned in mock pain. "Not now and maybe never," she said, explaining her abstinence in terms of the quantity she had consumed the evening before.

Tad grinned, looking up and down the beach at the young bodies sprawled in malaise under the buff-colored sun. "If you drink enough, you'll get so fat we won't want you to go nude next week," he said to her.

She poured a glob of suntan oil on her arm and began to massage it into the already bronze skin. "You know what would happen if I took off my clothes and did my thing like they're saying? The creeps with the cameras would be right here and I'd be the one in focus and, splat, there I'd be on the front page of *The Milwaukee Sentinel*."

"So what?" Tad asked.

"So daddy would be here in an hour and cut my throat," she said, falling back on the old Army blanket Tad had brought with him from his campus in Carbondale, Ill.

As another plane buzzed the beach, this one advertising $20 round-trips to the Bahamas for students, an advertising executive from Philadelphia closed his copy of *Portnoy's Complaint* and walked to the small bar beside the patio.

"Another one, please, Earl," he said, and the bartender accommodated him quickly.

"Your eyes are bleeding," said Earl, and the ad man acknowledged it had been a rough evening the night before. "You'll be O.K. after a couple more," Earl predicted confidently, and his customer smiled.

"Would anyone like to have a picture?" asked a pretty girl in shorts carrying a camera and a brown leather bag over her shoulder.

"Sure, baby," said a tall, stout man in plaid slacks and an open-necked sports shirt. "You come sit by me and we'll let Earl take the picture."

She smiled. "Then we'll send it to your hometown newspaper, O.K.?" she asked.

He scowled. "To hell with that. We'll pin it up on the bar as a portrait of the world's best-looking couple," he said.

The doctor who had been indignant about the nude wade-in had approached the bar and overheard the conversation. "Why don't you go down to the beach and get pictures of those naked kids," he said, but by then the photographer had disappeared behind the line of palm trees surrounding the patio.

"Hit me again, Earl," said an insurance man from Louisville, Ky., "and bring her one, too." He pointed to a raven-haired secretary from Washington. "You know how these girls from the capital drink," he said, and she smiled coyly.

"Why, thank you," said the girl from the capital. "My name is Jean, what's yours?"

An ambulance siren drifted across the tiled patio and faded in the direction of the beach, where it was picked up by five boys from Springfield (Mass.) College who sat cross-legged in the sand, downing their second six-pack of the day.

"Some broad cut her wrists," said Ron, a senior from Boston.

"What for?" asked Richard, a junior from Rowayton, Conn.

"Because she knows I'm here and she hasn't met me yet," Ron answered, and then fended off handfuls of sand thrown by his companions.

The siren died in the distance and the music of hundreds of portable radios on the beach crept through the shrubs around the hotel into the patio, mixing with the Muzak pouring forth from speakers around the pool.

"Body and Soul" merged with "Son of a Preacher Man" in a conflict of rhythm, lyric, and melody. "The music is one thing that's wrong with the kids," said the doctor. "It has no meaning, no real essence, no depth. How about another drink, Earl?"

The executive vice president of a shopping center corporation in Binghamton, N.Y., agreed enthusiastically. "You know, I hired one of those folk-rock-soul whatever you call those bands for our grand opening. It was an absolute tragedy," he said. "The music was so loud and weird we couldn't get anybody into the store to buy."

The secretary from Washington nodded. "I still feel young," she said, explaining she was 25 years old. "But I don't understand their music. It's . . . it's so senseless and sort of immoral, if you know what I mean."

The ad man had now moved to the stool next to her. "You're absolutely right, honey," he said.

The bartender approached them. "Another one?" he asked.

"By all means," said the young Philadelphian. "And what about you, darling?" he said to the secretary.

"By all means," she said.

Baptist "amens" echo in South

ROY REED

Jackson, Tenn.
November 12, 1970

Sin—not war, crime, or social discontent, but old-fashioned sin—is hanging heavy over Southern towns like ambivalent Jackson this month.

This is the season when the Southern Baptists gather in their annual state conventions to attend to church business and reinforce their doctrine of hard work, clean living, and a very personal Satan who has to be firmly put behind a man every day of his life.

Half a dozen of these conventions are being held this week in towns that look and feel like Jackson, where the bright yellow leaves are still clinging to the maple trees and the air is touched with the first prolonged chill of fall.

As in the other places, the bartenders of Jackson are dispirited this week. Most of the convention delegates are teetotaling ministers, and even the laymen who come are not likely to take a drink with so many preachers around.

About 1000 of Tennessee's Baptist leaders finished a three-day meeting of the Tennessee Baptist Convention here today without passing any resolutions about the Vietnam war, crime in the streets, the race problem, or even the death of Charles de Gaulle.

The issue that almost tore the convention apart was dancing.

After 5 years of urging by the students, the board of trustees of Carson-Newman College, one of three colleges operated by the Southern Baptist Churches of Tennessee, changed the college's 119-year-old charter last spring to permit dances on the campus for the first time.

116

The executive board of the Tennessee Baptist Convention, which contributed $405,933 last year to the college, asked the board to rescind its action. The college board suspended the dances but refused to reamend the charter.

About 100 churches began to withhold money that was designated for Carson-Newman. Others threatened to do the same.

That was the way the controversy stood when the convention began Tuesday in the West Jackson Baptist Church, one of the largest of the 136 Christian churches in this city of 34,376 persons.

Aside from hearing reports on missions, Sunday school programs, and the like, most of the time at a state Baptist convention is taken up with preaching, singing, and praying.

Nineteen sermons were preached at this meeting, counting those at the preconvention pastors' conference.

Most were standard Biblical expositions, like the one on the second coming of Christ by the Rev. Hugh Van Eaton of the First Baptist Church of Lake Charles, La.

"There is no hope for this sin-cursed and Satan-blighted world unless Jesus comes again," Mr. Van Eaton declared near the end. A man in the back who resembled Senator Strom Thurmond (as did a large number of the messengers, as the delegates are called) led a chorus of "Amens."

Baptists are not without humor. Outside the door as Mr. Van Eaton's sermon passed the half-hour mark, two ushers stood shifting their weight from one foot to the other. One finally looked at his watch and said, "He's preaching on the second coming of Christ. You reckon he's going to preach till He gets here?"

The preachers and the deacons talked about the second coming behind the stained glass of the sanctuary, but out in the halls they talked about dancing. The rumblings and mutterings and the earnest, fretful looks (which many Baptists wear habitually) made it clear from the beginning that this would be the one explosive issue of the convention.

There was an early hint that not even the ministers were unanimous in their readiness to condemn "social dancing," as the church traditionally has referred to it while opposing it.

The Rev. Grant Jones, pastor of the First Baptist Church of Sevierville, Tenn., preached the official "convention sermon" Tuesday afternoon. He castigated his colleagues for refusing to follow "the implications of the Gospel."

"While our Roman Catholic friends seem to be opening the windows of their minds to some fresh ideas," he said, "we seem to be attempting to force our free denomination into an ecclesiastical straitjacket."

He did not receive many "Amens" when he sat down.

The big debate broke into the open the next morning. A committee of the executive board had tried to smooth it over by recommending that the matter be studied for a year. The majority would not agree.

When a mother of two college students tried to persuade the messengers to let the young "do what they want to do," she was greeted with a loud, collective "Ooohhh."

Another friend of the students, a layman, demanded scriptural proof that dancing was wrong, to which a preacher replied, "If it was wrong for 119 years, it is wrong now."

A second preacher, the Rev. John Buell of Knoxville, cited the Sermon on the Mount and quoted Matthew 5:28, in which Jesus said that a man who looks with lust at a woman commits adultery in his heart.

"Any man who says he can dance and keep his thoughts pure is less than a man or he is a liar," Mr. Buell cried, to a great chorus of laughter and "Amens."

No one rose to defend lust, and the convention voted overwhelmingly to ask the board of Carson-Newman once again to rescind its charter action.

Afterward, Robert L. Delaney, a conservatively trimmed and clothed student from Carson-Newman, talked of the students' disappointment.

"In an age when people are more concerned about the social and moral issues of the day—the Vietnam war, how people are going to relate to one another, black to white, man to man—the issue of dancing is absurd," he said, and shook his head sadly.

He said the college enrollment had dropped about 50 last year, partly because of boredom on the campus. Jefferson City, where the college is situated, does not even have a movie theater, he said.

The Carson-Newman problem may shed light on a larger one facing the Baptist Church in Tennessee and across the South. Southern Baptists are not gaining members nearly as rapidly as they did 10 and 20 years ago, and they are worried about losing many of their young people.

The decline was underlined at this convention. The budget adopted for next year is $5,675,000—exactly the same as last year's. And last year's was not met because contributions fell short by $135,000.

Ministers like Mr. Jones see a few hopeful signs. For example, several Tennessee Baptist Churches have begun to accept Negro members, he said. The new president of the convention, the Rev. Hayward Highfill, recently baptized a Negro boy in his church, the First Baptist Church of Clinton, the scene of violent racial disturbances during the 1950s.

But outreach comes hard to the Baptists. Inner discipline, or even tension, is still prized more highly, and the instilling of it begins early.

A choir of nursing students sang for the convention Tuesday afternoon. The girls were fresh, young, beautiful, and smiling, but their songs were somber. Two songs began with the line, "I am not worthy. . . ."

A girl who looks like a teen-aged Barbra Streisand stepped forward and made a little talk. She began, "Indeed, I am not worthy," and the messengers said, "Amen." The fretful lines were already beginning to form in her earnest, innocent face.

A Wallace backer stirred by busing

NAN ROBERTSON

Detroit
May 13, 1972

Dewey Burton is going to vote for George C. Wallace for President in the Michigan primary.

He is 26 years old, short and thick, with a gravelly voice and a gap-toothed grin. He lives with a warm-hearted, pretty wife, a rollicking 5-year-old son, and a scramble-footed Great Dane puppy in an immaculate bungalow he owns in Redford Township, a white working-class suburb on Detroit's western edge.

He struggles out of bed at 4 A.M. five days a week. He drives 20 miles to the Ford Motor Company plant at Wixom. His job begins at 5:42 A.M. as the first car moves past him on the assembly line. It ends at 2:12 P.M. after he has wiped clean one side of 217 Thunderbirds, Mark IVs, and Lincoln Continentals before their first coat of paint.

He then drives his beat-up 1960 Thunderbird back to the tiny house with the orchid-colored front door and a plaster reproduction of Rodin's "The Kiss" near the living-room sofa. After supper, he goes to his neighbor's garage to work long hours on the family heirloom—a shark-nosed 1963 Stingray he "customized" himself. The neighbor, thrown out of steady work 18 months ago, has posted a sign by his back entrance: "Our God Is Not Dead—Sorry About Yours."

Dewey Burton is a man of contrasts: independent, energetic, and sensitive, yet seeming old and trapped.

119

He is in love with cars; he hates his job at the auto plant, which he finds boring, brutalizing, and endlessly repetitive.

He is smart, driving, a compulsive worker, spilling over with ideas; he cannot be promoted.

He does not read newspapers; but he speaks his mind and his friends listen.

He resents welfare cheats; he was on welfare as a child after his parents deserted him.

He calls the black man who is president of his local union "the best president we've ever had." He has no qualms about his son David going to school with blacks. And if a black family moved on his block—and he would not object—he bets they would take better care of their home than the white folks on welfare down near the corner, whose conduct scandalizes him.

But he is violently opposed to busing, even one-way busing that would bring black children into his son's school three blocks away, saying:

"My child will never be bused into Detroit or anywhere for integration purposes. Busing—that's the only issue I'm interested in. It's the biggest issue in this campaign."

Like Dewey Burton, there are hundreds of thousands in the state of Michigan who will vote for George Wallace in the primary—and they make the Alabama Governor the most important political phenomenon in this traditionally liberal state.

Dewey Burton will count for not one vote but four. He is the undeniable head of an affectionate, trusting, but disheartened family that would include his wife, Ilona, a platinum blonde with a 5000-watt smile; his mother-in-law, Violet Kish, a lickety-split talker who makes Edith Bunker of "All in the Family" seem positively taciturn by comparison; and his father-in-law, Stephen Kish, who works at Detroit Edison by day and is a gas station attendant at night.

As Mr. Burton votes, so will the three others.

He buys a Sunday newspaper mainly to pore over the classified ads for hot rods.

But there are about 150 books in his house, ranging from Jean-François Steiner's *Treblinka*, through volumes on algebra and trigonometry, Erich Segal's *Love Story*, Gordon Seagrave's *Burma Surgeon*, and *Inside the Ku Klux Klan*.

Mr. Burton rarely watches television. Saturday nights, however, he and his wife invariably sit down to watch "All in the Family."

"We all call him Archie now," Mr. Burton said. "He's a fool. He's taken hate and bigotry and turned them into the most fun things I know. It's like Mark Twain's satire—it's hilarious."

It is one of his few diversions. He has not had a vacation since he and Ilona went to Niagara Falls on their honeymoon eight years ago. Work has been his whole life.

He was born in Detroit of Southern parents who were on the verge of divorce. When he was three days old, his mother turned him over to his grand-mother, who lived in Mount Vernon in southern Illinois.

It galls him to this day that, when he was 11, he and his grandmother spent Saturdays packing rice, beans, and flour at the welfare outlet to get a pound of cheese in pay. "Then those guys setting on their cans all week at home came in to pick up their food. We didn't get no meat or cheese because I wasn't her legal child," he said.

Now there is the white welfare family on Mr. Burton's block in Redford—an unmarried mother with eight children and many male visitors. Mrs. Kish railed against them: "Filthy-mouthed, busted for drugs, kicking in the storm doors, boys turning into girls. There she is, having a ball in bed every day, and we got to go out and work our tails off for them. They're giving America away free."

The young Burton was sent back to Detroit when he was 12, supported by an aunt. That year, he was putting roofs on houses for $1 a day. Other jobs followed: short-order cook, gas station attendant, playing drums and guitar in bars in a band that he formed at the age of 16.

He became a "line rat" at Ford's Wixom plant when he was 18 years old, full of hope for the future. His son David was born. Five years ago, he and his wife bought their bungalow for $14,800.

Dewey Burton, 26, and his family, at their Detroit home.
NYT/FRANK LODGE

"There are two things you buy a home for—how close you are to a school and how close you are to a shopping center," Mr. Burton said. "What burns me to the bottom of my bones is that I paid an excessive amount of money so that my son could walk three blocks to school. I'm not going to pay big high-school taxes and pay more for a home so that somebody can ship my son 30 miles away to get an inferior education."

But he also insists, "If a black mom and daddy buy or rent a house here and send their kids to David's school and pay their taxes, that's fine."

"Busing black kids to white neighborhoods and white kids to black neighborhoods is never going to achieve integration. It's upsetting. It's baloney," he went on. "Who's going to pick up the tab for the buses? I'm going to wind up paying part of it anyway."

Only his family and cars give him solace now. Mr. Burton spends almost all of his time outside the factory fashioning cars into wondrous shapes and painting them with exotic designs and colors: candy apple, diamond dust, metal flake, pearl. He can build a car from scratch.

For three years, while his wife took one job after another, including hiring out as a maid, Mr. Burton struggled toward an industrial management degree in a community college, going "half whipped" to his regular job. Often he would be able to snatch only two hours of sleep, parked in his car at the plant after the night shift before going to early morning classes. In late 1970, he quit six months short of "that piece of paper," and it almost broke his wife's heart.

Last year he spent six months trying to run a small bumper and paint shop —"Dewey's Custom Illusions"—on the side. It went bankrupt.

He passed tests for foreman and skilled trades apprentice, but he's never moved up. He's still at what Ilona bitterly calls "a dummy-type job."

"I hate my job. I hate the people I work for. I hate having to drive so far to work," he said. "I'm doing the same job as the fellow working across from me, and he quit in the eighth grade. It's kinda stupid to work that hard and achieve so little.

"Once you're there, there's no other way to make as much money and get the benefits. Ford's our security blanket. I'm a scaredy-cat. If I leave, I lose 8 years seniority."

During those years at Wixom, Mr. Burton has been given every kind of work on the line except what he wants to do most—the difficult status job of painting cars with a spray gun.

What his wife calls his "mouthing off" at the plant has led to a bad record of disciplinary actions for what seem to be minor infractions of the rules. His foremen find him "pushy" and much too outspoken about his complaints.

At the age of 26, Mr. Burton feels exhausted and deeply frustrated. He has arthritic gout. His wife has an ulcer.

The Burtons think his wages—his gross pay was $189.90 last week and his take-home pay $134.68—are enough to carry them. But "I don't have no self-satisfaction in my job," the husband said.

In 1968, Mr. Burton voted for Hubert H. Humphrey, "as a union man coming from a long line of F.D.R. Democrats."

"People have been telling me since I was a child that when the Democrats were in office, everybody was put to work," he said.

He thinks President Nixon means unemployment but he would not vote for Humphrey now. The reason is that he is convinced that Mr. Humphrey "said right here in Detroit, in simple, plain English, 'I believe in forced integration through busing.' I will not send somebody to the White House who doesn't represent what I believe in."

"I used to think Muskie was one candidate for me. He seemed to be a guy who could stop and look sensibly at things. But all of a sudden I began to feel it was just his way of talking around issues and not taking a stand. He's not a decision maker. If you're President, whether you decide right or wrong, you've got to make decisions 24 hours a day."

"McGovern to me is like a dark shadow—like McCarthy—he strikes me as the kids' candidate."

Mr. Burton, never a soldier, does "not give a deadly damn about the war."

"It has never concerned me," he said. "People getting killed concerns me. When this war is over, there'll be another one. Maybe it's because it keeps big industry going, keeps people employed."

"The trouble with this war is that we're not fighting a Hitler or Mussolini or little slant-eyed Japs who bombed Pearl Harbor," he said. "We're fighting a civil war. You see 30 Vietnamese running down a road in the newsreels and you don't know if they're friends or enemies."

Mr. Burton has never seen a Presidential candidate, or been to a political rally, or even put on a button or a bumper sticker.

But he'll vote Tuesday. He will vote against the dreariness of his dead-end job, the threat to take his child away, and the dollars he thinks he's forced to pay to support welfare drones.

Dewey Burton knows only one way to protest now:

"I'm voting for Wallace."

Woody Guthrie's home town is divided on paying him homage

B. DRUMMOND AYRES JR.

Okemah, Okla.
December 14, 1972

Out on the eastern edge of this little farming and ranching town, where the streets run to yellow clay and the yards are littered with broken-down cars on cinder blocks, there is a crumbling hillside shack with a high porch that commands the best view in Okemah.

A person can stand on this porch and take in a lot of what Oklahoma is all about—oil pumps rhythmically nodding like so many giant praying mantises, fat Black Angus cattle grazing in a pasture of frost-crumpled prairie grass, and wind, always the wind, rattling willows down in the bottom, flapping blue denim overalls on a galvanized line, kicking up a puff of dust on a distant tabletop butte.

Inside the old shack, there are four dank and empty rooms. The light is bad, but even in the semidarkness, the graffiti can be read:

"Hey, hey, Woody Guthrie, I wrote on your wall."

". . . and Woody, no one even cared."

Not until recently, anyway.

Now, however, five years after he died at the age of 55 and his ashes were scattered over the Atlantic, Woody Guthrie is suddenly the talk of Okemah (pronounced Oh-KEE-Muh).

Some of this town's 3000 residents have decided it is time to honor him as a native son who became the balladeer of the Depression and Dust Bowl

124

by writing 1000 heartfelt American folk songs, among them "This Land Is Your Land" and "So Long, It's Been Good to Know You."

Other residents are opposed to granting any honors because they remember Woody Guthrie as a left-winger who betrayed the conservatism of rural, east-central Oklahoma and wrote a newspaper column for the American Communist party.

Thus far, supporters of the dusty-voiced singer have managed to get "Home of Woody Guthrie" painted on one of the town's water tanks. They also have persuaded the local library to accept a collection of his records and books.

But the town is still holding out on the ultimate Guthrie honor—an annual Woody Guthrie Day.

"Commemoration just isn't justified because of Guthrie's Communist affiliation, whether he was active or duped," says Allison Kelly, a banker.

"Commemoration is justified because Woody was a great musician and a great individualist who nobody ever proved was a Communist," counters Earl Walker, a petroleum company owner who recently bought the old Guthrie house from another family for $7000 and hopes to turn it into a "living memorial" run by a nonprofit foundation.

Such give-and-take has caused memories of Woody to flood back in Okemah.

Suddenly, those who knew him and those who did not seem to remember the wiry, curly-haired boy who "blew out" of here at the age of 15, memories of the panoramic view from that high porch imbedded deep in his psyche, battered guitar slung across his back, "bound for glory, bound to win," as he put it.

Suddenly everyone seems to recall how Woody used to swing up on red-balling freights to escape railroad yard "bulls," how he joined with other Dust Bowl migrants to pick the grapes of wrath in California, how he used to sing out for the laboring man to "take it easy, but take it."

And of course everyone suddenly remembers that he wrote that column after his surfeit of social impatience boiled over.

Were it not for Earl Walker, the memories might have lain dormant.

But Mr. Walker is a staunch Guthrie fan, and he has pushed repeatedly for some sort of recognition.

For instance, he led the drive to have the water tank painted. (The two other towers already were labeled "hot" and "cold;" an indication that the water board does not always toe the conservative line that cuts through rural Oklahoma.)

Already some people are speaking out against the new paint job, done in black against a bright yellow background. Says a service station operator: "Woody was no good. About half the town feels that way. I knew him, went to school with him, used to whup him. He doesn't deserve to have his name up there."

Before persuading the water board to act, Mr. Walker joined with some of Woody's second cousins—the only kin left here—and led the fight that forced the local library to accept the collection of Guthrie records and books.

Initially the library board flatly refused, relenting only in the face of Mr. Walker's pressure and when Woody's widow, Marjorie, and his son, Arlo, also a folk singer, showed up in Okemah to hand over the gift in person.

Mr. Walker and his followers are now pushing for a Woody Guthrie Day.

"We'll get something through sooner or later, but there's no question that some people still don't fully accept Woody," says J. O. Smith, a hardware store owner.

One of those people is Mr. Smith's son, Mac, owner of a variety store. He says:

"We can honor him in some manner, O.K. But he did have that affiliation and we ought not to go hog-wild by painting his name all over the place."

Mr. Smith, who sells records, says he has never had a request for anything by Woody Guthrie despite the current furor over the singer.

The older folks around here are still trying to forget many of the things he sang about—the Depression and the Dust Bowl days, when half the town left, not bound for glory but simply searching for a place where there was money and topsoil.

Okemah's youngsters prefer to listen to the Top 40 out of Tulsa and Oklahoma City, where the disk jockeys play the Three Dog Night, the Rolling Stones, and, of course, Merle Haggard, a country and Western singer who put nearby Muskogee on the musical map by celebrating its supposedly upright Oklahoma ways in song.

"I know people around here say Woody Guthrie did some bad things, but about all I know about his songs is that he wrote 'This Land Is Your Land,'" says 14-year-old Marilyn Jones. She is standing in front of Powers TV on Broadway, staring at a display of guitars.

There are, nevertheless, usually a few youngsters in town who know all about Woody's songs.

They come by foot, by car, and by motorbike, one and two at a time, packs and guitars on their backs.

Somehow, they always find their way to the old Guthrie house, though they seldom ask directions from the local populace.

Then, they climb the rickety stairs, take in the view from the high porch, perhaps smoke a little grass, leave their respects on a wall and depart.

"Jai B" dropped by on 5/19/72. He wrote:

> Going down that hot dusty road
> Okie wind was ablowin'.
> I passed your only childhood home
> And Woody, I'm aknowin'.
> Well, Woody, I finally made it.
> Woody, I'm finally here.
> Woody, I finally made it.
> And Woody, no one even cared.

Football in the South: Happy link to a feared future

JAMES T. WOOTEN

Poplarville, Miss.
August 31, 1970

One day last week, as the high-school football team was practicing behind the gymnasium, a group of the town's businessmen gathered to watch.

Like most merchants in small communities all over the South, these men have an avid, almost proprietary interest in the fortunes of the team. So they come to the field nearly every afternoon and stand along the sidelines studying the adolescent athletes with the careful shrewdness of National Football League club owners.

For them, football is more than a game. It is a link with pure absolutes in a crumbling age of relativity. It is an assurance that despite pollution and assassination, autumn does indeed follow the summer; that, regardless of Vietnam, the best teams win and strength invariably beats weakness; that, in spite of the stock market, inflation, and tight money, a touchdown is still six points and 10 yards will get you a first down; that it's a good thing to be a white Mississippian regardless of what people say and think in Boston and Manhattan; and that some things, thank the Good Lord above and no thanks to the Federal Government, just don't change.

But, of course, some things do.

For the first time in its history, under order of the Federal courts, this little town's rigid social structure is being significantly altered and the 1970 Poplar-

127

ville Hornets, its beloved football team, are the vanguards of that change.

This year when the Hornets take the field, they will include nine young Negroes, and although the community is trying heroically not to appear excited or interested, here in Pearl River County, in southern Mississippi, this is the stuff of which history is made.

Approximately 365 Negroes are expected to begin classes with about 1400 white children today in the town's four schools. Although there is no obvious threat to the peace of the community, a grim streak of resentment lies just below the surface of life in Poplarville these days.

"It's just plain old fear," said Lee White, a local banker who once served on the town's school board. "All of this integration is new, and I think people are more afraid than anything else."

But despite its fears, Poplarville is integrating its schools, and its white leadership is persuaded that there is no prospect of violence.

"We don't like it, of course," conceded Mayor Thomas Rawls, the owner of a supermarket. "We don't believe in mixing up the races but a court order is a court order and we're a law-abiding people and always have been."

Theodore G. Bilbo, were he still alive, would have enthusiastically agreed with the Mayor. A Governor and later a United States Senator, Mr. Bilbo, a Poplarville native, spent most of his political career ranting against the evils of racial integration.

"There are higher laws than man's," Mr. Bilbo used to say, "and God was the first segregationist"—and that is the law by which the 1800 white people in this town of 2400 citizens have always abided.

Like Mr. Bilbo, who is to Poplarville what Sam Houston is to Texas, they believe that integration is intrinsically wrong and essentially evil. Segregation, for them, is a higher law and it is inscribed on their souls, and the courts and the Federal officials with their guidelines cannot erase it.

This loyalty to "a higher law" might also explain what inspired a mob of white men to storm the yellow brick jail at the county courthouse here in April, 1959. They pulled Mack Charles Parker, a young Negro awaiting trial for allegedly raping a white woman, from his cell, and a week later his body was found floating in the Pearl River. He had been shot.

The Federal Bureau of Investigation presented confessions from some members of the mob, but no indictments were returned.

That same year, 1959, the Poplarville school board built a new school for the Negroes, a sprawling, attractive one-story building that has been the academic home for the black children of the town ever since.

But this year, Todd Memorial, named for one of the first Negro educators in Pearl River County, will be used for all fifth- and sixth-grade children, black and white, and the new principal, Jack Mobley, a white man, is optimistic.

He seems representative of the teachers and administrators in Poplarville's school system. Eager but cautious, he believes "everything's going to be O.K. long as we forget about color."

The children, black and white, concur, and despite the tensions there is a feeling of hope in the halls of the schools.

At the practice field behind the gymnasium, the businessmen were speculating about the coming football season. There was no sense of history in the sultry air, only the unmistakable sounds of football—that solid thud of strong, young bodies joyfully colliding.

"Don't know hardly what to say, Hoss," said one of the merchants. "If the backfield's any count at all, we going to be as good as last year."

A friend agreed. "You mighty right," he said. "And if our nigras are tough as you say, we going to be clean mean."

A whistle knifed across the field, piercing the afternoon and punctuating the conversation on the sidelines.

"Oh, the nigras are tough, all right," responded another. "See that big one there? He's 200 if he's a pound and he runs the hundred in 10 seconds flat."

A skeptic spat in the grass.

"O.K. Hoss," the first man countered. "I'll lay you two to one by the end of the season you going to thank the Federal court for giving us a fullback."

Clam-digging controversy divides Down East towns

ROBERT REINHOLD

Jonesport, Me.
October 7, 1969

A large trailer truck, navigating down the narrow street of this tiny coastal town the other day, scraped some paint off the fender of a parked car. Wool-shirted old-timers, weather-beaten and leathery from decades of tending lobster traps or digging clams, put down their coffee cups and sauntered out of Ginnie's Food Shop to inspect the damage. It was about as much excitement as anyone could normally expect in this remote Down East town, where street crime and war, riots and hippies are only words—words of another society, another place.

Along the broken rocky coast, proud pines and spruce stand darkly against cotton-white clouds and near-azure waters as a cool salt breeze gently rocks ungainly lobster boats in the harbor.

For generations, Jonesport's fortunes have risen and fallen with the sea. Its 1500 taciturn but friendly residents—almost all of them Beals, Alleys, or Kelleys—live in a collection of simple frame houses and lead a quiet existence that has changed remarkably little since Colonial times.

Despite the surface tranquility and stability bred by decades of insulation from the unsettling winds of change, Jonesport is in the midst of a jarring confrontation—replete with civil disobedience, defiance of authority, seven arrests, and lengthy court appeals.

Vietnam? The draft? Racism? Hardly. It's clams. No other issue, except possibly lobsters, could stir such emotion here.

It all started a few months ago, when the neighboring town of Jonesboro started to enforce a municipal ordinance that restricted clam-digging on its tidal mud flats to residents.

This did not sit well with the Jonesport diggers, who have long been accustomed to digging wherever they pleased. Besides, Jonesport's own flats are largely polluted, while Jonesboro's are very clean.

So Arpie Alley and six other Jonesport diggers invited arrest recently by intruding on Jonesboro. They were duly apprehended by the Jonesboro clam warden and sentenced to 30 days in jail.

"Is it right for the state to sell you a clam license and you can't go anyplace clamming? That don't sound logical," groused Mr. Alley, a 39-year-old with rugged irregular features whose family has been digging clams for as long as anyone here can remember.

"We feel you should be able to dig anyplace you want to; that's the only way you can make a decent living at it," Mr. Alley continued. "One day we decided that the only way to get this thing moving was to go over and get arrested."

The result has probably been more commotion in this area than anything since local citizens defeated the British in the first naval battle of the Revolutionary War after a British captain had refused to allow them to erect a liberty pole.

It was perhaps the same Down East stubbornness and rugged individualism that led Arpie Alley and his group to defy Jonesboro.

While the case awaits appeal this month, a court test that Mr. Alley hopes will upset similar digging restrictions up and down the Maine coast, the Jonesport diggers are free on $10 bail each.

The issue is: Does a town have the legal right to exclude the holder of a $3 state license to dig and sell clams, quahogs, oysters, and mussels in accordance with the restrictions and traditions provided by law?

While the issue is being decided, Jonesport diggers are staying on the right side of the town line. The other day, as the tide ebbed and exposed the dark, glistening mud, Arpie Alley and six others were hard at work digging clams, strenuous work that provides only meager reward.

Arpie Alley planted his feet deep into the mud, hunched over and sliced down hard with his clamming hoe. In the same motion, he pulled forward and turned over the ink-black mud with a heavy slopping sound, reached down and deftly picked up a half-dozen grayish-white clams.

"When my father was first digging clams," he was saying, "there was no such thing as a clam law. I don't care if I go to jail—someone has got to support my family."

Even when the tides and weather are optimum, that is not easy. His take is seldom more than three to four bushels a day. At $6 a bushel, he must support his wife and children on about $20 a day.

Not far away, Richard Merchant, 28, brushed some mud off his face and put down his hoe. "If the law ain't broken, I don't know what we're going to do," he said. "In another two years we won't have any clams left here."

Since there is little else to do for a living here, more than just principle is at stake.

Across the channel from where the Jonesporters were digging, a man kept a lonely watch from a small boat. He was Johnny Cox, the clam warden from Jonesboro who had arrested the Jonesport men.

Jonesboro, like several other Maine coastal towns, has had shellfish restrictions for some time, but it could never enforce them because no one was willing to become warden. Last January, however, Mr. Cox, a digger who moonlights as a television repairman, took the job and began to enforce the rules with a vengeance.

And the Jonesporters may have met their match for Down East stubbornness in Mrs. Theone Look, the Jonesboro town clerk. A motherly-looking woman, she has run the town's affairs with an iron hand for 17 years from a small, cluttered office just off her kitchen.

Jonesboro, she said, has "the finest digging on the Maine coast," and intended to keep it that way.

"I feel this is a very great asset the town has—perhaps the only one. We don't have any town poor simply because in wintertime the people can go out and work on the flats."

"Furthermore," she added, "if Jonesport doesn't have any flats it's their own fault, because they haven't taken care of them."

Meanwhile, Mr. Alley has become something of a local hero in Jonesport. "To look at him you wouldn't think he knew enough to get in out of the rain," remarked a neighbor. "But he can really talk. He's even been on television."

But the mood is darkening. "If we don't beat this law, I almost hate to say what will happen—it's going to be a war," said Don Merchant, a tall, handsome man with a shock of thick graying hair and deeply suntanned skin.

Appalachia's hillbillies find a life in the North

WILLIAM K. STEVENS

Detroit
March 28, 1973

> Home folks think I'm big in
>   Dee-troit City.
> From the letters that I write they
>   think I'm fine.
> But by day I make the cars,
> By night I make the bars.
> If only they could read between
>   the lines.
>
>   I wan-na go home.
>   I wan-na go home.
>   Oh, how I wan-na go home.*

The song is sweetly plaintive, almost mournful, its melody suggesting down-home woods and fields, its rhythm just upbeat enough to avoid depression. It can be very affecting to the transplanted Kentuckians, Tennesseeans, West Virginians, and other white Appalachian folk whose feelings it expresses.

133

When they play "Detroit City" or "Green, Green Grass of Home" at Li'l Abner's Lounge in north-central Detroit, the dance floor fills with nostalgic, sometimes homesick hillbillies—for that is what they call themselves today, with a growing sense of pride. Those who don't dance just sit there over a bottle of beer, seemingly lost in varying states of reverie. "It really hurts," said one ex-Kentuckian.

For three decades and more the hillbillies have trekked northward from the green hills and coal country of job-poor Appalachia, seeking the steady employment and solid security offered by the industrial Middle West.

No one really knows how many there have been, but a conservative estimate says that at least 4 million have poured—at a somewhat lower rate in recent years—into such cities as Cincinnati, Akron, Cleveland, Dayton, and Chicago. And especially Detroit, with its bountiful supply of jobs in the automobile industry.

Though the vast interstate movement of these fiercely proud and independent but often shy and different people has paralleled that of the blacks, it has been much less noticed.

What has become of the hillbillies? How have they fared? What is their life like in the North?

One can start to get some answers by visiting Li'l Abner's, one of maybe 25 "hillbilly heaven" bars scattered throughout the metropolitan area. Together, these bars constitute perhaps the nearest thing to a unifying cultural institution that Detroit hillbillies have—apart, that is, from the city's fundamentalist churches that perpetuate the frontier faith of the hills.

The evening was still young at Li'l Abner's one recent Friday night, and the empty brown beer bottles were only beginning to accumulate in the half-darkness, when Jimmy Hardin, leader of a band called Country's Pride, welcomed the crowd back to "Dogpatch Country" and invited everyone to stay and get drunk.

Many did. But not Joe Petrey, a wiry, blue-eyed 25-year-old with short-cropped black hair and the angular features so common to the eastern Kentucky hills where he grew up. His character seems to be as straightforward and basic as the unfiltered cigarettes he smokes, and he nursed a beer only long enough to tell a visitor something about his life. It is a life that in many ways seems to represent the general Appalachian experience in the North.

First, it is an economic success story. The hillbillies for the most part have made it.

"My wife and me make more'n $25,000 a year now," Joe Petrey said, although he doesn't brag about such things and dislikes people who do.

He operates a radial drill for a company that makes spot welders for use on auto assembly lines. His wife, Eva, 22 years old from back home in Corbin, Ky., with a shy smile, a nearly flawless complexion, luminous blue eyes and long, light brown hair, sews vinyl seat upholstery at a Ford Motor Company plant. The Petreys work hard for their money, 10 hours a day, six days

Country's Pride, a hillbilly band, arrives to play at Li'l Abner's in Detroit.
NYT/GARY SETTLE

a week, getting up before dawn and quitting in time to eat supper, watch a little television, and fall into bed.

Second, most of the hillbillies have pulled themselves out of the inner-city ghettos that originally served as points of entry from the South. Although there remain pockets of Appalachian poverty near downtown Detroit, most of the migrants from the hills are evidently suburbanites today.

They live in modest frame-and-shingle houses ("This Family Will Not Be Bused," read signs on some of them) in such towns as Warren, just northeast of Detroit; Taylor, southwest of the city; and especially in the three towns of Madison Heights, Ferndale, and Hazel Park that adjoin each other on Detroit's north-central border.

The Petreys now live in a spotless three-room apartment in Madison Heights, with a color television set and a combination radio and eight-track stereo tape player that Mr. Petrey uses to record and play country-Western music.

He estimates that 100 people from his home county, including perhaps 35 of his relatives, live in adjacent Hazel Park. There are so many Kentuckians there that the town is nicknamed "Hazeltucky." It and the other suburbs favored by people from Appalachia now serve as way stations for the continuing migration from the South. Downtown Detroit is being largely by-passed.

Third, the Appalachian migrants appear to be developing an explicit sense of ethnic identity that was lacking in the past. "Hillbilly and Proud of It," reads a sticker on the rear window of Joe Petrey's Chevrolet pickup truck.

This perhaps does not seem like much until it is remembered that "hillbilly" was long a term of insult. But the new feeling of pride expressed by Joe Petrey's sticker does not mean that the hillbillies are about to create their own version of the black, Chicano, or Indian power movements.

That is just not their way. They have not generally proved to be the organizing or joining kind, so independent are they. Nor have they seemed to find a sufficient cause for grievance. They have never formed a cohesive voting or political bloc.

Fourth, and perhaps more striking, the hillbillies' strong sense of nostalgia for the homeland remains and grows. "Detroit City" expresses deep-running and widespread feelings, especially among the men.

Joe Petrey's roots in the land where his father still operates a logging business go very deep. "There's an old log house been in the family a hundred years, I guess," he said. "My dad, and I guess his dad, was raised in it, and it's still standin'.."

"I wouldn't give an acre down there for this whole state."

There is no question in Mr. Petrey's mind that he is going back for good. "I'm just workin' from week to week," he says, "tryin' to get enough ahead to go back, just like a lot of other people." He hopes that will be in four or five months, if all goes well.

If he does go back, he may be a bit unusual. For although many say that is their intention, Dr. James S. Brown of the University of Kentucky, one of the relatively few social scientists who have studied the migrants, says that "once they've been gone six months, they're gone for good."

Willard Brafford, a 30-year-old Kentuckian who has lived in the Detroit area 10 years, and in his own house in Warren for the last five, likes the city no more than Joe Petrey. "Too many people," he says. But he is doubtful about ever returning to the hills.

"If I could get some work down there, something dependable, in the next four or five years, I'd go back," he says. "But after that I couldn't afford to, with so much time in toward my pension."

While the nostalgia and desire to return are a dominant theme, there are variations on it and exceptions to it.

There is, for example, Ernest Trent, who sings country and Western music here under the name of Joe Pain. He is a native of Harlan County in Kentucky, a coal-mining region with little of the farming appeal of Joe Petrey's neighborhood.

"Even if I weren't having such a good time singing," Joe Pain says, "I'd never go back. There ain't nothin' there for me but a hole in the ground—I don't mean a coal mine—and I can get that here."

And there are many, many women who have gotten used to the amenities of urban life and are not anxious to give them up. Mrs. Linda Keelen, formerly of West Virginia and now of Warren, is proud of being a hillbilly and is teaching her 3-year-old son to be proud, too.

But, she says, "I can't picture bein' back on some farm, churnin' butter."

So mostly, despite the widely expressed desire of men like Joe Petrey to go back home for good, the hillbillies are here to stay. They have adapted as best they can to what they widely perceive as an uncongenial urban atmosphere, and in the process a kind of urban-hillbilly culture seems to have emerged.

It has emerged, for example, in the popularity of bars like Li'l Abner's, and particularly in a passion for the kind of neo-country music that is played there and over local hillbilly stations like WEXL.

The Appalachian migrants have reestablished, undiluted and unchanged, some aspects of their culture—for example, their churches, with their straight-from-the-shoulder fundamentalist message.

"You're goin' either to heaven or hell, and you're goin' to hell if you don't live right," the Rev. Charles E. Curtis told his somewhat sparse congregation at the Faith Pentecostal chapel in Hazel Park on a recent Sunday morning.

Mr. Curtis gave a classic sermon, punctuated by frequent "Amens" and "praise Gods." There was a hand-clapping, foot-tapping hymn session ("Are You Washed in the Blood of the Lamb?" and "Living by Faith" were two of the selections). And the service ended with a brief ritual in which Mr. Curtis laid hands on the heads of a child and a woman, asking the Lord to cure the child's rash and the woman's sore leg.

These are "old-fashioned holiness people" of the kind that Joe Petrey admires and values. "I believe in heaven and hell," he says. "There's a lot of hypocrites, but I wouldn't take nothin' for my raisin'."

There are those who predict that in a generation under the influence of mainstream urban pressures, the hillbilly identity will all but disappear. It is said that many of the younger people, those who were born in the North, identify as mainstream Americans—Detroiters—and want no part of being hillbilly.

Maybe so, but maybe, also, what happened at the Sunday afternoon jamboree at Li'l Abner's not long ago offers other clues.

Hillbilly music there was, and plenty. But when younger musical groups got up to play, there was rock music, too. The teens and preteens in bellbottoms and hip-huggers ate it up.

Then, well into the afternoon, a young girl of perhaps 10 stepped onto a bandstand and asked the master of ceremonies if she could sing a song.

In a high, thin voice that nevertheless filled the total hush that fell over the room, she slowly sang:

"Country road, take me home, to the place where I belong."

Where the elderly try to escape and be young once more

JON NORDHEIMER

Miami Beach
February 26, 1971

"Look at 'em," mutters the blonde in a see-through blouse and skintight black pants. "You can almost hear their joints creak."

On the floor of a beachfront auditorium near the southern tip of Miami Beach, several dozen couples dance cheek to cheek as a four-piece band plays "Lucky in Love." Outside a cold spell has dropped the temperature to 40 degrees, and the couples, all 60 years of age or older, appear to cling to each other more for warmth than pleasure.

The blonde in the see-through blouse digs through a pile of coats on a table near a door. "Aah, here it is," she says and shakes a squirrel wrap out of the pile. She is about 60 years old, and her home is in Chicago.

She and her husband spend every winter here. "He stays in the room at night, and I go out looking for a little fun," she said. "But here. . . ." She pauses and surveys the dancing couples.

"Who needs this?" she asked. "I went to school on a scholarship and I have to talk to these bums? Yeeech! A bunch of tailors. I'd rather stay home with my husband." She pulls the wrap tight at the neck and goes outside, leaning into the cold wind as she disappears around a corner.

Frank Fields, who once wrote music for a living in Bayonne, N.J., snorts with derision. "That's some tootsie," he says, nodding in the direction of the blonde who has been swallowed up by the night. "She's had her face lifted as many times as she's been married."

139

Glances are exchanged across the generation gap.
NYT/BOB SHERMAN

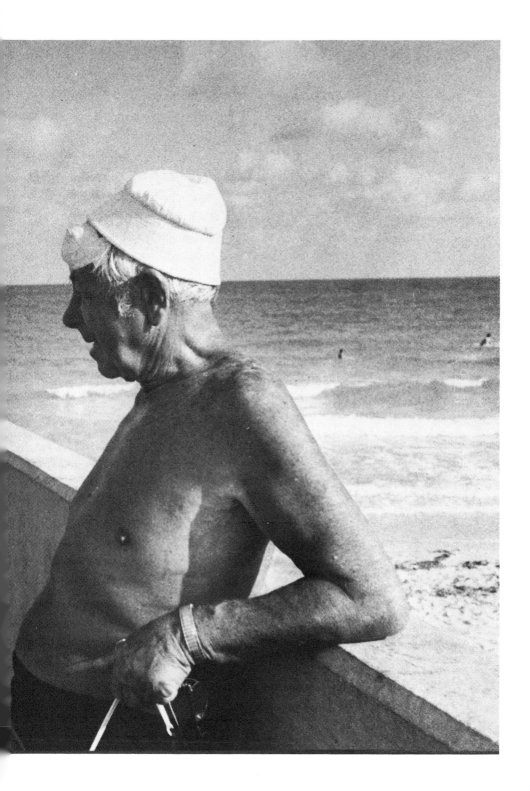

The blonde, he explains, is a regular at the dances held four nights a week at the city auditorium for the large elderly population of Miami Beach.

The band switches to a Latin tune, and the dancers break apart and try to pick up the beat. "Cha-cha-cha," grunts a gray-haired man in mustard yellow pants and shirt. "Cha-cha-cha," answers his partner. She wears a Shirley Temple wig with ginger-colored ringlets, a fringed dress, and go-go beads. Mr. Fields places her age at three score and ten.

These are the elderly who spend the winter months in the senior citizen enclave on the southern tip of Miami Beach, looking for suntans and romance.

The tans are vigorously pursued—and more easily achieved. But in the last 5 years, according to those who return here year after year, the love lives of the widowed and the lonely have improved dramatically.

The sexual revolution that has liberated much of the nation's youth during the last decade has also bestowed a measure of freedom on their grandparents. There are signs of a new understanding among people reaching retirement age today that sex no longer has to be discarded with the death of the marriage partner.

From November to May an estimated 25,000 men and women over the age of 65, mostly Yiddish-speaking Jews who had emigrated to this country from Eastern Europe in the early decades of this century, crowd into South Beach, living alone in rundown rooms in paint-peeling boarding houses and hotels that no longer can attract the moneyed tourist.

Oddly, hippies and surfers gather here, too. The City, fearful that its image as a resort suffers from the impoverished, young or old, has tried to discourage both groups from moving out of South Beach, which has been officially designated as a poverty area. Merchants along the Lincoln Mall, a shopping strip, once wanted tacks fixed to a large ornamental fountain to keep the old folks from sitting on it.

For the elderly, the main source of income is the Social Security check that arrives in the mail around the third day of every month.

The week before the checks arrive, many of the South Beach residents exist on a diet of bagels or go without eating altogether. A few can be seen slipping into alleys behind supermarkets to scavenge for food from the garbage piled outside.

Hot plates are used for cooking in the rooms and are usually the only source of heat. When the temperature drops, the city is plagued with an outbreak of fires caused by hot plates that were left to burn all night.

Conditions like these create an emotional need for companionship that bring the elderly together on the shuffleboard courts, at senior citizens' societies (there are more than two dozen), and at dances like the ones held at the city auditorium at Lummus Park. The dog track, Hialeah race track, and the golf clubs frequented by the wealthy are greatly beyond their means.

Hand-holding affection, more than passion, directs affairs of the heart in South Beach. But occasionally passion drives the elderly into trouble. There was a 78-year-old man arrested here recently after he tossed a fire bomb made from a kerosene-filled prune-juice jar into the apartment of his gray-haired girlfriend who had jilted him. Another man in his 70s shot and wounded his wife who had run off with someone else.

Some years ago it was disclosed that many unmarried couples, mostly widows and widowers, lived together here. Social Security laws at the time penalized couples who had remarried by reducing the size of the widow's benefits. The law was changed and the obstacle removed, but there was no stampede to the altar.

The "sinning seniors," as they were called, were comfortable with illicit love.

"There is very little promiscuity," explained Bernard Baron, director of social services for the city. "But a lot of them crave companionship. They're lonely. Their children dumped them down here and they feel neglected.

"A lot of them figure it's easier to live together in sin than face tremendous pressure from their children if they try to remarry. Almost always the children are dead set against remarriage. Sometimes the only time a child will come down here from New York to visit his parent is to prevent a marriage."

Phil D'Andrea, manager of the Governor's Cafeteria across the street from City Hall, corroborates Mr. Baron's views. "Some of these people are too hungry to care about sex," he says. "Most of them live on fixed incomes, and the cost of renting a room in South Beach now is about $300 a month. It used to be half that. They live together so they can share the rent—and maybe give each other some kindness."

Sylvia Henig, who says she is 79, sits at a table in the cafeteria, sipping coffee. Her home is in Brighton Beach in Brooklyn, but she would like to move permanently to Miami Beach.

"I'm a widow for eight years, so that makes me a member of the wolf pack," she says with a smile. "These women are looking for a man, and they don't care how they get him. Anything that walks or is still above ground is considered a bachelor.

"And the men? They're just as bad," she continues. "I've had lots of propositions but no proposals. The deal usually works like this: You dance, there is an invitation to coffee and Danish, and then, your room or mine? You say no, and there's no more dancing or Danish. He wants a return on his investment."

She gets up to walk back to her rented room. "Back in Brighton Beach," she says, "I'm just another middle-aged Jewish woman plodding along in life. But here . . ." she shrugs her shoulders, "I can escape that and try to be young again."

"Where else would a woman like me who looks like a stuffed sausage wiggle around in a pair of pants three sizes too small? It's a new life. When I came down here I put a picture of my dead husband in my Bible, and when I stepped off the plane I said:

"Well, Izzy, we finally made it to Florida."

Cajuns celebrate crawfish at an exuberant Louisiana festival

ROY REED

Breaux Bridge, La.
April 30, 1972

La Poussiere is a dance hall at the edge of town. To understand what is happening in Breaux Bridge this weekend, one must understand La Poussiere.

It is a Saturday night. The people have eaten dinner—that is important—and now they are sipping whisky, listening to a loud Cajun band and dancing. At least 200 people from 16 to 80 years of age are crowded onto a barely lit wooden dance floor that is no more than 40 feet by 40.

A man who appears to be in his mid-70s explodes from the crowd, fixes a wild eye on a good-looking woman who appears to be in her mid-20s and without introduction sweeps her onto the dance floor.

"Are you married?" he asks.

"Yes, yes," she replies. She is lying, but it does not matter; he ignores her reply.

He swings her lustily to the middle of the floor, into the relative anonymity of the crowd, and immediately makes a bold proposition with his body. She reproves him sharply.

"Well, some womens likes it, some womens don't," he said in a Cajun accent and dances on, utterly unabashed.

The biennial Breaux Bridge crawfish festival going on this weekend is Saturday night at La Poussiere multiplied by one hundred. Officially, it is held to pay homage to the crawfish (crayfish, as it is spelled among out-

144

The first crawfish across the outer ring wins this early event in the two-day Crawfish Festival. But it was music, food, drink, and other attractions which swelled Breaux Bridge, Louisiana, from 5,000 population to 50,000 for the occasion.
NYT/CHRISTOPHER HARRIS

siders), a freshwater crustacean resembling a small lobster that the people of this region not only eat but have also turned into a $50-million-a-year business. But in fact, the festival is two days of almost uninterrupted music, food, drink, dancing and the play, if not the actuality, of sex.

This lusty celebration of the senses is carried on with a wholeheartedness that may be peculiar, among Americans, to the people of south Louisiana. The crawfish festival is one of dozens of spring festivals held each year in the villages and towns of French-speaking south Louisiana, where the Mediterranean outlook still prevails.

But there is trouble in paradise. Some believe it is serious enough to threaten the future of the festivals.

The long-standing rites of spring in this area have been discovered by the young from other regions. The young outsiders, turning the puritan ethic of their fathers on its head, try to outcelebrate the Louisians. Some of the thousands who come inevitably end up in orgies of drunkenness and destructiveness that appall the residents. Two towns, Mansura and Pierre Fort, abolished their festivals this year because of the influx of young people.

Breaux Bridge, a 113-year-old town of 5,000 persons on the slow, winding Bayou Teche, is a relative late-comer among the festival towns. It started the crawfish festival in 1960. But vandalism and rampage by outsiders have caused so much anxiety already that the town's leaders have considered abolishing it. They decided to try again this year with more policemen and a prohibition on glass bottles.

"This is a conservative town," Woodrow Marshall, an organizer of the festival, said today. "Of course, there's no conservatism in the good time—clean good time."

And what is clean good time?

"Dancing, guzzling," he said. "Guzzling to the point you're good and happy. But drunkenness is not looked upon as a good time."

So far this weekend, drunkenness and destructiveness have been minimal, even though thousands of young men and women have come from other places in old automobiles and vans and on motorcycles. The town officials estimated yesterday's crowd at 50,000.

That included a few dozen elderly couples who are members of an Airstream trailers club. They park their expensive trailers under the large oaks at the home of Mr. and Mrs. Harris Champagne. While the younger crowds on the packed streets downtown ate boiled crawfish, peeling the shell, eating the tail and throwing the discarded red heads in the gutters, the guests of the Champagnes sat on the quiet bank of the bayou and ate a gourmet dish called crawfish étouffé, which, according to her friends, Mrs. Champagne invented about 1949.

There is continuous live music from at least two places downtown, and occasionally from three or four. Crawfish, beer and wine can be bought about every 50 feet.

The festive activity has not stopped for two days, except for a few hours early today for sleep and church. There has been a parade with the newly elected Cajun Governor, Edwin Edwards, as the main participant.

A crawfish queen was crowned and there were crawfish eating and peeling contests, crawfish races.

Northern interests have had mixed luck. A native of Pitman, N.J., named Chester McGear won the eating contest by putting away 20½ pounds of crawfish (weight before peeling). But in the races, a visitor's entry named Allenous refused to leave the starting post and was defeated by a large and rather aggressive crawfish named Snaggletooth from Metairie, La.

The festival is supposed to end tonight, but no one seems to know that.

At La Poussiere, the old man has delivered the young woman to her waiting friends at the edge of the dance floor. He pauses to chat.

"I made a lot of money in my life and now I'm a, how you call, playboy," he says with a broad and disarming smile. "I don't have much time left so I'm going to take some of it with me."

He heads back into the crowd like a bull, his eye searching.

*Shifting patterns of immigration
add new flavor to New York City's
melting pot*

JOHN L. HESS

New York, N.Y.
Sept. 25, 1972

In subtle and in startling ways, the flavor of New York is changing.

Japanese spitted meats at the San Gennaro festival in Little Italy . . . the soft accents of Afro-French and Afro-British on the subways . . . lamb turning on vertical barbecues in Times Square snack bars . . . graffiti blazoning names like Toni and Michele . . . an uproar of Spanish as well as Italian on the bocci courts on Houston Street . . . a proliferation of Latin-Chinese chop suey-and-cocino joints and of more or less authentic Mandarin and Cantonese restaurants. . . .

As ever, New York is a prism that refracts the shifting pattern of American immigration, now being transformed by the reform act of 1965. Until then, a national quota system heavily favored the British Isles and the countries of Northern Europe—where the pressure to emigrate was lowest.

Today, the inflow more closely responds to the pressures of the world's population and poverty. The main tide of immigration comes from the Mediterranean, Asia and, above all, Latin America.

A survey of the statistics and a tour of some of the new foreign communities lay to rest some popular miconceptions, however. For example, fears that the racial and cultural mix of the United States would be radically transformed have proved groundless.

Historically speaking, the tide of immigration is hardly more than a trickle,

148

In the decade that followed 1900, when the population of the United States was 76 million, a total of 8.8 million immigrants arrived. In the decade that followed 1960, when the population was 179 million, immigration totaled 3.3 million.

These figures exclude illegal immigration, which some authorities suspect may exceed a million a year—nearly triple the present legal rate. Because of the reluctance of the poor, the illiterate, the foreign and above all the "illegals" to respond to census takers, all estimates must rely heavily on guesswork.

The Very Rev. Dr. John A. Poulos, the ebullient pastor of St. Demetrios Greek Orthodox Church in Astoria, Queens, says humorously that he has devised his own census: "If I have five funerals a week, 10 christenings and seven weddings, then I must have 38,000 to 42,000 people in my parish."

While the effect of immigration upon the United States as a whole is minimal, its impact on New York City is evident. But it is a matter of mix rather than an increase in the number of foreign-born.

In fact, the 1970 census showed a decline in the metropolitan area's "foreign stock"—persons of foreign birth or with one or both parents foreign born. The 1970 figure was 4,561,286; in 1960 it was 4,893,341.

These figures exclude Puerto Ricans, whose number is now thought to exceed a million, and, of course, American blacks "immigrating" from the South.

The Dominicans form one of New York's fastest-growing communities. Of 71,437 aliens legally admitted into New York City in fiscal 1971, they led with 8,217 entries. But the actual number is thought to be far larger, and members of the community think it now totals 200,000.

City planners seeking to cope with the social and educational problems of immigrants estimate the foreign communities as far larger than the census estimates but somewhat below the estimates of community leaders. At any rate, the Greek community growing in Astoria and Woodside, Queens, and in Chelsea, Manhattan, is visibly greater than the census figure. Queens political leaders on a ceremonial pilgrimage to Israel recently added Athens to their itinerary.

With waiting time for legal visas running to 18 months, impatient foreigners arrive as tourists and stay on. Many Haitians buy forged visas or take an "underground railroad" through Canada; Dominicans go as tourists to Puerto Rico, where they shed their nationality; South Europeans enter marriages of convenience with American citizens, and many Greek and Chinese seamen jump ship.

But inquiry tended to refute another widely held notion: that immigrants are lured by New York City welfare.

Speaking of the illegals, Sol Marks, the district director of the Federal Immigration and Naturalization Service, said in an interview:

"Contrary to some public impressions, the people we encounter are generally gainfully employed, their employers speak highly of them, and they're

A bocci player on East Houston Street; A. Socrates Torrez, co-owner of an upper Broadway Dominican Bakery; and shoppers in Little Italy.
NYT/NEAL BOENZI, WILLIAM SAURO

not of the criminal class. Most of them are law-abiding, hardworking people who have been drawn here by economic conditions in their countries."

Perhaps the most dramatic effect of the 1965 act has been the mushrooming of the city's Asian communities. The trend actually had begun earlier; the census showed 27,909 residents "other than black and white" in 1950, then 53,391 in 1960 and 177,906 in 1970.

The explosion is most visible in the spread of Chinatown north through Little Italy. The Italians, still the most numerous segment of New York's "foreign stock" and still arriving from the old country in large numbers, have in the main quit this old neighborhood and Red Hook (now Puerto Rican) for the outer reaches of Brooklyn, Queens and the suburbs.

But old traditions and old ties remain. As a result, Little Italy and Chinatown co-exist in a curious harmony. The stroller may see an Italian religious procession on Mott Street, with nearly all the onlookers Chinese, or glimpse Italian barbers shearing Asian locks. In one store, Italians are playing cards; next door, Chinese are playing mah-jongg.

Farther east, on Houston Street, three of the five public bocci courts are abandoned to weeds and beer cans. The other two are tended impeccably by a Russian concessionnaire; the players shout, in mock anger or triumph, as often in Spanish as in Italian, with broken English serving as a lingua franca.

On Mott Street, an elderly man in an employment agency confides that there is a shortage of help for Chinese restaurants—"at least for us because if you don't have the green card, we can't send you."

A cook estimates that there are now at least 2,000 Chinese restaurants in New York with new ones opening as fast as cooks can be imported from Hong Kong or stolen from competitors. Thanks to the 1965 immigration act, the supply of talent seems excellent; Mr. Chin said the cooking was sometimes as good as in Hong Kong, although the variety of foods available here was more limited.

The new arrivals are mostly Cantonese, from southern China, with a sprinkling of Northerners. In this connection, the rash of restaurants offering the cuisine of the western province of Szechwan draws crinkly smiles in Chinatown. It appears to be a polite Oriental response to a demand inspired by the Beautiful People and their emulators.

The Latin-Chinese diners have a different history: They are an import from Latin America and especially Cuba where Chinese have lived for generations and there became assimilated both in language and cuisine.

The hand laundry has fallen on lean times, owing to the washing machine and the drip-dry shirt. A growing number of shops in Chinatown provide needlework for women, subcontracting for the garment industry uptown. But the prosperity of the community, whose population is now thought to have reached 100,000, rests on the prosperity of the Chinese restaurant business.

The term is subjective. Mr. Chin says those with jobs make "good money."

Even dishwashers, he said, earn $500 a month, working the standard 10 hours a day, six days a week. But many are unemployed.

Far different is the situation of the new Japanese community, now about 10,000. A majority represent Japanese companies here, commuting to downtown offices from homes in Forest Hills and other neighborhoods. Many of them have box lunches—typically rice, pickled vegetables, teriyaki and tamago yaki dishes—delivered by such office catering services as Matsuya in Maiden Lane.

Most of the Japanese expatriates plan to return home some day, and their chief problem seems to be a sense of isolation and nostalgia. This led some time ago to the suicides of several wives.

Some 500 Japanese artists also are thought to have settled in the New York area, many of them in the loft district of SoHo. Taxie Kusunoki, a Nisei—an American born here of Japanese immigrant parents—who is an editor of the weekly *Japanese American News*, commented about the Japanese-born artists working here:

"Most of them are painting in the Western genre—in fact, the work of some Nisei artists is more Oriental."

The effort to excel in Western art forms was visible—or rather, audible—at a recent Korean concert on the Mall in Central Park. It featured, in addition to dazzling native songs and dances, arias from *Rigoletto* and *Il Trovatore* and a Korean opera in the Western mode.

On another level, youths of many immigrant communities were found to be going in for rock and other elements of the American juvenile scene, including gang fighting and delinquency.

There are exceptions, such as a few Haitian combos, creole folk artists and soccer leagues and West Indian steel drum bands and cricket players. But the rapid Americanization of the young is a common preoccupation of all national groups here.

Community leaders complain that there are few or no youth centers and gymnasiums in many of the new communities. Several Greek, Haitian and Chinese civic leaders volunteered that an even more urgent need was for the establishment of day-care centers.

Many immigrant women take outside jobs when they can find them, breaking with custom in the home country. Elias Betzios, president of the Greek-American Neighborhood Action Committee, told a visitor to his pizza factory in Astoria:

"In a lot of families, the salaries are so small that the wife has to work. Many women here send their children back to Greece to live with relatives. One came back recently with a 5-year-old who almost didn't recognize his mother. And believe it or not, a lot of families just leave their children alone."

"The big one takes care of the little ones," said Mrs. Irene Ekos, a vivacious young mother of two. She was interviewed beside her hot-dog cart outside Macy's in Herald Square. Her husband, Alex, a slender man from Salonika, had just pulled his cart alongside for a family chat. He looked weary.

"Too many hours' work," he explained. "Eighteen blocks I push this. I'm exhausted."

"We are in the streets so our kids can go to school," Mrs. Ekos said. She was flustered at how they might react if their parents' picture was in the paper.

"They don't know that we may be worth more than those who work in an office. If you come first, the spot belongs to you, so you've got to be every day here."

A "good spot," in the Greek community, means a place where a hot-dog stand does active business. Rights to a spot are honored by seniority within the trade, although not by the police.

Despite frequent fines for unlicensed peddling, it appears that hot dogs can yield a surprising income. Father Poulos says he knows a young man who found a good spot by a hospital, and bought a $68,000 home after three and a half years.

Asked why so many Greeks in America had entered the restaurant business, he replied: "That's easy—because they could start as dishwashers, and then buy the business."

The Greek drive to succeed and to acquire property is personified by Mr. Betzios. He arrived virtually penniless in 1955, and found a job as a machine designer. "But after 5 p.m., I couldn't stand still," he said, so he opened a pizzeria. "I'd never eaten a pizza," he confided.

Today, he runs a large, spotlessly automated plant, Ellio's Pizza House, where 115 employes turn out 40,000 frozen pizzas a day. And he has completed his Americanization by merging his pizza plant with the Purex Corporation.

"I'm very happy in this country," he said. "We're doing very nicely here. If we're missing a lot of things, we missed a whole lot over there."

Relatively speaking, the new Greeks are a success story in American immigration. They have their problems, but are well on the road to prosperity and assimilation that many other ethnic groups have taken before them.

Less fortunate, and less optimistic, are the new arrivals from Latin America, who straddle the color line and face graver handicaps in findings jobs and housing. Many look home with nostalgia, and despair.

Said a Dominican tailor on Amsterdam Avenue: "Go back? Not now. When I find something to do."

Integration: Mississippi town "Isn't like it used to be"

JAMES T. WOOTEN

Hot Coffee, Miss.
January 8, 1970

Thirsty visitors here may choose between water or soft drinks or, rumor has it, high-quality moonshine whiskey, but the steaming liquid for which this tiny village was named is not available.

"No, you can't buy no ready-made coffee," R. J. Knight said this week amid the incredible clutter of his general store. "Used to keep it for folks but they made such a mess, leaving the cups around and spilling it and all such stuff as that, I don't fool with it anymore."

His town's name grew out of another storekeeper's custom generations ago of providing coffee for his customers.

"Folks would say 'Let's go get some hot coffee,'" Mr. Knight said, "and pretty soon they were just saying 'Let's go to Hot Coffee,' and it sort of stuck.

"Seems a downright shame not to do it anymore," he continued, nodding toward a large percolator perched idly on a shelf, its black cord wrapped around its spout.

"That thing used to cough and splutter all day long," he said. Now it stands as a silent, stainless-steel symbol of just one more thing that "isn't like it used to be."

Cotton is about gone, and so are Sunday morning buggy rides to church, and so are the mules Mr. Knight's father once sold "on the credit" to farmers who raised cotton and sent their children to segregated schools. Now those

155

schools are gone, too, erased by a Supreme Court ruling that includes Mr. Knight's county and 29 other Mississippi school districts.

"Been reading where they claim integration's going to work down here," Mr. Knight said, polishing his spectacles and peering through them at arm's length. "I'd like to know what they mean by 'work.' Guess they mean the niggers will be marrying white folks before long. That's what some of them want and reckon now that's what they'll get."

He sighed and settled back in an old lawn chair near the blue flames of a gas heater and gazed out the window at the empty house across the road where he was born 58 years ago.

Hot Coffee's population is no problem for the decennial census takers. They can drive here in a few minutes from Collins, the seat of Covington County, and begin counting at the first house they see when they reach the intersection of highways 532 and 37.

That would be C. J. Pridgen's home, and they might find the 85-year-old widower out in his yard puttering around the bushes and shrubs. It is less than a mile from there to the white frame home of Mr. and Mrs. James H. Carter, and in between they would count but 14 other people in six other houses.

"But it's hard to say just how many people do live here," Mr. Knight said. "See, we got people that live four and five miles out in the country who call Hot Coffee their home."

It is an understandable claim, for, in addition to their traditional Saturday shopping trips to nearby Mt. Olive or Laurel or Collins, most of them wind up three or four times a week at Mr. Knight's store.

They buy gasoline, usually a dollar's worth at a time, and serve themselves from the two pumps out front. They munch bologna and crackers and drink root beer or some other "soda water."

They squat in the gravel outside in the summer or around Mr. Knight's blistering heater at this time of year and exchange views and discuss politics and religion and talk about hunting and maybe pick up a few groceries before they leave.

Mr. Knight's clientele is integrated and he knows all their names, and they call him "Mr. Dutch." They are farmers who grow soybeans and a little bit of cotton and quite a bit of timber, and there are calluses on their hands, whether they are black or white.

They are people who know the land and depend on it for their livelihoods and respect it for its constancy and sometimes curse it for its demands on their bodies, and none of them wants to move into town.

It was late in the afternoon, and Mr. Knight's plate-glass windows were covered with steam. Stacy Burnham and his freckle-faced, 7-year-old son, Joey, climbed down from their pickup truck, which had two rifles in a rack behind the seat, and hurried in to the store, rubbing their hands and stomping their feet.

"I mean, it is going to be bad out there," Mr. Burnham said as he turned his back to the heater.

He is a tall, sturdy red-faced man with 1000 acres of good Mississippi land, a wife who drives a school bus, a quick laugh, and a great love for Joey.

"The boy there was supposed to go to the nigger school this year," he said. "He ain't, though. Gonna get him in the private school up at Mount Olive."

The boy, wearing a miniature copy of the brown hunting cap on his father's head, squinted up at him and asked whether they were going to buy ammunition for his rifle.

"That's against the Federal law," Mr. Knight told the youngster. "Not supposed to sell you any shells, ain't that right, Stacy?"

Mr. Burnham winked. "That's right, Mr. Dutch."

"Going to anyway," Mr. Knight said. "Law don't do nothing but protect criminals any way."

The two men looked at each other and smiled. Mr. Knight and the boy went to the back of the store, and Mr. Burnham returned to the subject of his son's education.

"He ain't goin' over there to nigger school," he said, "that's all. Not right." He said that everybody else he knew felt the same way and that some people were planning a demonstration "with pickets and boycotts and such stuff as that" in Collins when the school opened this week.

The boy returned with his shells and a box of caramel-coated popcorn. He and his father left in their truck.

"Good folks," Mr. Knight said. "They live about four miles out. Ain't the boy something? Come around here last summer chewing tobacco. Yessir, had him a package of Red Man in his back pocket, bigger than everything. He's a good one, that boy is."

Mr. Knight settled back in his lawn chair near the heater and polished his spectacles again. "Sure am glad they got a place for him to go to school with white people."

Troubled America

Memorial Day at Arlington: "Our only son"

JAMES T. WOOTEN

Arlington, Va.
May 31, 1971

At the crest of the great green hill, a slight figure moved haltingly among the white marble stones, stopping and stooping at each one, then stepping on toward the next, cradling a small wreath of red roses against her dark frock. "I only get to come from Richmond once a year, and I always get mixed up about just where he is," she explained apologetically.

The soft sod squished beneath her feet as she walked from one row to another until, finally, she knelt in the damp ground above the grave of Pvt. Roy W. Maclan Jr., a teen-aged infantryman who died in Korea 20 years ago.

"He was our only son," she said, planting the wreath's wire tripod beside the stone. She smoothed the grass at its base with that quick tenderness mothers learn and when she arose her eyes were moist with remembering.

"This makes the 20th year, now," she said as she left. "You'd think I'd remember where he is, wouldn't you? But there are so many here like him."

A delicate spring rain was falling this morning when the big black gates of Arlington National Cemetery creaked opened to admit a tiny group of waiting, shivering visitors. As Memorial Day grew older, however, the shreds of charcoal clouds skittered away and, by midday, the little lanes and walkways that

161

ramble through the 518 rolling acres were like rush-hour expressways for pedestrians.

On any day, the cemetery attracts hundreds, but today, as on this holiday in past years, there were thousands—and across the country, from here on the banks of the Potomac to the Punch Bowl, a national cemetery high above Pearl Harbor, thousands of other Americans made quiet visits to the graves that held meaning for them.

For some who came to Arlington, it was the Tomb of the Unknown Soldier where, after the traditional wreath-laying, Gen. Leonard F. Chapman Jr., the Marine Corps commandant, told a large crowd that the latest of this nation's wars had been its most unselfish.

For others who came here, the focal point was an elliptical walkway that brought them to the eternal flame burning over the body of President Kennedy and to the small graveside of his brother Robert.

For many others, tourists in a tourists' town, coming to Arlington was much like going to the Smithsonian—a part of the prepaid bus tour.

"It's a tourist attraction just like the rest of Washington," a veteran employe at the cemetery's visitor center said. "For most of these people, it's just one more stop."

Mr. and Mrs. Lyle Bacon were standing at the back of their car in the newest section of the cemetery when the thunder of the salute at the Tomb of the Unknown Soldier reverberated across the valley.

She shuddered and looked inquisitively at her 41-year-old husband, an accountant in Baltimore. He placed his arm on her shoulder.

The last time they came to Arlington was to watch the burial of their 18-year-old son, William, a Marine private killed last October near Danang by a Vietcong booby trap.

They both were torn by what has become a common schism in the soul of the American parent. "I would have been ashamed if he hadn't wanted to serve his country and I don't think I could have stood it if he had cut and run," his father said. "But, God, how do I explain his death to myself? I mean, can anybody tell me what difference it made?"

Mrs. Bacon wept softly while he spoke. Then, suddenly, as though he had uttered some posthypnotic suggestion, her face was contorted in rage and her eyes flashed with a deep anger.

"Yes, that's right," she snapped. "Can anybody tell me? Me! Me! I'm his mother. Why shouldn't I be told?" Mr. Bacon wrapped his arm around her as she began to sob and they walked off into the line upon line of marble markers.

At the grave of a fellow Army major who was killed in the 1968 Tet offensive in Vietnam, a stocky career soldier with graying hair stood at attention and saluted the small American flag flapping beside the stone. He said:

"It's an honor to die for the right thing, and I'm convinced that this country, with all of its problems and sins, is still worth dying for."

Then, like the Bacons, he turned and strode away.

At an intersection, not far from the grave of President Taft, a florist's van pulled to the curb and a young man alighted with a basket of flowers.

"Can't talk," he said hurriedly. "Busy day. People phoning in orders from all over the place. Biggest day we've had this year. Bigger than Easter."

As large as it is, Arlington National Cemetery has almost reached its capacity and there is serious discussion in the Army and in Congress about closing its lots forever, a move already made at eight other national cemeteries. There is no room for expansion. The Pentagon is on one side, Fort Myer sprawls on two other sides, and the Potomac curls along in front.

The road alongside the newest section, where most of the Vietnam dead are being buried, will be closed tonight, and tomorrow the asphalt will be removed to make room for more graves. After that, the cemetery officials say, there is no place else to go.

"Wouldn't it be nice if when it's all full," 17-year-old Richard Billingsley of Silver Spring, Md., said wistfully, "they'd just stop having wars. I mean, like you'd just say, 'Well, I'm sorry but we can't get in this war because we don't have any more room left in Arlington.' "

Fate deals a last blow to
Vernon McCall of Balsam Grove

ROY REED

Balsam Grove, N.C.
June 13, 1971

The trials of Vernon McCall came to an end here last night in one more unmanageable act of fate of the kind that had puzzled and overwhelmed him all his life.

He was the frailest of the McCalls, a clan that makes up more than half of the once hundred families in this isolated little valley in the Blue Ridge Mountains south of Asheville.

Most of the McCalls are archetypal Southern mountaineers: tall, lean, sturdy, pale-eyed, wry-humored, quick to take offense, and not much inclined to reveal themselves to strangers.

Vernon was thin and had pale blue eyes, but beyond that was not like the others. He was short, stooped, diabetic, and epileptic. He was more likely to laugh at himself than at someone else, if he could forget his worries long enough to laugh at all. He did not seem to know how to get angry, and he trusted strangers.

It was this 40-year-old waif who turned out to be the principal target when the United States Government exerted its awesome authority in Transylvania County.

The trouble blew into the open Feb. 22, the day the Government destroyed Vernon's home. But it had been building for a year before that.

164

The people here once considered the United States Forest Service their friend. That was fortunate, because the valley of the north fork of the French Broad River, which Balsam Grove straddles, is completely surrounded by Forest Service domain, the huge Pisgah National Forest.

The community and the Government agency had had many years of peaceful coexistence. That meant the people avoided the old mountain practice of setting fires in the forest, and in return the Government blinked most of the time when the residents hunted and fished illegally in the federally protected woods.

About a year ago, the Forest Service ended the practice of live and let live. It began sending its surveyors onto the private property adjoining the national forest to recheck old property lines.

In a year and a half of resurveying, the Government has yet to discover an error in a private property owner's favor. On the other hand, it has raised the threat of extending the national forest boundaries onto land used as farms and pastures by distances ranging from a few feet to many yards.

The methods did not help matters. On one wooded piece of property, a surveyor ran a line, painted a row of trees to mark it, then decided he had made a mistake. He had the painted trees sawed down, then ran a second line. Once again he had erred, and that row of trees was cut. He finally settled on a third line. The Forest Service has not offered to pay the owner for the cut trees.

In the midst of the resurveying, the Forest Service began the controversial practice of clear-cutting in the Pisgah National Forest.

The residents have found at least seven patches of mountainside surrounding balsam groves that have been peeled of every tree and bush, then bulldozed, to prepare the cleared land for planting white pine seedlings.

The Forest Service is trying to increase its stands of pine, which grows faster and is in greater commercial demand than hardwoods.

The seedlings are not yet in evidence, but the effect of the clear-cutting is very much so. One mountain-top tract of about 100 acres had been stripped to the red clay subsoil and is visible for miles from the high, winding roads in the surrounding mountains.

Richard McCall, an older community leader, pointed out some of the clear-cut patches one day last week. He drove first down a steep dirt road and stopped to gaze down into a wooded draw that had not been molested.

The oaks reached up more than 100 feet and many were 15 to 18 inches in diameter at the trunk. An ovenbird's sharp call rose up from the dark floor of the hollow, up through the sunlight's spots, and out the roof of the oaks.

"This was cut over the last time about 50 years ago," Mr. McCall said. "It took it this long to get back like this."

Then he drove to a clear-cut patch half a mile down the road. The trees and saplings, even the wild azaleas, rhododendrons, and mountain laurel bushes that are blooming in this area now, were all lying in brown piles, waiting for the bulldozer.

"They're just about to ruin this country, the way I see it," Mr. McCall said.

The residents complained that the clear-cutting had already bared so many steep slopes to the spring rains that red clay was washing into the creeks and rivers, threatening the fish.

Cutting the hardwood also alarms the hunters.

"Can't nothing live in a pine thicket—deer, squirrels, not nothing," said Spurgeon McCall, one of the community's angry young men.

He is an unabashed violator of the game laws. He has served time in Federal prison for his repeated incursions on the national forest and swears he will continue to hunt there, if they do not cut it all down.

In the growing hostility over clear-cutting and resurveying, the Forest Service made its move against Vernon McCall.

The agency decided that the one-acre tract that his house trailer sat on, in a woods with the mountains rising in the background, was legally part of the National Forest.

It sent a letter in January to Cannon McCall, Vernon's 89-year-old father, who claimed ownership of the acre, and warned him to take everything off the property by Feb. 22.

The father did not respond.

Vernon, who lived alone in the trailer, was away from home much of the day Feb. 22. He had no regular employment. He worked at odd jobs in the winter, and in the warm months he picked and sold blackberries and sprigs of mountain laurel.

Dan W. Hile, the district ranger, arrived at Vernon's trailer that day with eight workmen and a bulldozer. Finding the trailer locked, they broke in and removed a bed and two or three other items and put them down in the mud outside. Then they dug a huge hole with the bulldozer and shoved the trailer in and covered it up.

Vernon also had a small barn, a hogpen, and a wooden milk box over the spring that provided his water. These, too, were destroyed and buried.

An angry crowd of neighbors gathered, but the workmen and Mr. Hile went on with the job.

"My orders came from Atlanta and this property must be cleared before we leave here," he told Cannon McCall.

Spurgeon McCall, 27, his blue jeans and T-shirt dirty from working on a machine, his felt hat bandless and slouched around his dark hair, long sideburns, and lean face, talked with a visitor recently about what happened at Vernon's place Feb. 22.

Spurgeon, whose friends call him Spug, and Glenn McCall, one of Vernon's brothers, had gone to the scene together, he recalled.

"Vernon was sittin' under a tree lookin' dazed. Hile walks up to Glenn, says, 'Glenn, I hope there ain't no hard feelin's over this.' Glenn didn't answer, just looked at the ground.

"Hile come over to me. 'Spug, ain't no hard feelin's, is there?'

"And I says, 'Well, Danny, you just went an' buried a man's dwellin' place. It had everything in it belonged to his dead momma and his two dead brothers. Then you knock down his barn and hogpen and buried them, too. What you figger you got to do to cause hard feelin's—spit in a feller's face?' "

The community was enraged. Vernon, at the urging of his friends, swore out a warrant charging Mr. Hile with destruction of his property.

The young men were especially angry. Many talked of taking guns after the Forest Service men, even weeks afterward.

"It's a wonder they didn't get this country burnt down," Spurgeon McCall said last week, referring to purposely set fires in the national forest, a possibility that is still discussed quietly.

The effect on Vernon was different. He did not get angry.

"Vernon's bad to drink," said Mrs. Leonard Griffin, a community leader, "and he's been drinking a lot more since they buried his trailer."

Friends set up another trailer for him on the highway right-of-way in front of the disputed acre. He plowed a garden and planted six rows of potatoes on the land the Forest Service claims.

Last week, he showed a stranger the bowl of plastic flowers he had placed on the "grave" of his old trailer. The trailer contained mementos of his dead mother and two dead brothers, the brothers having frozen to death beside a whisky still in 1970. He pointed to pieces of the milk box the workmen had left beside his spring.

"I kept milk and butter both in there," he said, proudly and sadly.

That was Friday. Yesterday, just at nightfall, he and three young men from another community walked along state highway 215, drinking.

A quarrel began. A passing motorist saw blows being struck.

Another car came along a few seconds later. The driver saw something in the middle of the highway but in the dimness realized too late that it was two men, lying crosswise.

The younger man escaped. Vernon, as usual, did not. He was killed.

The Government's little acre, or Vernon's, or Cannon's, or whomever it belongs to, was quiet today. If the Government comes again to claim it, its agents will have to move not only Vernon's potato plants but also his chair, which he left sitting under a shade tree, noticeably over the property line.

For a proud Bronx couple, place called home is a car

PAUL L. MONTGOMERY

New York
June 4, 1971

Up near the end of the Bronx, where the sludgy Hutchinson River curves out to Eastchester Bay, there is an area of lots and junkyards that seem sooner or later to contain all the worn-out discarded parts of the city.

Almost every day for the last eight months, in the snow and the rain and now the summer sun, a 1966 Dodge has been parked on a little-used road by the side of the river.

Mr. and Mrs. Chester Konarsky, who were born in the Bronx before World War I and who have seen most of the things they worked for slip away, have been living in the car, sitting in it by day and sleeping in it by night; they think it must have been in September or October because the weather was still warm.

They remember unusual things—the dates that Mrs. Konarsky, who cannot walk, has to go to the hospital for treatment; the time the ice melted so Mr. Konarsky could again dig for steamer clams, the couple's staple food; the time last month they were down to their last can of beets and decided to forget their fierce pride and go to the Welfare Department for help.

Mr. Konarsky, soft-spoken man with mechanic's hands who worked in the City Island boatyards until the arthritis in his right arm hurt too much, remembers that the welfare office was on Bainbridge Avenue.

168

"They told me I couldn't get any because we didn't have a permanent address," he recalls.

A welfare spokesman said the Konarskys had not been processed because they refused to answer questions about their backgrounds.

The spokesman also said their car seemed so well kept ("I don't have much else to do but keep it nice," Mr. Konarsky says) and their clothes so neat ("We got some water from the hydrant and got fixed up to go down there") that officials found the couple's story hard to believe.

The Welfare Department is now looking into the couple's case again. The Federal Social Security office is also seeing if Mrs. Konarsky qualifies for disability payments, a process that can take as much as five months. Meanwhile, the couple, who have been married 35 years, still live in their car.

Yesterday was not a bad day for them. The weather was nice and there had been no trouble at the motel lot where they park to sleep. They still had a little gas so they drove down to the river at 6 A.M. for breakfast—bread from the day before and instant coffee cooked in a Sterno stove in the grass.

In the afternoon, there was good luck clamming in Mamaroneck and they came back with two buckets for supper. "I don't know what we'd do if it wasn't for the steamers," Mr. Konarsky says.

The Konarskys' only source of income since last fall, when Mr. Konarsky's boatyard job ended, has been unwinding copper wire from electric motors in abandoned cars in the neighborhood. The wire can be sold for 40 cents a pound.

"Some days I can do 20, 25 pounds," Mr. Konarsky says. "Some days the arm hurts and I can't do any."

The last time the couple slept in a bed was the week before Christmas.

Aside from the car and a radio and the few bits of furniture, they have little else to sell. "There's Alice's engagement and wedding rings," Mr. Konarsky says matter-of-factly, "but her finger's too swollen to get them off."

It began, as nearly as Mrs. and Mr. Konarsky can remember, in August, 1969. They were having trouble with the heat and hot water in their apartment, the landlord wanted to raise the rent from $60 to $80 a month. Mrs. Konarsky was not feeling well, so they decided to move to a friend's boat on City Island.

Mr. Konarsky, who is 59 years old, and his wife, who is 55, met through a friend of his at the City Island boatyard where he had worked since he was 16.

During the war, Mr. Konarsky worked at building PT boats on City Island, and afterward rose to be a foreman, earning as much as $200 a week. Then shipbuilding declined, Mrs. Konarsky's health deteriorated, and Mr. Konarsky found he could not work regularly because of his arm. So they moved to the friend's boat.

"It was comical, really," Mr. Konarsky says. "I had a lot of time so I fixed up the boat. Then somebody saw it and bought it, so we were out of a place to stay. That was the first time we went to the car."

It was last spring, and they lived in the car for about two months. The reasons they chose the car seem hard for them to express.

Part of it was the difficulty of finding a place at reasonable rent where Mrs. Konarsky would not have to walk up steps. For the rest, all they know is that they had been brought up on the belief that hard work was a virtue and it was a disgrace to be on relief.

"We never asked for anything until last month," Mrs. Konarsky says. "It just seemed like we could make it without it."

After the two months in the car, a friend offered them a room at the back of a vacant store and they took it gratefully. Mr. Konarsky again set to work fixing up the place, using scrap lumber from the multitudinous dumps in the neighborhood. In the fall, the store was rented, and they went back to the car.

They rise every morning with the sun on the motel lot, Mr. Konarsky sleeping in the back seat and Mrs. Konarsky in the front.

Then they go down to park by the river for breakfast and, if they are feeling well, a day of breaking open starter motors and windshield-wiper motors with a jacknife and a ball peen hammer for the copper wire inside.

Their meals are simple, usually clams or canned goods cooked over the Sterno. If there has been a good day for copper, they have a hamburger or a sandwich at a stand. One day, several months ago, they spent $4 in a diner for a meal and still remember it.

Mr. Konarsky showers and shaves in the boatyards, where he is still known. For Mrs. Konarsky, he boils water over the stove and she washes in the car.

The winter was not pleasant. They remember sitting together for hours huddled under blankets and old clothes; some nights, when Mr. Konarsky had the gas, he kept the motor going all night to keep off the cold.

"It's better now," Mr. Konarsky said yesterday. "It looks like it's going to be a nice summer."

"We're down now, but we still have some pride left," Mrs. Konarsky said in the car by the Hutchinson River. "We'll get up again."

Newnan, Ga., hopes to hold on to its traditions

JAMES T. WOOTEN

Newnan, Ga.
December 30, 1969

Each morning at nine, the old men come to the weather-scarred courthouse as though answering a Pavlovian summons from the clanging clock in the dome.

They walk the halting, shuffling walk of the aged past the Confederate monument and the row of recruiting posters—reminders of wars' too early and too late for their services—up the chipped steps and into the dim, dingy hallway where they spend their day hunched around a ragged checkerboard, playing a while, watching a bit, laughing, coughing, talking, or gazing silently out the fly-specked window.

"Them checkers, they don't never really stop," one of them explained. "When a fellow gets beat or quits or maybe gets sick or dies or something, somebody else just scoots his chair over and don't nobody notice the difference." The constancy of their game is characteristic of life in this pleasant, prosperous little city—and when this decade dies, it is entirely possible that the next one will simply scoot its chair over and few here will notice the difference.

"Not much to notice, is there?" snorted J. T. Pike, a stern-faced short-spoken octogenarian whose job as the Coweta County Ordinary makes him custodian of the area's vital statistics.

It is to his cluttered, high-ceilinged office, just around the corner from the old men and their checkers, that the young men bound for military duty come for their birth certificates. "Volunteers or draftees, it doesn't matter. They've all got to have proof of their birth," he reminded a recent visitor—and in his nearly 30 years on the job he has provided that documentation to hundreds of Newnan men.

Since 1960, 16 who came to Mr. Pike's office for proof of their birth have subsequently died in combat. Halfway around the world from this city of 16,000 and the rolling red clay hills of northern Georgia, the 16, half of them white, half black, were killed in such places as the Iadrang Valley and Khesanh and Danang and Bienhoa, victims of a war that many believe has changed the complexion of America's politics and altered the postures of its people.

But the city they call home has felt little impact from that war.

"Nope, other than losing those boys, we haven't noticed it one way or the other," said Ernest W. Barron, the city clerk. "I didn't realize there were that many killed. I guess you get used to it after a while," he said and then apologized for using those terms.

One who didn't come back was Timothy Cole Jr. He enlisted in the Army after two years in an engineering program at Georgia Tech in Atlanta and shortly after his father, a dairyman, had died in Newnan.

"He saw the need and believed it was his duty," his mother said. "He had two cousins who'd served over there and he just felt that the right thing for him to do was to do his part."

On Oct. 18 last year, two months before his twenty-second birthday, Warrant Officer Cole, a helicopter pilot, was killed near Chulai when his craft was hit by Vietcong fire.

"He'd been married a year and two weeks when it happened," his mother said.

Had Timothy Cole Jr. survived what his mother calls "that useless war," his plans were to transfer to Auburn University in Alabama to study dairying and to keep his hand in flying.

"His death seems useless but there's more to it than that," she continued. "He even said so in his letters. He said it was the war that is ruining the country and making a mess of so many people's lives, Americans and Vietnamese, and that we just refuse to go in and win it and if we weren't going to win it we were just losing it day by day and he believed that losing is useless—and so do I."

But the passion in her voice is absent in the conversations of many neighbors; instead, there is an echo of the view of Mr. Barron, the city clerk. Their community has not really noticed that Mrs. Cole's son or the 15 other men will not be coming back to Newnan. Perhaps that is because this city has always been generous with its sons in time of war. A plaque at the courthouse lists separately the 21 white men and 13 Negroes who were killed in World War I. More than 80 died in World War II, and Korea claimed 40.

"The casualty rate in Newnan is extraordinarily high," a Marine officer said not long ago.

In addition to the 258 draftees who have left Newnan in the last five years alone, recruiting for other services is and always has been booming. "I think that's because boys around here grow up knowing it's their duty to serve their country, and a great many of them not only are willing to do it but eager to do it," said Mrs. Sylvia Neal, the mother of an 18-year-old who will leave Newnan in January for the Navy.

"Some people would call us squares, but we're happy squares, and we don't have our children out in the streets or tearing down the schools or smoking marijuana or anything like that," she said. "We're squares who are proud of our kids."

Earlier this year the city honored Maj. Stephen Pless of the Marine Corps and Lieut. Col. Joseph Jackson of the Air Force, both former residents of Newnan and both winners of the Medal of Honor for bravery in Vietnam.

"I don't know how one little town can produce courage in such quantity," President Lyndon B. Johnson told the nation the day he presented the two men with the medal.

"I know how," Mrs. Neal said. "We teach our children right and wrong. That's the only way—and I hope and pray we aren't going to change that in the next 10 years or ever."

She and most of her neighbors are satisfied with their city and believe it would do well not to change during the 1970s.

"It's true that we're changing in some ways," Mr. Barron conceded. "But I'm pretty much sold on this place the way it is now."

In 1960 the official population count was slightly more than 12,000. Now about 16,000 people live in Newnan. During the seventies that number is expected to increase by at least 25 percent.

An interstate highway, now 12 miles away, will soon be but four miles away, and as a result Atlanta will be less than an hour's drive from the old courthouse. "I think the city will soon become a 'bedroom community' for Atlanta," predicted the Rev. Walton Peabody, the associate minister of the First Methodist Church.

"It's probably true that even the war hasn't made much of an impact on this place," he went on. "But the next 10 years will—and they will be significant changes."

More than a third of the city's residents are Negroes. Next year all Negro students are to be assigned to previously all-white classrooms. Two are on the local police force and one ran for City Council last fall. He lost by a small margin.

Most of Newnan's Negro citizens are poor, and if their economic plight is one of the things Mr. Peabody believes will be changed by the end of another decade, another young man, Milliard C. Farmer Jr., vigorously disagrees. He thinks that a 10-year span of effort would hardly touch them.

"The cycle is too well established," he said. "Their education has been atrocious, and we're not going to correct the wrongs of generations and generations by 1980."

Not long ago, Mr. Farmer was in the sparkling new Federal building in Newnan and noticed a group of draftees mingling with a collection of men about to be sentenced by the Federal Court for manufacturing illegal whiskey.

"They were all predominantly black and all predominantly uneducated," he said. "It struck me as peculiar that it was difficult for me to distinguish between the ones being drafted and the ones about to go to jail for moonshining."

Although exact statistics are not available because of the Army's aversion to racial identification, most of Newnan's draftees are thought to be Negroes.

Mr. Peabody said that, perhaps as a result of the war, there has been a change in the relationship between Newnan's adults and its young people. "There's been a marked increase, I think, over the past few years, in the adults' understanding that the problems and questions of their children are just not the same that they faced when they were young."

From this understanding could come a new "quality of family life which would, in turn, lead to a new quality of community life," he speculated.

Mrs. Florence Grogan, the librarian at the Carnegie Library, shares in the optimism for Newnan's future: "I don't mean in terms of more and more people and more and more industry. All I'm really hopeful about is that in the next few years the quality of life in Newnan will improve.

"New things aren't always given the warmest of receptions," she said, frowning. "Things are changing, though."   If they are, Mr. Farmer doesn't recognize them. "Most white adults just are not capable of understanding the undercurrents of the young and the minority groups," he said.

If change does occur, in areas of race and politics and social traditions, it will occur because Newnan is a place to which young people return. "They come back here from college and from the service, and they either fall into the same old patterns or they get fed up and move though there aren't many of them, or they start working on the changes that need to be made," Mr. Farmer said.

As Newnan approaches the end of the decade, it is able to recognize in itself that it has remained untouched by most of the frenzies of the past years chiefly because its people are insulated from the impact of those frenzies. This is not an unusual circumstance for a small city—yet here, among the Civil War monuments and the steeples and the statues, there is a conscious effort to avoid being touched by the events of the world, and, in the 1960s, even with the war that took 16 of its sons, it was a most successful effort.

Obituary of a heroin user who died at 12

JOSEPH LELYVELD

New York
January 12, 1970

Walter Vandermeer—the youngest person ever to be reported dead of an overdose of heroin here—had been identified by many of the city's leading social service agencies as a child in desperate need of care long before his body was discovered in the common bathroom of a Harlem tenement on Dec. 14, two weeks after his twelfth birthday.

For most of these agencies he never became more than one case among thousands passing through their revolving doors. Others tried to fit him into their programs but lacked the manpower or resources to focus on him effectively. Eventually he would be shunted off to yet another institution.

It was not heartlessness or malfeasance that explains why he usually went unnoticed, just overwhelming numbers. As one school official expressed it, "There are thousands of Walter Vandermeers out there."

Along the way his case was handled by Family Court, the Society for the Prevention of Cruelty to Children, the Department of Social Services and its Bureau of Child Welfare, the Board of Education's Bureau of Attendance and Bureau for the Education of Socially Maladjusted Children, the Wiltwyck School for Boys, and the Office of Probation.

Most of these agencies have refused to discuss their actions in the case on the ground that their relationship with the boy was confidential.

175

But interviews with neighbors, relatives, and individuals in the schools and agencies through which he passed have made it possible to retrace the course of his short life and his efforts to find a foothold in a world that always seemed to him on the verge of collapse.

The agencies had exhausted their routine procedures before he died; only his file continued to move. For his last 14 months he was left to himself, with no consistent supervision or counseling of any kind, on the decaying block where he lived most of his life and died—117th Street between Eighth and Manhattan Avenues.

There he was in intimate daily contact with addicts and pushers, as if none of the overstrained agencies had heard of him or even existed. After his death, one of the block's junkies paid him this discerning tribute:

"Walter lived to be 30 in 12 years. There was nothing about the street he didn't know."

In those months he slept at home only sporadically and attended school for a total of two and a half days.

Walter would be out late at night hawking newspapers in bars or begging for coins at the corner of Eighth Avenue. In the daytime, when most children were in school, he would station himself near a radiator in a grocery store for warmth until chased or borrow a couch to catch up on the sleep he had missed.

His diet was made up of Yankee Doodle cupcakes, Coca-Cola, and, when he had the change, fish 'n' chips.

It was a life of frightening emptiness and real dangers. The only regular thing about it was a daily struggle for survival.

"Walter didn't do too bad," a junkie on the block remarked when he was dead.

"He didn't do too good," retorted a black youth, full of bitterness over what heroin has done to Harlem. "He won't see his thirteenth birthday."

"He didn't do too bad," the junkie repeated. "He looked after himself."

The one thing the court and the various agencies to which it referred his case never knew was that he was experimenting with drugs. But even this probably wouldn't have mattered, for no treatment centers have yet been authorized for narcotics users under the age of 16, although youths under 16 in the city are dying of heroin overdoses at the rate of one a week.

Two sides of Walter Vandermeer are remembered on his block.

One was the apprentice hustler, an angry, mistrustful youth given to violent rages in which he hurled bottles and flayed about with iron pipes.

The other was the small child who cried easily and searched continually for adult protection and warmth. Some of the older addicts into whose orbit he gravitated in the last months of his life say he would sometimes call them "Mommy" or "Daddy" and fantasy a household into which he could move as their child.

"Walter wanted a lot of attention," said his oldest sister, Regina Price. And there were those in his family and neighborhood who tried to extend it, when they could. Given the stress of their lives, that was only now and then and never for long.

Survival on 117th Street is a hard proposition at best, and Walter's circumstances were already far from the best when he was born Dec. 1, 1957.

His mother, Mrs. Lillian Price, had come to New York from Charleston, S.C., with her husband, Cyril, in 1947, when she was 22. Her schooling had never got beyond the third grade and she was on welfare within a year (21 years later, she is still there).

In 1949, Mrs. Price had her first children—twins—and her husband moved out.

By 1957 she was, in social-work jargon, the nominal head of a growing, desperately disorganized "multiproblem" family. Walter was her sixth child; there had been four fathers. Five more children (one of whom died in infancy) were to be born in the next seven years to Mrs. Price and a Liberian immigrant named Sunday Togbah.

Walter's father, known variously as Robert or Willie Vandermeer, entered the country illegally from Surinam, having jumped ship here in 1947. Six months after Walter was born, he was found by immigration authorities while he was working as a counterman at a midtown pharmacy and deported.

But by then, it appears, Mr. Vandermeer and Mrs. Price had separated, for hardly six months after he left the country she gave birth to the first of the children she was to have with Mr. Togbah.

Only one other Vandermeer was left in the family, a brother, Anthony, three years older than Walter.

In those days, Mrs. Price and six of her children were squeezed into one room of a three-room apartment at 305 West 117th Street they somehow shared with a couple with two children of their own. (Another of Mrs. Price's children, a daughter named Beverly, was being raised by a friend.)

According to the recollection of neighbors, Walter was sniffing airplane glue by the time he was 6 and sitting in on card games on the stoops when he was 8. In school he was marked as a disruptive child who could not be contained within a classroom's four walls unless permitted to fall asleep, which he did regularly, a sign to his teachers that he was staying out nights.

Public School 76 on West 121st Street gave up on him in early 1967, when he was in the third grade, soon after his ninth birthday. Walter had been out of school more days than not that year. When he was there he seemed locked in an aggressive pattern, roaming the halls and throwing punches at teachers who sought to restrain him.

Sometimes his violence could be seen as a stifled cry for attention and help. On one occasion he stormed out of an art class, only to fly into a rage because his teacher had not pursued him.

Walter was repeatedly warned to behave better, then suspended on March 2, 1967. It does not appear that the school ever attempted to arrange psychological consultations for him or his mother with the Board of Education's Bureau of Child Guidance.

After Walter's death, Assemblyman Hulan E. Jack was to charge that the school had "put the child out onto the street."

In fact, it did just the opposite by referring his case to the Society for the Prevention of Cruelty to Children, which then brought it up in Family Court on a neglect petition.

On March 14, both Walter and his brother Tony—the two Vandermeers—were placed in the Society's Children Shelter in Queens. Later they were shifted from there to the Children's Center at Fifth Avenue and 104th Street.

An attendance teacher, as truant officers are now called, had singled out the older boy as a youth of unusual intelligence and promise. Six months later, Tony was assigned to a home operated by a private agency in Yonkers, where he made what is regarded as a highly successful adjustment.

But Walter got lost in the judicial maze. While one branch of Family Court found Mrs. Price unable to care for Tony, another decided in August to release Walter—the younger and more disturbed of the two boys—to her care.

He had been classified as a "person in need of supervision" rather than a "neglected" child—a narrow legal distinction that has the effect of blaming the child and not the parent for his difficulties.

The fact that the law forces the judge in such cases to an implicit finding of blame, a court officer said, places a tremendous psychological pressure on parents to resist help for their children: It does not seem to be offered as help but as punishment for having failed them.

Releasing Walter to Mrs. Price was tantamount to releasing him to the street (by now the family had shifted to a top-floor apartment at 2124 Eighth Avenue, near 115th Street).

The court expected Walter to go to Public School 148, a special school for disturbed and socially maladjusted children at West End Avenue and 82nd Street. But there was no response to repeated notices sent by the school to the boy and his mother.

Meantime, members of the family recall, Tony was attempting, without success, to interest the agency that looked after him in his younger brother's plight.

Stranded, Walter at 10 was reaching for his own solutions.

One involved Mrs. Barbara Banks, who had regarded him as a godchild ever since she accompanied Mrs. Price to the hospital at the time of his birth. Around Christmas, 1967, she said, she told Walter he could move in with her and three of her children, since her eldest son was going into the Army.

"A whole lot of people told me, 'Ain't no hope for that boy,' " she said. "But I believed I could save him. He was so inquisitive, he could have been anything."

Although Walter eagerly seized the invitation, she said, she was soon forced to withdraw it, for her son was never inducted. Walter felt rejected.

Late one night he made that clear in his own way by climbing to the roof of a tenement across 117th Street and hurling a bottle through Mrs. Banks's window, raining glass on her bed.

The boy spent most of his time on the streets until April, 1968, when the Family Court assigned him to the Wiltwyck School for Boys, a treatment center for disturbed youths from the slums that had enjoyed the patronage of Mrs. Eleanor Roosevelt.

The idea was to place Walter at the school's main center at Yorktown Heights in Westchester County, but the center was full and cutting down on its staff because of a budget crisis. As a temporary alternative—to get Walter off the streets—he was put in Patterson House, at 208 East 18th Street, a "halfway house" run by the school for youths returning to their communities from the main center.

Dr. Howard A. Weiner, a psychiatrist who was then in charge of Patterson House, remembers that Walter was "extremely bright verbally" but says he was "as disturbed as any kid we had."

Like many maladjusted children from the poorest, most disorganized families, he would erupt into towering rages when he felt himself under pressure and he had to be held till he regained control. Usually that took at least an hour, so it was decided to give him 50 milligrams of the tranquilizer Thorazine four times a day.

At first, Walter showed his suspicions about his new surroundings by taking food from the table in a napkin and hiding it under his bed.

After his wariness subsided, he permitted himself to draw close to his child-care counselor, John Schoonbeck, a recent graduate of the University of Michigan. Learning that they both had Dutch names, Walter eagerly proclaimed that they were "soul brothers."

Mr. Schoonbeck, who now is on the staff of *Time* magazine, says Walter was "a great little kid." Dr. Weiner credits him with giving Walter the warm, reliable affection he had rarely found in an adult.

Encouraged by his counselor, Walter finally put in an appearance at P.S. 148. In fact, in May he went to school there regularly—his first stretch of steady school attendance in more than a year and the last in his life.

Flora Boyd, a teacher at the school, says Walter had never learned to read beyond the first-grade level but thought he could catch up. "He was an intelligent little boy," she recalls. "Of course, he had a lot of problems. But he could learn."

Every afternoon when he returned to Patterson House, he would insist on doing his homework before anything else, according to Mr. Schoonbeck.

In the evenings and on weekends, he regularly made quick, unauthorized expeditions to Harlem to check on his family and block, but always returned to Patterson House.

Children like Walter, Dr. Weiner said, need to go back regularly to their home environments, however disturbed these may appear, "because their identities are bound to their communities—they need to reestablish who they are."

Finally a place opened for him at Wiltwyck's pastoral upstate campus, and on June 20, Mr. Schoonbeck accompanied him to Yorktown Heights—the fifth separate institutional setting in which he had been lodged in 15 months.

Walter felt that he had been betrayed and trapped. He had never been told that his stay at Patterson House would be temporary. It was a repetition of his experience with Mrs. Banks and, predictably, he flew into a fit of anger on his first afternoon at the school.

Wiltwyck's troubles, meantime, had gone from bad to worse. In May, a third of its staff had been suspended after protesting that students were receiving inadequate clothing and food in the wake of the economy drive.

In the next two months, Walter ran away at least four times. As justification, he told his family he had been beaten at the school. Wiltwyck concluded that it could not hold Walter without his mother's cooperation and that this was unavailable.

On Oct. 10, 1968, Wiltwyck turned Walter back to Family Court, which meant he was where he had been more than a year earlier, only more frustrated and "street-wise."

His involvement with institutions was now nearly ended.

It took warrants to bring him and his mother to court so that he could be ordered to go to school, or to Harlem Hospital for psychiatric counseling, or to one of Haryou-Act's "self-help teams."

Asked why the court had not placed him in a state institution—a training school or mental hospital—in order to take him off the street, a judge replied that Walter, who was too disturbed for Wiltwyck, did not seem disturbed enough.

In fact, the probation officer assigned to the case recommended last spring that he be detained in a training school. But Walter's sister Regina insisted that her mother oppose the recommendation in court. In the back of her mind were recollections of the state institutions in which she was placed after she became pregnant at the age of 12.

She knew that a youth in detention had to "stay by himself" to survive, she said, for there were always homosexual fellow inmates threatening to "mess up his mind." Regina wanted Walter to receive care, but she thought the probation officer only wanted to "criticize him" and "lock him up." In her view, state institutions were no less dangerous than the streets.

On his own, Walter continued to search out adults he felt he could trust.

In November, he went down to East Sixth Street to call on John Schoonbeck, who had quit Patterson House in discouragement and was packing for a trip to Africa. Walter asked plaintively if he could come along.

On the block he had a half-dozen households where he dropped in regularly at unpredictable hours to cadge food, coins, an undemanding hour in front of a television set, or sleep.

One addict said Walter tagged along after a gang that called itself Bonnie and the Seven Clydes. The gang specialized in auto thefts and shoplifting, and he accompanied it on several forays downtown.

He also teamed up, it was said, with some older youths who conducted raids into Morningside Heights and learned to snatch purses.

According to Regina, he bought most of his own food and clothes and sometimes had as much as $50 in his pockets. But it is doubtful that he had any regular income as a drug courier, as has been alleged, for he continued until his last days to hustle for small change, selling newspapers and delivering groceries.

In his last months, Walter's already disastrous family situation deteriorated sharply.

Last summer, Mrs. Price was living most of the time on 117th Street, although her younger children were still in the apartment on Eighth Avenue. Walter stayed on the block, too, although not with her, sometimes sleeping on a fire escape above a warehouse.

When his mother saw him, she would shout, "Go home!" Walter would shout back, "Go home yourself!"

Sometimes, neighbors say, she would call the police on her son.

In September, an 18-year-old half-brother, Reggie Brooks, was arrested for robbery. Five days before Walter's death, he was sent to the Rikers Island reformatory.

In October, another half-brother, Eugene Price, 19, was shipped back to Vietnam, where he had already served a year, for an involuntary second tour of duty.

In November, the whole family was evicted from the Eighth Avenue apartment because Mrs. Price had not paid the $73.10 monthly rent for seven months out of her $412-a-month welfare checks.

She said she was holding the money in escrow because the toilet hadn't worked for a year and a half, but never got to Rent Court to explain this to the judge, perhaps because she no longer had the money.

Tony Vandermeer became distraught when he heard the news and got permission to come down from Yonkers for a day. It was not only the eviction that alarmed him—word had also reached him that Walter had started to take drugs.

The chances are negligible that any child on 117th Street could retain much innocence about narcotics, for the block is wide open to the traffic.

"I can go to my window any morning and see a man hand somebody some money and get his little package in return," a resident said. The fact that the police regularly manage not to see the same thing convinces the residents that they are indifferent, at best.

Walter's brother Reggie had long been using narcotics. Sometimes he would show his "works"—the eyedropper, needle, cord, and bottle cap that are the tools of the addict's vocation—to his younger brothers. Once Walter found an empty glassine envelope on their tenement stairway, filled it with salt and sold it to Reggie as a $3 bag of heroin.

Interviewed briefly after Walter's death, when he was brought to the funeral home from Rikers Island, Reggie said he knew who had first given drugs to his brother and named a 17-year-old addict on 117th Street, who shall be called Theresa here.

When she was visited the next day, Theresa was sitting next to a stove with all its burners on, the only warm corner in an apartment that had been without heat all winter. She readily acknowledged that she had been on drugs for 2 years, had been close to Walter and had known him to be using them.

Although she denied ever having given him any herself, Theresa said she had often seen him "skin" (inject the drug beneath the surface of his skin) but had never known him to "main" (inject it directly into a vein). Usually, she said, he skinned at the top of the stairs at 303 West 117th Street or in an apartment next door at 301 shared by two of her fellow addicts.

At 301, the two addicts—call them Mary Lou and Lizzie—also denied ever having sold or given drugs to Walter, but Mary Lou said he would often ask for them. She said that she had seen him "snort" (inhale heroin) and that she had occasionally allowed him to watch while she "mained."

Sometimes she would think of Walter as "a little man," Lizzie said. At other times, she would see him as an abandoned child and haul him to the bathroom to scrub him in the tub. Treated like a child, he would behave like one, she said.

The two addicts said they found it hard to imagine his locking himself in the bathroom across the street to "shoot up" by himself.

"Walter was scared of the needle," Lizzie said, laughing indulgently as one might in recalling a baby's first steps. "He'd always say, 'Wait. Don't hurt me. Let me get myself together. Please wait!' "

It was their expert speculation that he might have tried to "find the hole" where he had been "hit" earlier in the evening.

After the funeral, Tony Vandermeer rushed Lizzie, overturning a floral wreath and shouting, "You killed my brother!" He had heard stories on the block that Lizzie and Theresa had dragged his brother's body on the morning of Dec. 14 from 301 and across 117th Street to 310, where it was found.

Lizzie acknowledged that she had a loud argument with Walter the night before he died over $9—the change left from $25 he had given her to buy him some clothes—but insisted she had not seen him after that.

"Tony really didn't know me at all," she said. "He just had nobody else to blame."

Another addict—known here as Sugar—moved off the block as soon as the body was found. Walter had been especially close to him since the summer, it was said, and sometimes called him "Daddy."

A lanky, good-looking youth who now works at two jobs to keep up with the "Jones" (his habit), Sugar still returns to the block late at night to make his connection.

The other night at about 12:30 A.M. he came ambling into Mary Lou's apartment on the heels of two pushers—one wearing a leather tunic, the other done out in a frilly shirt with lace cuffs like an eighteenth-century gentleman.

After an interlude in a bedroom, Sugar appeared, rolling down his sleeve and adjusting his cuff link. Behind his dark glasses his eyelids were drooping.

His only response to a question about Walter was a perfunctory expression of "shock" over his death.

"But something had to happen," Sugar drawled sleepily. "He was always hanging around."

Dr. Michael Baden, an assistant medical examiner, who examined the body at the scene, said it looked to him like "a typical overdose case." But he cautioned that his office never classified narcotics overdoses as homicides, suicides, or accidents, for medical evidence on this point is invariably moot.

Curiously, chemical tests failed to reveal any trace of heroin in the eye-dropper found next to Walter in the sink—a hint, by no means conclusive, that it might have been planted.

The autopsy proved that Walter had been using drugs for at least three months—possibly longer—but the absence of any track marks on his arms indicated he had probably yet to become a full-fledged addict.

He had also yet to give up on himself. About a month before he died, Walter received a new pair of shoes from Mrs. Carletha Morrison, one of the women on the block whom he would allow to mother him. He said he would save them for going back to school.

According to both Regina and Mrs. Morrison, he seemed to think he could not go to school until his mother took him to court. No one seemed to realize that he was still enrolled at P.S. 148, where he had appeared only three times the previous year.

Friends and family gather at funeral service for Walter Vandermeer.
NYT

When the school reminded the Bureau of Attendance of his truancy, it was told to stop sending in reports on the boy because Family Court had his case "under advisement"—a bureaucratic formula that seemed to have no specific application.

Occasionally last fall, Walter would drop into the class of his younger brother "Doc" at P.S. 76 and would be allowed by the teacher to stay. He even asked his brother to teach him reading.

"I gave him my book and any words he didn't know I told him," said Doc, who is 11.

He was also looking forward to Christmas. Regina had promised to buy him a pair of expensive alligator shoes and a blue pullover. In addition, she said she would treat him to ice skating in Central Park and a movie downtown, probably *The Ten Commandments*.

Everyone noticed a macabre touch in a legend stamped on the cheap "Snoopy" sweatshirt Walter was wearing when he died.

"I wish I could bite somebody," it said. "I need to relieve my inner tensions."

"When I heard that I broke down," Regina said. "That was him. That was the way he felt."

Neighborhoods: Ozone Park's stability belies its uneasiness

MURRAY SCHUMACH

New York
December 6, 1971

The three men were early for the funeral service. So they strolled about the area around the church and parochial school. One of them, about 30 years old, beamed as he watched children playing in the school yard.

"Same good old neighborhood," he told his companions. "Just like it was when I lived here and went to this school."

He was not quite right. Like most visitors to Ozone Park, Queens, a middle-class area between the Brooklyn border and Aqueduct racetrack, he was judging too much by appearances.

For beneath the outward serenity—the City Planning Commission calls the area "stable"—is widespread uneasiness dramatized by a near-riot in the junior high school, the death of a youth from narcotics overdose, sporadic purse-snatchings and robberies.

The contrast is illustrated in two comments. Joe O'Boyski who has lived here for 50 years, says: "I love this place. I'm gonna die over here."

But a mother waiting to pick up her child at parochial school says:

"I can't wait for her to graduate and get my kids out of here."

For a stranger it is much easier to believe the first remark than the second. The yellow brick Roman Catholic Church of the Nativity of the Blessed Virgin Mary and its school remain community anchors at Rockaway Boulevard and 91st Street. The one-family and two-family homes of brick and frame look as sturdy and neat as ever.

In the bar of the Polish National Hall, at 97th Avenue and 90th Street, lights glow softly, pool balls click, and upstairs on Saturday nights the polkas are exuberant.

The strong aroma of cheeses hangs over Italian grocery stores—the new Bohack's supermarket caters to the dominant ethnic group with a section of Italian foodstuffs. In storefront clubs, men play briscola, scopa, and tre sett.

Pedestrians seem to know one another. Streets, on weekends, are sports arenas. At night, when the weather is not inclement, adolescents gather, as they have for years, in front of the United National Bank of Long Island.

"I've been here three years," says the Rev. Francis Romanowski, pastor of St. Stanislaus Roman Catholic Church. "The few people moving out are quickly replaced by other Poles, usually from East New York. There is no blighted area in Ozone Park. Our school is wall-to-wall kids, 50 to a class, and people pounding on our doors. We have no room."

And then there are the symbols of tension. First is the storefront chapter of the Italian-American Civil Rights League, spearhead of the community's determination to resist erosion of its special middle-class character.

Second is Junior High School 210, which seems to residents the epitome of their fears. This school was the scene of a recent outburst in which white students fought blacks, who are among the 1400 bused into the school as part of the borough's largest feeder pattern.

"These bused-in kids, they don't care about the neighborhood," says Vincent Miceli, president of the Italian-American branch that, he says, has risen sharply from 300 to 3000 members. There are about 30,000 residents in the neighborhood.

"The bused-in kids don't live here," he says. "They don't care if they cause trouble. If our kids cause trouble, they hear from their families. But not these kids. They ought to abolish junior high schools and have only elementary schools and high schools and build minischools in black neighborhoods so they wouldn't have to bus them here."

Many of the bused children are white. But residents say the fights are between blacks and whites. Teachers support this statement.

The acting principal brought in since the disturbances, Alfred S. Freed, says much of the trouble has subsided but the situation is still "volatile."

"But one important thing we have going in our favor," Mr. Freed said, "is that the parents—the white ones from the neighborhood and the black ones from outside—are all agreed that the most vital thing is the safety of their children."

The school has parents on post or patrol in the corridors. And in the afternoon, when buses arrive, a teacher with a bullhorn and policemen are on hand to prevent disorder. The school was intended for about 1600 and now has about 2000 students—about 30 per class.

"You hear a lot about the black kids," says a teacher "But these white kids are pretty tough too. That's one reason for the fights."

It is not only the youngsters who are tough. At the Italian-American League men tell how they protect the area against marauders.

One night, they say, they got a call about 2 A.M. from a resident, saying that two black men were wandering about the neighborhood.

"A few of us went out and found them," a member recalled. "We were delicate. We asked them what they were doing there. They told us they were looking for some street. We told them they were in the wrong section. They went away."

One of the major reasons for this aggressive policy toward any strangers is the increase in drug addiction among youthful residents. The general assumption is that no man from the neighborhood would be a pusher among the children of his friends.

However, Queens District Attorney Thomas J. Mackell, after looking over crime statistics, says that while addiction has risen in the area, it is not nearly as high as in other sections.

"But these people are so concerned, any addiction is too much," Mr. Mackell said. "It's a very stable neighborhood."

In a modest beauty parlor, one woman, after fixative was sprayed on her hair, remarked:

"The people here have been close-knit for years. We like it that way."

In the Italian-American storefront, Mr. Miceli pointed to a bullet hole in the wall. Two shots had been fired through the window one night after Joseph A. Colombo Sr. was shot in Columbus Circle last June.

"We stood guard with rifles in the store and on the roof after that," said Mr. Miceli. "We weren't looking for trouble, but we would have loved to catch them. The time has come to realize we cannot ask anyone else to give us our due respect unless we respect ourselves first."

A troubled patriot's life and death

JON NORDHEIMER

St. Joseph, Mo.
January 28, 1973

The House on Penn Street where Charley Stockbauer used to live sits near a historic crossroads of America.

It was from St. Joseph that the pioneers who won the West a century ago set out across the prairie in rough wagons drawn by mules and oxen and gritty conviction.

They came here by railroad and steamboat in the waning days of winter and huddled in muddy encampments on the gray bluffs above the Missouri River, waiting with mounting excitement for the floodwaters to recede from the Kansas plain.

As with most American schoolchildren, the seeds of patriotism were planted deep in Charley Stockbauer, and he grew to manhood in St. Joseph surrounded by the ghosts of nineteenth-century heroes and the legends of the days when men strode boldly toward an uncertain horizon, enduring hardship and fear on the impulse of duty or national destiny.

These values are still enshrined, but they have been questioned as never before by Charley Stockbauer's generation during the turbulent years when the vagaries of the war in Vietnam challenged traditional American attitudes about sacred abstractions such as patriotism.

Charley Stockbauer was a confused and reluctant warrior in a conflict that al-

188

most nobody fully understands, and that confusion and reluctance are mirrored here in the town that was his home before he died in Vietnam. Patriotism has not died in St. Joseph, but here, as elsewhere across the country in these days when war has at last come to an end, there is a reticence about it all, a nervous hesitance about parading the flag.

The myths and the legends persist. Buffalo Bill and Wild Bill Hickok were raw-boned riders from the Overland Pony Express, and the mail they carried westward started out from a brick building that still stands on Penn Street. Indian-fighters purchased, with leather pouches of gold, guns and knives from St. Joseph merchants, and Jesse James was shot dead in a weather-stained dwelling about half a mile from Charley Stockbauer's home.

But had he lived, Charley Stockbauer might have had trouble defining patriotism for anyone who asked.

By most standards of his community, Charley Stockbauer was a patriot. The President said so, in a letter of consolation to the Stockbauer family. So did the Secretary of the Army, the Army Chief of Staff, and a half dozen other generals.

But the Stockbauers do not think of Charley as a patriot in the usual sense, and they certainly do not believe that he sacrificed his life for his country and its ideals.

Specialist 4 Charles T. Stockbauer was killed in action three years ago when he was 23 years old, one of 26 young men from St. Joseph to die in the Vietnam war—one of America's 46,000 dead.

What makes Charley Stockbauer's story more illuminating than most is an 18-page letter he wrote on lined notebook paper the night before he was scheduled for induction in the Army. In it he expressed his concepts of freedom, patriotism, and love of country, and left it on the kitchen table so his family would see it after he had gone. But instead of heading for the induction center, Charley Stockbauer fled his country that day and crossed the border into Canada.

"I heard the door close in the middle of the night," his mother recalls. "I didn't know what it was. In the morning I found the letter, and only then did I realize the agony he was suffering. I prayed he'd realize his mistake and come home and do his duty."

Charley did return from Canada, five days later, saying that his conviction that Vietnam was an immoral war remained unchanged. Yet it was abhorrent for him to bring grief and shame down on the house on Penn Street. He reported for induction and one year later he was dead in a Vietnam jungle.

That was 3 years ago, and if time has not silenced the grief of the Stockbauer family, it has at least muted it. Charley's memory is now likely to produce fond smiles instead of hot tears. And the only time his mother has been moved to anguish in when a politician or a general has called for victory in Vietnam so that the sacrifice of Charley Stockbauer and the other dead Americans will not have been in vain.

In the entrance of Central High School is a World War I marble plaque that reads: "In Memory of Our Boys Who Gave Their Lives for Humanity." Farther down the hall, across from the principal's office, is a bronze plaque dedicated to the memory of students who died in World War II: "He Does Not Die Who Can Bequeath Some Influence to the Land He Knows."

There is no memorial for the Vietnam dead. If one is eventually put up no one seems to know what should be inscribed upon it. "What do you say about nothing?" said a girl in blue jeans in response to a visitor's question.

Mrs. Carol Pittman, a teacher of Latin who was a student at Central High at the outbreak of American involvement in Vietnam, can remember the fear that touched the boys in her graduating class when it began to penetrate their consciousness that they might be asked to go to fight in an obscure place called Vietnam.

"Sure," added James Rosenburger, a math teacher in his thirties, "the kids were downright scared in 1966 because most of them were going straight to Vietnam and they knew it.

"Only I wasn't too sympathetic," said Mr. Rosenburger, a baldish man with glasses who sipped coffee in a faculty lounge, "because I had just done 2 years' time in the Army and I figured it was everyone's patriotric duty to serve."

He put down his cup and looked at the other teachers. "If the President says it's your duty to go, you go. Even if it's a mistake. A blunder. You go. You don't stand around asking questions."

"Hell, when we marched off to the South Pacific in the Second World War," injected Frank Baker, the principal of Central High, "there was a highly patriotic feeling among us soldiers. It was like a football game and we felt we were fielding the best team. 'Let's get at 'em! Let's rack 'em up!' That sort of thing. It was a game of matching our equipment and the know-how against the gooks. It was that good old American competitive spirit."

Mrs. Pittman, who had listened silently to the men, said attitudes among the young were changing rapidly and she did not know if the Vietnam experience had fostered the changes or if there was a more fundamental cause.

"Take the other day in the student senate," she remarked. "Some kids made a motion to abolish the morning flag-raising ceremony." The motion was defeated, she went on, but now three boys in her room refuse to stand for the ceremony, an act of defiance that is tolerated.

"When I was in high school," she said, "we wouldn't dare do something like that. As a matter of fact, the idea wouldn't have entered our heads. And that," she said, looking at the older men, "was only 7 years ago when hardly anyone knew where Vietnam was."

"Dear Mother," Charles Stockbauer wrote in his letter when he fled to Canada, "By now you realize what I have done and you are probably upset. Well, I can't console you. This was not a decision I made with little thought.

I have hardly thought about anything else. . . . I've thought over the matter and I'm sorry that by this I'll be hurting you. But it has to be. I can't justify any other action. War is only a word to soothe our conscience. But it doesn't work. War is still nothing more than murder. And murder is wrong no matter who says it can be justified.

"I realize that war will possibly never cease as long as we live in this world, as long as there are flags, there will be war. . . . The trouble in America is that because freedom is written down we think we have it. But to quote Goethe, 'None are more helplessly enslaved than those who falsely believe they are free.'"

Young people from St. Joseph drive across the Missouri River bridge to Wathena, a farm community in Kansas where it is legal for 18-year-olds to drink 3.2 beer. On Fridays and Saturdays, the taverns fill up with teen-agers with long hair, beards, and ragged denims—the new dress style only recently approved by the police, educators, and blue-collar fathers in America's heartland.

"These kids just don't have respect for anything any more," muttered Paul Walts, the lean and leathery 62-year-old owner of The Keg. "Nothing means much to them any more. The war has a lot to do with it, sure, but there's a real dope problem now and the kids have all moved away from religion."

His son, Gary, who works the noisy bar on weekend nights, said that even he, at 28, felt alienated from the younger crowd. "For example," he said, "the war has made a negative attitude about serving in the Army. When I was their age everyone was willing to fight for the country. Hell, now everyone has to look at each war and figure out if it's really worth it."

"The way I look at it," Mr. Walts continued, "is that anybody that would run off to Canada is what I'd call a great big coward. We've had some come in here who'd done that, gone off to Canada. It's all wrong."

His wife nodded in agreement. "That's the way our generation was raised," she said. "We were a patriotic people. I can remember back as a little girl in Grant City in Missouri how the American Legion always had their parades, with all those flags flying. My, what a pretty sight it was!"

The Waltses were uncertain if there were any flag-snapping parades still held in St. Joseph. If there are, they do not watch them, and neither do the young people unless they are in a school band and obliged to participate.

About the only time anyone hears the national anthem these days is when a television station signs off for the night and distant jets barrel-roll across the flickering screen.

Charles Stockbauer, son of a stockyard worker, went off to a Roman Catholic seminary near Warrenton, Mo., at the age of 13, eager but scared, taking the first step toward a childhood ambition to become a priest. He went on to Jesuit College near Louisville but returned home in 1965 filled with doubts about the priesthood.

Charley Stockbauer: Catholic seminarian and reluctant G.I. A single word, Peace,
marks the stone at his grave in Mount Olivet Cemetery in St. Joseph, Missouri.
NYT

His older brother, Joe, was away in the Navy at the time, a volunteer, and
the young seminarian was the focus of attention of his parents and four
sisters in the frame house on Penn Street.

"He was such a bright boy, he spent all of his money on books on history
and architecture," said Mrs. Stockbauer, a registered nurse who worked at
St. Joseph's State Hospital, a mental institution. "He even went out and
bought a piano for the house and at night he'd play for the family." She
paused for a moment and ran her fingers over the kitchen table where the
letter written by a son had once been placed, and a furtive recollection made
her smile. "The house was filled with his music. He was the source of a heck
of a lot of joy for all of us."

He went to the local community college, but by 1967 he didn't have the
money to continue his education. His deferment ended, and he was drafted.
After his brief flight to Canada, he entered the Army and became a medical
corpsman attached to the 101st Airborne Division. He wrote home that if
he had backtracked on the convictions that sent him to Canada, at least as a
corpsman he would not have to hurt anyone. Perhaps, he wrote, he might
even help humanity. He began to keep a diary:

1 January. New Year's Day—It's good to be in 1969. It's going to be my year—I hope. Boy, am I looking forward to '70.

17 January. Again I find myself intrigued with T. S. Eliot. He begins: "Time present and time past/And both perhaps present in time future/And time future contained in time past." I don't understand why he says "perhaps" . . . why perhaps?

20 January. Convoy went smoothly. I see more beauty each day in the road we take.

25 February. Good day so far. *Ulysses* not moving as well as hoped.

14 March. Ambush last night—again a failure. Finished *Anna Karenina*—a great delight in reading. A beautiful portrayal of the main issues in a seemingly impossible existence. Spec/4 as of March 10. A little more money. I won't complain.

19 March. St. Joseph's Day. Many thoughts today but all seem to turn me to St. Joe. Oh! I really can't see living anywhere else.

29 April. Isn't life beautiful/Isn't life gay/Isn't life the perfect thing/To pass the time away?

2 May. Another ambush. One day less. Oh God, please help me.

19 June. Ambush tonight. What will it bring?

25 June. Not so hot last night. Nice headache. Sending in for *Selected Plays of Eugene O'Neill.*

28 June. Narcissus and Goldmund [by Herman Hesse]. Ends beautifully. "But how will you die when your time comes, Narcissus, since you have no mother? Without a mother, one cannot love. Without a mother, one cannot die."

8 July. August 23 [R. and R. leave] and away we go—must write home. Glad to hear that St. Joseph is showing some sign of progress.

He was killed on July 10 by enemy fire when his unit was in a night defense position near a town called Bou Aie Ha. He went to the aid of three wounded soldiers, treated them and was shot as he searched in the dark for more wounded.

"We were just leaving for church—it was a beautiful July morning and we thought we would have a picnic afterwards," Mrs. Stockbauer remembers. "A station wagon pulled up and an Army officer got out and I suddenly felt like running away and never stop running. I turned to my husband and I said, 'God I know what that is. Oh God, I know he's here to tell us our Charley is dead.' "

A flood of official condolences from the White House, the Army, and from Missouri politicians streamed into the house on Penn Street, all standard form letters sent to the next of kin of dead soldiers, extolling Specialist 4 Stockbauer's courage and military conduct. Some samples:

"In Vietnam today brave Americans are defending the rights of men to choose their own destiny and to live in dignity and freedom. You can cherish the thought that for his sacrifice your son is forever noble."—Gen. William C. Westmoreland.

"Charles was indeed a fine soldier who fought with courage and determination for his country and his ideals. He was brave in battle. He inspired confidence in all his associates by his dedication and strength of character." —Maj. Gen. John M. Wright Jr., commanding officer of the 101st Airborne.

"I pray for the day when this war can be ended, and peace restored. I wish that your son could have lived to see that day. His courage, his devotion and his sacrifice have brought it closer."—President Richard M. Nixon.

The words were bitter to the Stockbauers and they wrote back: "He lived what he believed and he died for it. By applying the principles he had been taught all his life he found himself at odds with his country and its policies on war. Our reaction when he applied these beliefs show how little we actually believe what we teach our children."

After Charley's death the women of the Stockbauer family joined the Fellowship of Reconciliation, a peace group, and on Wednesday afternoons they marched in small weekly antiwar protests on the steps of the downtown post office, like Greek women mourning their dead.

"He died and it's up to us to make his life worth while," says Janice, the oldest of the sisters. "People tell me I shouldn't think about it any more, that it's been 3 years and it's not healthy for me to still grieve.

"They say he died for his country and that's enough—that's something to be proud of—he was a patriot."

And there was no more music in the house on Penn Street.

Charley Stockbauer, posthumous winner of the Bronze Star, was buried in Mount Olivet Cemetery in St. Joseph. The women visit the grave on these gray winter days, with the biting wind out of Kansas whipping their coats, and drop to the hard ground in prayer before a simple marker.

The single word PEACE is inscribed in its cold granite face and below that is the peace symbol, the only tribute to the patriot lying in the ground above the bluffs where a young America once massed in excitement and hope.

Aged wait in stony solitude, but not for buses

MCCANDLISH PHILLIPS

New York
May 13, 1970

Two kinds of people wait in the Port Authority bus terminal near Times Square. Some are waiting for buses. Others are waiting for death.

At times transients cannot get a seat because so many of "the regulars" are there: old people, from about 61 to 90 years old, who have made the waiting room a kind of club. Some come almost every day, to sit and wait, but not for buses.

Most sit alone, in silence. A few read. Some are convivial and gabby. "Once you start to talk to somebody, you have to talk to them every day," one of the quiet ones said, explaining his social reticence.

Max Cohen struts around the waiting room with four or five cigars in his jersey shirt pocket and one stuck in the side of his mouth. He is a very small, wiry man with plenty of vinegar who wears his bristly white hair cut short. He worked for 50 years as a newspaper deliverer and now often comes to the terminal twice a day.

"Why don't you go home, Max?" he was asked.

"What, to lay down and look at four walls?" he shot back. He lives in a small, sparsely furnished room that rents for $7 a week. "Later on, I'll go out and sit in the park, when it gets a little warmer," he said.

To old people whose dwellings are tiny or dreary or places of endless boredom, the waiting room is a kind of indoor park. It never rains in the Port

196

Authority bus terminal. The overhead bulbs are as steady as the sun in a cloudless sky.

From 200 to 250 old men and women are known to come to the terminal regularly. Many more come now and then.

Occasionally the Port Authority police come in to clear the room, but it is a futile game, the rules of which are known to both sides.

Two policemen arrived at 1:20 P.M. the other day and stood in the center of the room. One of them spoke in a loud, brassy voice:

"Ladies and gentlemen. This here area is for people with tickets only. If you have a ticket, fine. If not, please get up and leave. Now show us your tickets."

There was a shuffling exodus as the ticketless drifted out into the concourse or the public toilets. For several minutes the room was the preserve of the ticketed minority, but within six minutes things were back to normal.

At 2:04 the police came again and, immediately, three old people departed. There was no announcement this time; the blue shadow was enough.

Some old people come and go like characters in a drama, having fixed roles to play. Two are known as "the lovers." They come in separately, meet, sit and hold hands a while, then leave.

Romeo is in his early 70s, a tall, spare man with bony shoulders that seem like pipes under his jacket. Juliet is in her late 60s, short, round-faced.

"You would think they were 16 years old and just in love," a woman said. "She always wears a veil on her hair. He wears a little cap, a couple of sizes too small, and they sit and hold hands."

Some sitters look invincibly alone—severe, motionless, figures in stone.

It was 5:55 P.M. For two and a half hours now, a tall, elderly woman with fluffy white hair had been sitting alone in a pink jacket and blue miniskirt, gazing straight ahead. Thin lips, painted a bright orange-red, stood out in a rougeless face powdered white.

"Never marry an old bachelor. They never change their ways," a woman in a red hat was saying to a woman named Mary. "I married an old bachelor. Selfish! Leave all kinds of pots and pans. He was terrible. I had to get rid of him."

For more than an hour, Red Hat ran on and Mary was held to brief expressions of assent.

"Don't forget this town is made up of all the little towns in the country," a woman nearby in sunglasses said. "It's just another little town, except it's bigger. Everybody came here from somewhere."

The watchers are watched three days a week, from noon to 4:30 P.M., by the friendly eyes of Mrs. Stella G. Trebony and Mrs. Mary Butler. The Port Authority, which regards the visitors as a mild form of nuisance, like an excess of pigeons on a veranda, has sanctioned a long-term study of the phenomenon, which began last June and looks as though it may run on for years.

The presence of the two watchers goes back a little over a year to the point at which the perplexity of Port Authority officials led to a call for help to Travelers Aid, which led to a plea to the New York City Office for the Aging.

Mrs. Stella B. Allen of the West Side Office for the Aging met with Marvin Weiss, the terminal manager, and five others to talk about what could be done.

"They wanted to get them out, but without being too harsh," Mrs. Allen recalled. "We decided we were not going to throw them out. That we knocked off the agenda first."

It was decided to put a table in the waiting room and to let it be tended by Mrs. Trebony and Mrs. Butler of Project Find, 1966 Broadway.

"Two chief terrors haunt the minds of older people," Mrs. Allen said. "One is placement in a home for the aged. The other is going on welfare."

One of the regulars is a woman who carries two bottles of wine in a shopping bag. She comes in and sips on them during the day and sometimes, when she is feeling loose, she stands up and sings "Moon River," a little bit off key.

Another steady sitter, of a bouncy, outgoing sort, speaks five languages "and he comes in and says 'good morning' in all five languages," an elderly woman said.

At 7:15 P.M., the woman with the white fluffy hair was still fast in her place. It had been almost four hours now.

A few of the sitters seem to have stepped out of a George Price cartoon. Their attempts at elegance are irreparably gauche. Several old sitters are alcoholics. Yet a surprising number, over half, dress and behave like solid members of the middle class, the upper middle class at that.

One man cuts the figure of a diplomat. He wears striped trousers, a dark blue coat with vest, and a black hat that stands out against a thick fringe of white hair. He looks as though he might have been at the Versailles conference. He sits erect, like a man posing for an oil portrait. He does not talk to strangers.

Mrs. Trebony, who still has the soft accents of her years in Savannah, Ga., offers assistance to any who need it and will take it.

Most of the regulars are from the West Side of Manhattan.

Mrs. Trebony nodded toward a male sitter. "He's here because he and his wife sat here," she said. "He goes around to all the places where they used to go, hoping she'll come to get him. He says: 'Why do you think she never comes?' He goes every Tuesday to the grave. People say he's crazy. Now, you know, I don't think he's crazy. Do you?"

A woman who is 90 and beyond the joys of living said: "I really just wish I would die, Stella. I wonder when my husband will come and get me?"

"You better be careful now," Mrs. Trebony said. "Which one of them do you want to come and get you?" The nonagenarian has been married three times.

Mrs. Trebony told of an old woman who came at last to the point at which she knew she needed public assistance, a day she had hoped never to see. "She wasn't even getting enough to eat," Mrs. Trebony said. "She had spent her reserve."

The woman held out for a while more, but finally agreed to make out forms for help. "I hoped I wouldn't live this long," she said. The next morning she was dead.

A few months ago an 86-year-old man named August went into a hospital for seven weeks. When he came out, he had lost his rented room.

With residential hotels quoting $14-a-day rates, or $70-a-week, there were terrors in it for him.

Mrs. Allen, commenting on why the elderly fear being sent to a home for the aged or being put on welfare, said:

"They feel that either just cancels them out as a person. They feel that this is the end of them. That's why they struggle so hard to stay independent, 'to be free,' as they put it."

"They can live in the crummiest little hole in a third-rate hotel, with pipes on the ceiling and holes in the floor, but they'll hold onto it," said Elizabeth Stecher of Project Find. "They only need a little bit of help to stay free— just a little bit of help."

At 8:45 P.M., the woman with the white fluffy hair wrapped her black coat around her and drowsed, her head slumping to her shoulder. A policeman walked behind her. Gently he touched her shoulder. "Mom," he said. "Mom, wake up." She brought her head up straight.

The illusion that one is waiting for a bus is made less credible by an attitude of slumber.

Few mourn Yuba City's faceless men

DOUGLAS E. KNEELAND

Marysville, Calif.
May 31, 1971

Nobody much missed the faceless men who disappeared from Lower D. And nobody much mourns them now as their hacked-up bodies are dug from the soft loam of peach orchards in the outskirts of Yuba City across the Feather River from here.

More than 20 of them dropped out of sight in the last two months from the four- or five-block Skid Row here that is anchored by the lower end of D Street. Hardly anybody noticed. Perhaps because if the men existed at all in the minds of Marysville and Yuba City, they were already lost, already dead.

They were the men New Yorkers stare hard not to see on the side streets off Times Square. The men Chicagoans brush by on Division Street. The men San Franciscans avoid in the Mission district.

The weaving, tattered men with the red eyes and the stubby beards. The ageless men, all old beyond their years. The thousands and thousands— nobody knows how many—who drift endlessly, aimlessly across the underside of America. The men who are as invisible in the small towns and cities as they are in the big ones.

Every day they turn up dead in the dank doorways of the cities, behind a shabby village saloon, beside a lonely railroad track.

It took a lot of them dead in one place to make anyone notice much at all. But 23 bodies have been dug from the orchard graves during an investigation led by Sheriff Roy D. Whiteaker, and Juan V. Corona, a 37-year-old farm-labor contractor with a history of mental illness, is being held on murder charges.

Now the nation is watching and asking how so many could have been so forgotten.

Actually, one of them was missed—one of the 14 murdered men identified so far.

Sigrid (Pete) Beierman, also known as Pete Peterson, a short, 63-year-old disability pensioner, was not a drifter. He was a long-time habitué of Lower D, the Skid Row of the twin cities of Marysville and Yuba City.

Early in May, according to Roy DeLong, another one of "the boys," as they call themselves, Pete Beierman got into a truck belonging to Mr. Corona. When he didn't show up the next day at the Marysville Men's Day Center, a dreary storefront shelter where he usually spent his time, he was reported missing. Mr. DeLong was arrested Saturday as a material witness.

On May 4, a Marysville police report noted, Mr. Corona was stopped on the street and was asked if he knew what had happened to Mr. Beierman. When he denied that he did, the matter was apparently dropped.

"Everybody says nobody is concerned about these guys," said Chris Bergtholdt, a slim, nervous, graying man who runs the center sponsored by this community of 20,000 for the homeless, the drifters, the winos. "But when Pete Beierman didn't show up, they reported him. He was supposed to go out and just work for the day, but when he didn't come back the next day, we turned him in."

As for the others, those who were not missed, Mr. Bergtholdt blamed the times, the unemployment in the country. He said that more drifters than ever were showing up in Marysville, looking for work in the fields and orchards.

"How can I keep track of all these people?" he asked. "One week in April, every day that week we had 80 men. This is something we've never had before."

And if the others are not mourned, Pete Beierman is, after a fashion.

"I don't think old Pete had any relatives," said Enoch Heath, an elderly, toothless man. "But we knew each other years and years. Used to live together for a while. He was a good guy. A nice guy. If he had the money, he'd pop for a drink."

Pete Beierman was known, a little. He lived in Marysville, sort of.

But the drifter's life is a hard one.

As Mr. Bergtholdt locked the door of the center a few minutes before the regular 4 o'clock closing time, five bleary-eyed men stood hesitantly on the sidewalk in front.

"The only thing they talk about," Mr. Bergtholdt said, "is a couple of their friends who are missing."

At the Twin Cities Rescue Mission, the Rev. C. W. Renwick remarked on how odd it was for people on Lower D to even think in terms of one of "the boys" being missing.

"I know of two who had been coming in here every day recently and suddenly we didn't see them anymore," the wrinkled, 65-year-old minister said, "but that's nothing to get excited about around here because a lot of them get discouraged and grab a freight and go down to Stockton or someplace."

The mission is a two-story, gray frame building on First Street, deep in the jumble of secondhand stores such as Joe's No. 2, of cheap barber shops, of Mexican, Chinese, black and Anglo bars, of card rooms such as the Nugget and the Bonanza, of vacant lots littered with the remains of Petri Tokay and Franzia white port bottles.

And the mission serves its purpose in Marysville, where the Lower D Skid Row is a hangover from the historic wide-open days when the town catered to gold diggers and lumberjacks as well as the field hands and pickers needed by its peach and prune and rice growers.

The growers prefer migrant Mexican laborers for their harvest seasons because they think they are more stable and will horde their money for the day when they return home. But there are times when they are happy to pick up whatever hands they can find.

So the drifters come from all over the country, from Connecticut and Texas, from Indiana and Arkansas, from everywhere, sometimes to get away from the chill Northern winter, sometimes to try to pick up a few dollars in the orchards and fields.

On the freights they come, as they always did, and on the freights they leave, riding the rods of the Southern Pacific and the Western Pacific, which cut through Marysville a few blocks from Lower D.

And when they are cold or hungry or desperate for a bed, they turn up at the Twin Cities Rescue Mission. Many of the 14 murder victims who have been identified slept or ate there in the past, some off and on for several years. They came and went, from where and to where nobody knew, often with lapses of months or years.

"We had Jonas Smallwood," Mr. Renwick said, thumbing a stack of index cards. "He was here—slept here the ninth of the month and the seventh of last month. Beierman was here around the first of the month. When they didn't have any money, they came here.

"A fellow can stay here for five nights in a row and then he's got to wait a week before he comes back, unless he gets special permission. It all depends who it is. The Weary Willies and the Tired Tims who have no intention of working have to wait a week."

To earn their bed and their beans or stew, served in bowls on bare tables in the dark chapel with its cheap stained-glass windows, "the boys" must arrive before 7:30 P.M., without a bottle, and sit on the hard folding chairs through an hour's sermon, songs, and testimony.

At about 8:30, when the service is over, they eat.

"They can come up and get their bowls filled as many times as they want," Mr. Renwick said. "Some of them are hungry. They've just come off freights from all the way to Salt Lake City.

"We don't let them come in if they have a bottle. We tell them if they've got enough money to buy wine, they don't need our help. If they say they're really hungry and would rather have the food than the wine, we tell them to pour it out in the gutter and we'll let them come in. But very few of them do."

Mr. Renwick, who has been in the rescue missions for 18 years, the last five here, knows his men well, and for good reason.

"I was saved in a rescue mission," he said. "I went in as an alcoholic and a bum and after 15 years I got my license."

After the meal, the men are led across the street to an old building with a cavernous room about 15 feet wide by 50 feet long that is lit by two bare bulbs hanging from the ceiling. It has six double-deck beds, seven single beds, two ancient couches, and a stack of well-worn extra mattresses.

No-smoking signs are painted on the dirty beige walls. Flypaper dangles from the light cords, and a can of roach killer sits on a battered bureau.

At 9:30 P.M. the lights are put out, and at 5:30 A.M. the men are awakened and taken back across the street for hot cereal, doughnuts, and coffee.

By the time they have finished, those who want work shuffle out to stand on a nearby corner to wait for a labor contractor such as Mr. Corona to drive by and offer them a job in the orchards.

If they are hired, they can make up to $18 to $20 a day during the peach harvest, which starts in July.

"The winos will work three or four days, then come in and spend it," Mr. Renwick said. "Others will stay through the picking, then come in and go on one big spree."

When they are flush, "the boys" often avoid the mission with its sermons and no-bottle rules. They will spend $2 a night for a bed in the dormitory of the old U.S. Hotel and maybe even buy their wine by the shot at the Colver Club or the Nugget instead of picking up a 39-cent bottle to drink in a vacant lot.

At this time of year, green peaches are being thinned on the trees. The men are paid 75 cents for a small tree and $1.50 for a large one. It is hard and demanding work, especially for the out-of-staters who have never thinned peaches. And work is scarce.

Still they come, more every day, dropping off the slow freights and then drifting out when they can't find work or their welcome is worn out at the mission.

The day center is crowded. The mission is feeding about 50 meals a day. It is a difficult time to keep track of men whose identities are elusive at best.

"On Skid Row you never pry into a man's background or you'll get a reputation as a stool pigeon or something," Mr. Renwick said, "so you never ask questions. If a man wants to volunteer something, that's different.

"The only questions we ask are what the Federal authorities make us ask, his name, Social Security number, where he was born and when.

"Every once in a while, you'll get somebody who'll try to tell you he was somebody in the past. A lot of fellows, if they have been somebody, they won't admit it. But we do get lawyers and fellows who have had businesses and schoolteachers.

"Quite a lot of these fellows have had college educations. Not a big percentage, but quite a few."

Which reminded him of Overcoat Shorty, who had graduated from a college in Canada and had taught high school in Hannibal and Independence, Mo.

"We used to call him Overcoat Shorty," Mr. Renwick said, "because he was about 5 feet 5 inches tall and always wore an overcoat—even in the hot weather—because he used to go in the jungles and sleep in the overcoat. I can't remember his name now. Hughie, his first name is."

Still pondering a few minutes later, he added:

"His right name was Hughie, but I can't think of his last name. They just called him Shorty. There are a lot of Shortys on Skid Row, so they called him Overcoat Shorty."

The Overcoat Shortys of this world have a tenuous hold on their identities. And like many others, Overcoat Shorty has drifted in and out of Marysville for years. He may be riding a freight in tomorrow. He may be in a peach-orchard grave.

Mr. Renwick grew thoughtful and a little sad as he recalled one of the men who had been missing from the mission for the last couple of weeks, a young man as Skid Row transients go, only 24.

Then Mr. Renwick's eyes brightened as he considered the ways of the drifter.

"These fellows are subject to whims," he said hopefully. "They could be standing out here by the freight yard and suddenly move on. Sometimes the whistle of that engine just whistles them out, makes them move on."

Lonely death closes a woman's lonely life

JOHN CORRY

New York
November 7, 1971

June Nector died in Roosevelt Hospital last week. When she died, she was alone, and a doctor said that she had really just wasted away.

The doctor did not know her age, and neither did anyone else on 85th Street between Central Park West and Columbus Avenue, where she had lived. Everyone agreed, however, that Miss Nector was at least 80 years old, even though in the last months of her life she had become so small and thin that she looked like a child.

"I don't have the picture that this happened to her overnight," the doctor said. "She had pneumonia, and you might say that was the end cause of death, but there was also severe malnutrition. The main problem was that she was old. I see a lot of them like that."

Miss Nector had lived in a rooming house, and because she did not invite friendships she had no friends. She had no visitors, and she received no mail, either.

When she went about the neighborhood, she carried shopping bags instead of purses, and the shopping bags would be full, but no one, of course, ever knew what was in them.

Sometimes, however, Miss Nector wrote notes to the owner of her building. Almost always they were full of fanciful grievances, and often they would be written in the third person.

After her death, a note that Miss Nector apparently had written to no one but herself was found in her room. It told of travels about Europe, and of what had happened to the girl who made them.

"This little friend of mine," it said, "is from abroad, Oslo, the cleanest and most beautiful city in the world. Intend stay there one week, were there six, hated to leave. Her family noble and very wealthy. Entertained us lavishly, met royalty from all over the world.

"Told little girl, New York, see world, come back home. Lived the way she was accustomed to on Park Avenue. Her millions dwindled to almost nothing. She didn't go home, but took job with wealthy families as nurse, companion, secretary. Moved over to West Side. Took this little room. Kept it."

Now, in fact, Miss Nector was from Oslo, and she had worked for wealthy families, one of which had lived on Park Avenue, and she had taken her own little room on the West Side 25 years ago.

In the 10 days before she was taken to the hospital, she did not leave the room, and she had survived only because workers from something called Project Pilot, a part of Selfhelp Community Services, had visited her, fed her, and sometimes crouched on the floor next to the bed and held her hand.

Stefan P. Herz, the director of Project Pilot, had heard about Miss Nector after she had collapsed in the hallway of the rooming house and been taken to Roosevelt Hospital for the first time.

She had, however, refused to stay, and so she had been sent back to the rooming house, where she collapsed again.

Every day after that, either Mr. Herz or Mrs. Nusser, another member of Project Pilot, had visited Miss Nector. If she wanted to die in her own room, they thought, they would help her to do it with dignity, but as the days went on it became harder for Miss Nector to find even the simplest dignities.

For one thing, she would fall out of bed and lie on the floor, too weak to rise. A trip down the hall to the bathroom was out of the question, and despite anything that Mr. Herz or Mrs. Nusser could do, the room became foul.

Still, in those last days of Miss Nector's life, and for possibly the first time in that small room in 25 years, there was laughter.

"June, what beautiful teeth you have," Mrs. Nusser said. "Where did you get them?"

Miss Nector stared for a moment, and then she grinned, and then she laughed out loud. After all, she had dentures.

"Did you ever get married, June?" Mrs. Nusser asked, and Miss Nector shook her head. "Well, you can, you know," Mrs. Nusser said, and Miss Nector, who had never been known to even smile, laughed again.

Mr. Herz visited Miss Nector for the last time in her room on a Sunday. He arrived with soup and with orange juice that he had filled with vitamins, and he found Miss Nector on the floor, unable to do anything except to try to say: "Go away."

She knows she's dying, Mr. Herz thought, and she doesn't want anyone to see her. Mr. Herz knew that Miss Nector did not want to go to a hospital, but it seemed indecent to leave her in the fetid air, amid the stained sheets and clothing, and so he made a decision.

"Miss Nector," he said, "I hope you won't think I let you down."

He called 911 from the phone booth at Columbus Avenue, and within 10 minutes a squad car had arrived. He met the policemen on the street and took them to Miss Nector's room. They went in, and quickly backed out.

"God," the older one said, while the younger one started to retch.

Ten minutes later an ambulance arrived. The ambulance attendant, however, wanted nothing to do with Miss Nector, and he said he could not possibly get her down four flights of stairs.

"Look, I'll carry her myself," Mr. Herz said, "in my arms. All right?"

One of the policemen told the driver of the ambulance to get a wheelchair. The driver did not even glance at the attendant, and went downstairs and got it. Then, the driver, the policemen, and Mr. Herz wrapped Miss Nector in a blanket and lifted her into the wheelchair.

She was unconscious, and her head was thrown back, while very carefully the driver and one of the policemen carried her down to the street.

A few neighbors stood about, watching and mostly silent, while Miss Nector was placed in the ambulance. A woman who, in fact, lived only three houses away, pursed her lips and said, "Who's she?"

When the ambulance reached the emergency room at Roosevelt Hospital, Mr. Herz was only seconds behind it. A guard motioned him into a waiting room, and Miss Nector was wheeled into an examining room.

In the next hour, nurses, doctors, and attendants moved in and out of the examining room perhaps 20 times, and Miss Nector herself was taken out and back in again once. Finally, a young doctor summoned Mr. Herz.

"There's severe muscle wastage, dehydration, malnutrition, and a very low body temperature," he said. "Has she been complaining of anything?"

Twenty minutes later, the doctor emerged again, and said Miss Nector would be admitted to the hospital. She was taken to the women's ward on the third floor, and put in a bed. Needles attached to tubes were in both her arms, and she lay with her eyes closed, her head thrown back, breathing through her mouth.

"Miss Nector, Miss Nector," Mr. Herz said.

For just a moment, Miss Nector opened her eyes, and for just an instant there was comprehension. Then she closed her eyes again.

All the next day, Miss Nector lay in bed that way, never moving, never talking, slowly dying. Great red and purple bruises had spread around the needles in her thin arms, and if there was any other apparent change in her at all, it was only that her breathing seemed more labored.

"She's a very tough lady," a doctor said, "but you've got to look at her as a medical problem. It hurts when you stick needles in someone, and there comes a time when death is better than the pain of staying alive. Then you

An old photograph, carefully preserved by June Nector, was found in her effects. Almost certainly the little girl in the picture is June Nector.

don't fight as hard for the patient anymore, and they slip away."

The next morning, Miss Nector died. That afternoon, Mr. Herz and Mrs. Nusser, hoping to find the name of some relative or friend, went through the things in her room. They found no name, and indeed they did not find much of anything.

There were, however, four postcards—from Paris, Lake Placid, Pittsfield, Mass., and Miami Beach. They were all impersonal, the last one had been mailed in 1961, and apparently Miss Nector had once worked for the people who sent them.

Buried in a box of shabby clothing, wrapped in tissue, were two pairs of white gloves. On a table there was an address book, its pages absolutely blank. In an otherwise empty closet there was a mottled, rolled-up reproduction of a painting called "China Dream," and in a plastic bag full of what once might have been blouses there were four neatly folded lace handkerchiefs.

There was not much to connect Miss Nector to her past except for one small, very neat package. There were five photographs inside, all mounted on cardboard, and Miss Nector evidently had taken pains to preserve them.

Only one of the photographs was dated, and it said 1899. The largest photograph showed a man, his wife, and a girl of perhaps 10. The little girl had a ribbon in her hair and a sash around her waist, and she was holding her father's hand. She looked quite happy and almost certainly she was the little girl who had grown up and who had died in New York that morning.

From Dakto to Detroit:
Death of a troubled hero

JON NORDHEIMER

Detroit
May 25, 1971

A few tenants living in the E. J. Jeffries Homes, a dreary public housing project in Corktown, an old Detroit neighborhood, can still remember Dwight
Johnson as a little boy who lived in one of the rust-brown buildings with his
mother and baby brother. They think it strange, after all that has happened
to Dwight, to remember him as a gentle boy who hated to fight.

Dwight Johnson died one week from his twenty-fourth birthday, shot and
killed as he tried to rob a grocery store a mile from his home. The store
manager later told the police that a tall Negro had walked in shortly before
midnight, drawn a revolver out of his topcoat, and demanded money from
the cash register.

The manager pulled his own pistol from under the counter and the two
men struggled. Seven shots were fired.

Four and one-half hours later, on an operating table at Detroit General
Hospital, Dwight (Skip) Johnson died from five gunshot wounds.

Ordinarily, the case would have been closed right there, a routine crime
in a city where there were 13,583 armed robberies last year.

But when the detectives went through the dead man's wallet for identifica-
tion, they found a small white card with its edges rubbed thin from wear.
"Congressional Medal of Honor Society—United States of America," it said.
"This certifies that Dwight H. Johnson is a member of this society."

210

CONGRESSIONAL MEDAL OF HONOR SOCIETY
UNITED STATES OF AMERICA

CHARTERED BY CONGRESS
AUGUST 14, 1958

This certifies that

Dwight H. Johnson

is a member of this society

Donald A. Gary
Secretary Treasurer

Tom Kelly
President

Dwight (Skip) Johnson, Medal of Honor winner, in a snapshot from the family album. The card was found in his wallet by police who shot and killed him as he tried to rob a grocery store a mile from his home in Detroit.

The news of the death of Sergeant Dwight Johnson shocked the black community of Detroit. Born out of wedlock when his mother was a teen-ager and raised on public welfare, he had been the good boy on his block in the dreary housing project, an altar boy and Explorer Scout, one of the few among the thousands of poor black youngsters in Detroit who had struggled against the grinding life of the ghetto and broken free, coming home from Vietnam tall and strong and a hero.

The story of Dwight Johnson and his drift from hero in Dakto, Vietnam, to villain in Detroit is a difficult one to trace. The moments of revelation are rare. There were, of course, those two brief episodes that fixed public attention on him: 30 minutes of "uncommon valor" one cold morning in combat that earned him the nation's highest military decoration, and the 30-second confrontation in the Detroit grocery that ended his life.

Oddly, they are moments of extreme violence, and everyone who knew Dwight Johnson—or thought he did—knew he was not a violent man.

Now that the funeral is over and the out-of-town relatives have gone home and the family conferences that sought clues to explain Dwight's odd behavior have ended in bitter confusion, his mother can sit back and talk wistfully about the days when Skip was a skinny kid who was chased home after school by the Corktown bullies.

"Mama," he would ask, "what do I do if they catch me?" His mother would place an arm around his thin shoulders and draw him close. "Skip," she would say, "don't you fight, honey, and don't let them catch you." The boy would look downcast and worried. "Yes, Mama," he'd say.

"Dwight was a fabulous, all-around guy, bright and with a great sense of humor," reflected Barry Davis, an auburn-haired Californian who flew with his wife to Detroit when he heard on a news report that Dwight had been killed. Three others who had served with him in Vietnam, all of them white, also came, not understanding what aberration had led to his death.

"I can remember our first day at Fort Knox and Dwight was the only colored guy in our platoon," Barry Davis recalled. "So we're in formation and this wise guy from New Jersey says to Dwight, 'Hey, what's the initials N.A.A.C.P. stand for?'

"And Dwight says, 'The National Association for the Advancement of Colored People.'

"And this wise guy from New Jersey says, 'Naw, that ain't it. It stands for "Niggers Acting As Colored People." '

"And I said to myself, 'Wow, those are fighting words,' but Dwight just laughed. From then on he was just one of the guys. As it turned out, Dwight liked this wise guy from New Jersey in the end as much as he liked anybody."

Most of the men who served with Sergeant Dwight Johnson remembered him that way—easy-going, hard to rattle, impossible to anger.

But Stan Enders remembers him another way. Stan was the gunner in Skip's tank that morning in Vietnam three years ago, during the fighting at Dakto.

"No one who was there could ever forget the sight of this guy taking on a whole battalion of North Vietnamese soldiers," Stan said as he stood in the sunshine outside Faith Memorial Church in Corktown three weeks ago, waiting for Skip's funeral service to begin.

Their platoon of four M-48 tanks was racing down a road toward Dakto, in the Central Highlands near the Cambodian border and the Ho Chi Minh Trail, when it was ambushed. Communist rockets knocked out two of the tanks immediately, and waves of foot soldiers sprang out of the nearby woods to attack the two tanks still in commission.

Skip hoisted himself out of the turret hatch and manned the mounted 50-caliber machine gun. He had been assigned to this tank only the night before. His old tank, and the crew he had spent 11 months and 22 days with in Vietnam, and which had never seen action before, was 60 feet away, burning.

"He was really close to those guys in that tank," Stan said. "He just couldn't sit still and watch it burn with them inside."

Skip ran through heavy crossfire to the tank and opened its hatch. He pulled out the first man he came across in the turret, burned but still alive, and got him to the ground just as the tank's artillery shells exploded, killing everyone left inside.

"When the tank blew up, Dwight saw the bodies all burned and black, well, he just sort of cracked up," said Stan.

For 30 minutes, armed first with a .45-caliber pistol and then with a submachine gun, Skip hunted the Vietnamese on the ground, killing from five to 20 enemy soldiers, nobody knows for sure. When he ran out of ammunition, he killed one with the stock of the machine gun.

At one point he came face to face with a Communist soldier who squeezed the trigger on his weapon aimed point-blank at him. The gun misfired and Skip killed him. But the soldier would come back to haunt him late at night in Detroit, in those dreams in which that anonymous soldier stood in front of him, the barrel of his AK-47 as big as a railroad tunnel, his finger on the trigger, slowly pressing it.

"When it was all over," Stan said, walking up the church steps as the funeral service got under way, "it took three men and three shots of morphine to hold Dwight down. He was raving. He tried to kill the prisoners we had rounded up. They took him away to a hospital in Pleiku in a straitjacket."

Stan saw Skip the next day. He had been released from the hospital, and came by to pick up his personal gear. His Vietnam tour was over and he was going home.

No one there would know anything about Dakto until 10 months later, at the White House Medal of Honor ceremony.

Sergeant Johnson returned home in early 1968, outwardly only little changed from the quiet boy named Skip who had grown up in Detroit and been drafted. Even when he and other black veterans came home and could not find a job, he seemed to take it in stride.

He had been discharged with $600 in his pocket, and it was enough to buy cigarettes and go out at night with his cousin, Tommy Tillman, and with Eddie Wright, a friend from the Jeffries Homes, and make the rounds to the Shadowbox or the Little Egypt, to drink a little beer and have a few dates.

And at home no one knew about the bad dreams he was having. They would have to learn about that later from an Army psychiatrist.

If anyone asked him about Vietnam, he would just shake his head, or laugh and say, "Aw, man, nothing happened," and he would change the subject and talk about the girls in Kuala Lumpur where he went for R. and R. or the three-day pass he spent in Louisville, Ky., drinking too much whiskey for the first time in his life and ending up in jail.

He returned home just as the Communist Tet offensive erupted in Vietnam, and everyone talked about how lucky he had been to get out before things got hot. They teased him then about his lackluster military career.

"When he came home from Vietnam he was different, sure, I noticed it, all jumpy and nervous and he had to be doing something all the time, it seems," said Eddie Wright. "But mostly he was the same funtime guy."

Carmen Berry, a close friend of Katrina May, the girl Skip started dating after his discharge, thought she detected nuances of change she attributed to the same mental letdown she had seen in other Vietnam veterans.

"They get quiet," she said. "It's like they don't have too much to say about what it was like over there. Maybe it's because they've killed people and they don't really know why they killed them."

"The only thing that bugged me about Skip then," reflected his cousin Tommy, "and the one thing I thought was kind of strange and unlike him, was the pictures he brought back. He had a stack of pictures of dead people, you know, dead Vietnamese. Color slides."

In the fall he started looking for a job, along with Tommy Tillman.

"We'd go down to the state employment agency every day and take a look at what was listed," his cousin recalled. "Skip was funny; he wouldn't try for any of the hard jobs. If we wrote down the name of a company that had a job that he didn't feel qualified for, he wouldn't even go into the place to ask about it. He'd just sit in the car while I went in.

"Or if he did go in some place, he'd just sit and mumble a few words when they'd ask him questions. It was like he felt inferior. He'd give a terrible impression. But once we got back in the car, it was the same old Skip, laughing and joking."

One day in October two military policemen came to his house. His mother saw the uniforms and before opening the door whispered urgently, "What did you do?"

"I didn't do nothing, honest, Ma," he answered.

The M.P.s asked Skip a few questions. They wanted to know what he was doing and if he had been arrested since his discharge. Fifteen minutes after they left, the telephone rang. It was a colonel, calling from the Department of Defense in Washington. Sergeant Johnson was being awarded the Medal of Honor, he said. Could he and his family be in Washington on November 19 so President Johnson could personally present the award?

One week later, on Nov. 19, 1968, they were all there in the White House, Skip tall and handsome in his dress-blue uniform, his mother, Katrina, and Tommy Tillman. The President gave a little speech. The national election was over, the Democrats had lost, but there were signs of movement at the Paris peace talks.

"*Our hearts and our hopes are turned to peace as we assemble here in the East Room this morning,*" the President said. "*All our efforts are being bent in its pursuit. But in this company we hear again, in our minds, the sound of distant battles.*"

Five men received the Medal of Honor that morning. And when Sergeant Johnson stepped stiffly forward and the President looped the pale blue ribbon and sunburst medal around his neck, a citation was read that described his valor.

Later, in the receiving line, when his mother reached Skip, she saw tears streaming down his face.

"Honey," she whispered, "what are you crying about? You've made it back."

After he officially became a hero, it seemed that everyone in Detroit wanted to hire Dwight Johnson, the only living Medal of Honor winner in Michigan. Companies that had not been interested in a diffident ex-G.I. named Johnson suddenly found openings for Medal of Honor Winner Johnson.

Among those who wanted him was the United States Army.

"The brass wanted him in the Detroit recruiting office because—let's face it—here was a black Medal of Honor winner, and blacks are our biggest manpower pool in Detroit," said an Army employe who had worked with Skip after he rejoined the service a month after winning the medal. "Personally, I think a lot of promises were made to the guy that couldn't be kept. You got to remember that getting this guy back into the Army was a feather in the cap of a lot of people."

Events began moving quickly then for Skip. He married Katrina in January (the Pontchartrain Hotel gave the couple its bridal suite for their wedding night), and the newlyweds went to Washington in January as guests at the Nixon inaugural. Sergeant Johnson began a long series of personal appearances across Michigan in a public relations campaign mapped by the Army.

In February, 1500 persons paid $10 a plate to attend a testimonial dinner for the hero in Detroit's Cobo Hall, cosponsored by the Ford Motor Company and the Chamber of Commerce. A special guest was Gen. William C. Westmoreland, Army Chief of Staff and former commander of United States forces in Vietnam.

"Dwight was a hot property back in those days," recalled Charles Bielak, a civilian information officer for the Army's recruiting operations in Detroit.

"I was getting calls for him all over the state. Of course, all this clamor didn't last. It reached a saturation point somewhere along the way and tapered off."

But while it lasted, Skip's life was frenetic. Lions Clubs . . . Rotary . . . American Legion. Detroit had a new hero. Tiger Stadium and meet the players. Sit at the dais with the white politicians. Be hailed by the black businessmen who would not have bothered to shake his hand before. Learn which fork to use for the salad. Say something intelligent to the reporters. Pick up the check for dinner for friends. Live like a man who had it made.

But Leroy May, the hero's father-in-law, could still see the child behind the man.

"Dwight and Katrina were a perfect match—they both had a lot of growing up to do," he said. "They didn't know how to handle all the attention they got in those early days. They'd go out to supper so much Katrina complained she couldn't eat any more steak. I had to take them out and buy them hot dogs and soda pop. They were just like a couple of kids."

Bills started piling up. "They were in over their heads as soon as they were married," Mr. May said.

Everyone extended credit to the Medal of Honor winner. Even when he bought the wedding ring, the jeweler would not take a down payment. Take money from a hero? Not then. Later, the Johnsons discovered credit cards.

At first they lived in an $85-a-month apartment. But Katrina wanted a house. Skip signed a mortgage on a $16,000 house on the west side of Detroit. Monthly payments were $160.

In the spring of 1970, he wrote a bad check for $41.77 at a local market. The check was made good by a black leader in Detroit who was aghast that the Medal of Honor winner had gotten himself into a financial hole.

"I went to see him and told him he couldn't go on like this," said the man, a lawyer who asked to remain anonymous. "I said he was young and black and had the Medal of Honor. He could do anything he wanted. I tried to get him to think about college and law school. The black businessmen would pick up the tab. He wouldn't have any part of it."

Looking back on this meeting, the lawyer said he suspected Skip was burdened by a "ghetto mentality" that limited his horizons. His world had been a public housing project and schools a few blocks away. Now, suddenly, events had thrust him outside the security of his boyhood neighborhood into a world dominated by whites.

He was paralyzed, the lawyer speculated, by an inability to formulate a plan of action in this alien culture that he had been transported to by something that happened on the other side of the globe.

"What does he do when he's introduced to Bunkie Knudsen, the president of Ford?" asked the lawyer. "Does he come across strong and dynamic because he knows there is a $75,000-a-year job waiting for him if he makes a good impression? And what happens to him when he just stands there and fumbles and doesn't know if he should shake hands or just nod his head? He was forced to play a role he was never trained for and never anticipated."

Tommy Tillman remembers how Skip would take several friends downtown to the Pontchartrain Hotel for an expensive meal and sit fumbling with the silverware, watching the others to see what fork to use first. "I'd say to him, 'Shoot, man, what do you care? Go ahead and use anything you want.'

"I wondered how he must feel when he's the guest of honor at one of those fancy meetings he was all the time going to."

It was about this time that the stomach pains started.

"It was all that rich food he was eating," said his father-in-law. His mother recalled that "Skip always did have a nervous stomach."

He began staying away from his job as a recruiter, missed appointments and speaking engagements. "It got so I had to pick him up myself and deliver him to a public appearance," said Mr. Bielak. "I had to handcuff myself to the guy to get him someplace. It was embarrassing. I couldn't understand his attitude."

Last summer it was decided that Sergeant Johnson should report to Selfridge Air Force Base, not far from Detroit, for diagnosis of stomach complaints.

From Selfridge he was sent in September to Valley Forge Army Hospital in Pennsylvania. An Army psychiatrist later mulled over his notes on the patient and talked about them:

Maalox and bland diet prescribed. G.I. series conducted. Results negative. Subject given 30-day convalescent leave 16 October 1970. Absent without leave until 21 January 1971 when subject returned to Army hospital on own volition. Subsequent hearing recommended dismissal of A.W.O.L. charge and back pay reinstated. Subject agreed to undergo psychiatric evaluation. In cognizance of subject's outstanding record in Vietnam, the division's chief psychiatrist placed in charge of the case. Preliminary analysis: Depression caused by post-Vietnam adjustment problem.

In February, Eddie Wright bumped into Skip on a Detroit street.

"Hey, man, where've you been?"

"I just got out of Valley Forge on a pass."

"How things going there?"

"They got me in the psycho ward."

"Huh, you got to be kidding."

"No, man, they think I'm crazy."

During the convalescent leave, Sergeant Johnson borrowed $4992 from a Detroit credit union. In his wallet he had a cashier's check for $1500, the back pay the Army had awarded him. Most of his time he spent at home on the pass, but when he went out, he would drive to the Jeffries Homes and play basketball with the teenagers after school.

"He was a big man down there with the kids," recalled his cousin. "We had all lived in the project and had been on welfare, just like these kids there today, and we were like heroes because we had broken out of there. We had made it to the outside world, and to them we were big successes. We had made it.

"Skip was something special. He had that medal, and they were proud of him. He'd be down there five minutes and the kids would come around and say, 'Hey man, ain't you Dwight Johnson?' "

His old high-school crowd was concerned about some of his new friends, though. "They were strung out on drugs, and they just seemed to be hanging around Skip for his money," said his mother. "I asked him one night if he was taking anything, and he rolled up his sleeves and showed me there were no tracks [needle marks]. 'Ma,' he said, 'I'm not taking a thing.' "

On his return to the hospital, he began analysis with the chief attending psychiatrist.

Subject is bright. His Army G.T. rating is equivalent of 120 I.Q. In first interviews he does not volunteer information. He related he grew up in a Detroit ghetto and never knew his natural father. He sort of laughed when he said he was a "good boy" and did what was expected of him. The only time he can remember losing his temper as a youth was when neighborhood bullies picked on his younger brother. He was so incensed grown-ups had to drag him off the other boys. In general, there is evidence the subject learned to live up to the expectations of others while there was a buildup of anger he continually suppressed.

The Army hospital is actually in Phoenixville, Pa., several miles from Valley Forge. It is the principal treatment center for psychiatric and ortho-pedic patients in the Northeast, with 1200 beds now occupied.

Because of the large number of amputees and wheelchair patients, the hospital has only two floors and is spread over several acres. Long oak-floored corridors run in all directions, connected by covered walkways and arcades. Someone once measured the hospital and found there were seven miles of corridors in a mazelike jumble. To prevent patients from losing their way, wards are painted different colors.

Dressed in hospital blue denims, the warrior-hero walked the labyrinth late at night, wrestling with the problems that tormented his mind and drained his spirit.

"The first day Dwight arrived here, the hospital's sergeant major brought him to us," said Spec. 6 Herman Avery, a tall Negro with a flat face and close-set eyes, who was master of the ward Dwight was first assigned to at the hospital. "It was the first time the sergeant major ever did that. We got the message. This guy was something special.

"Well, practically the first night he's here they dress him up and take him over to the Freedoms Foundations in Valley Forge to shake hands. When he got back he told me that if they ever did that again he would go A.W.O.L."

There was further psychiatric evaluation.

Subject expressed doubts over his decision to reenter the Army as a recruiter. He felt the Army didn't honor its commitment to him. The public affairs were satisfactory to him at first, but he started to feel inadequate, People he would meet would pump his hand and slap his back and say, "Johnson, if you ever think about getting out of the Army, come look me up." On several occasions he contacted these individuals and they didn't remember him. It always took several minutes to remind them who he was.

Back in Detroit on leave on one occasion his mother asked him to drive her to a doctor's appointment. In the office, an off-duty Detroit policeman, Ronald Turner, recognized the Medal of Honor Winner. When he asked for an account of his experience in Vietnam, Skip replied: "Don't ask me anything about the medal. I don't even know how I won it."

Later, the policeman reported, Skip complained that he had been exploited by the Army. He told him that ever since he won the medal he had been set on a hero's path as an inspiration to black kids.

Others recalled how upset he had become when his recruiting talks at some black high schools in Detroit had been picketed by militants who called him an "electronic nigger," a robot the Army was using to recruit blacks for a war in Asia.

With his psychiatrist, he began to discuss his deeper anxieties.

Since coming home from Vietnam the subject has had bad dreams. He didn't confide in his mother or wife, but entertained a lot of moral judgment as to what had happened at Dakto. Why had he been ordered to switch tanks the night before? Why was he spared and not the others? He experienced guilt about his survival. He wondered if he was sane. It made him sad and depressed.

Skip signed out of the hospital on March 28 on a three-day pass to Philadelphia. The next day the newspapers and television were filled with reports of the conviction of First Lieut. William L. Calley Jr. on charges of murdering Vietnamese civilians. Skip turned up in Detroit a few days later and never returned to the Army hospital.

He settled in at home once again and dodged the telephone calls from the Army.

"How can you take punitive action against a Medal of Honor holder?" asked a major at the hospital who tried to convince him to return.

The Army did contact the Ford Motor Company, however, which had been letting Skip use a Thunderbird for the past two years. Ford picked up the car on the theory that without it he might be inconvenienced enough to return to the hospital. Instead, he cashed the cashier's check for $1500, his Army back pay, and bought a 1967 Mercury for $850. He changed his unlisted phone number to avoid the Army callers and a growing number of bill collectors.

By April, his house mortgage had not been paid for the previous nine months, and foreclosing proceedings had been started. He owed payments on his credit union loan. The car had to go into a garage for brake repairs on Wednesday, April 28, and Skip was told it would cost $78.50 to get it out. The same day, Katrina entered a hospital for removal of an infected cyst, and he told the admitting office clerk he would pay the $25 deposit the next day.

Lonely and depressed at home, Skip telephoned his cousin. "Let's go out and grab some beers," he said. But his cousin was busy.

He made another phone call that night and spoke to a friend in the Army. "I have a story I'm writing and I want you to peddle it for me," he said. "It starts out like this:

"Sergeant Dwight Johnson is dead and his home has been wiped out. . . ."

On April 30, Skip visited Katrina at the hospital. She said they were asking about the hospital deposit. He left at 5:30, promising to return later that evening with her hair curlers and bathrobe.

"He was just the same old Dwight, just kidding and teasing," his wife recalled. "When he was going, he said, 'Ain't you going to give me a little kiss good-bye?' He said it like a little boy with his thumb in his mouth. So I kissed him and he went."

When Eddie Wright got home from work that night about 9 o'clock, he got a call from Skip. He said he needed a ride to pick up some money someone owed him and wanted to know if Eddie could get his stepfather to drive him. He said he would pay $15 for the ride.

Around 11 o'clock, Eddie, his mother, and his stepfather picked up Skip at his home. At his direction they drove west for about a mile to the corner of Orangelawn and Prest.

"Stop here," Skip told him, getting out of the car. "This guy lives down the street and I don't want him to see me coming."

The family waited in the car for 30 minutes. They became nervous, parked in a white neighborhood, and as Eddie explained later to the police, it may have looked odd for a car filled with blacks to be parked on a dark street. "So we pulled the car out under a streetlight so everybody could see us," he said.

At about 11:45 a police car pulled up sharply and two officers with drawn pistols got out. "What are you doing here?" they asked.

"We're waiting for a friend."

"What's his name?"

"Dwight Johnson."

"Dwight Johnson's on the floor of a grocery store around the corner," the officers said. "He's been shot."

"I first hit him with two bullets," the manager, Charles Landeghem, said later. "But he just stood there, with the gun in his hand, and said, 'I'm going to kill you. . . .'

"I kept pulling the trigger until my gun was empty."

Skip's psychiatrist recalled one of the interviews with him.

The subject remembered coming face to face with a Vietnamese with a gun. He can remember the soldier squeezing the trigger. The gun jammed. The subject has since engaged in some magical thinking about this episode. He also suffers guilt over surviving it, and later winning a high honor for the one time in his life when he lost complete control of himself. He asked: "What would happen if I lost control of myself in Detroit and behaved like I did in Vietnam?" The prospect of such an event apparently was deeply disturbing to him.

The burial at Arlington National Cemetery took place on a muggy and overcast day. The grave, on a grassy slope about 200 yards east of the Kennedy Memorial, overlooks the Potomac and the Pentagon, gray and silent, to the south.

The Army honor guard, in dress blues, carried out its assignment with precision, the sixth burial of the day for the eight-man unit, while tourists took photographs at a discreet distance from the grieving family.

For a few days after the burial, the family weighed the possibility that Skip had been taking narcotics in the last few months of his life and the demands of drugs had sent him into the grocery store with a gun. But the autopsy turned up no trace of narcotics.

Eddie Wright and his family were released by homicide detectives after questioning, even after Eddie could not produce any plausible reason why his best friend had carried out a bizarre crime and implicated him at the same time.

The dead man's mother was the only one who uttered the words that no one else dared to speak.

"Sometimes I wonder if Skip tired of this life and needed someone else to pull the trigger," she said late one night in the living room of her home, her eyes fixed on a large color photograph of her son, handsome in his uniform, with the pale blue ribbon of his country's highest military honor around his neck.

Emerging
America

Motel mania: Traveling America never leaves home

DOUGLAS E. KNEELAND

Overland Park, Kan.
July 6, 1970

As the prairie sun swings to the west, still high but slumping behind the wispy afterthoughts of clouds in the all-consuming sky, the dusty cars start peeling off the highway.

From California, they come. From New York. From Texas, Georgia, Wisconsin, and Nebraska.

And out of their crowded interiors, heavy with luggage, Thermos jugs and travel games, stained by drinks and popcorn and potato chips, spills America. Summer-struck, road-caught middle America.

The men, blinking their strained eyes behind sunglasses, easing the cramps in their weary legs under pastel slacks and plaid bermuda shorts. The women, tight in the mouth, their hair windblown, their culottes wrinkled. The children, sullen, explosive-looking.

Wearily, they file into the Glenwood Manor Motor Hotel. A stop at the registration desk and back they traipse to the cars to search out their rooms among the 275 in the sprawling two-story complex of cellblocks with picture windows.

Once in the rooms, experienced eyes search out the expected. Paneled walls setting off the papered or painted ones. Firm mattresses on two double beds. Decorator-coordinated drapes and spreads and wall hangings. Color television,

225

hidden in a cabinet above the low bureaus. Bathrooms with sink and shower. A separate lavatory and the vanity table beside it.

Then a flurry of changing to bathing suits and a rush to the pool, already reconnoitered by the children. The men stroll expansively. The women, tugging at straps to cover white streaks on their tanned skin, sigh. The youngsters, the prison of their cars forgotten, prance.

Middle America is home again—until tomorrow.

Glenwood Manor is a Best Western motel. But it could be a Holiday Inn, a Howard Johnson's, a Ramada Inn, a Downtowner, or any one of many of the 6500 motor hotels—at least 50 rooms—with 675,000 units, or 44,000 motels or tourist courts—fewer than 50 rooms—with 1,274,000 units, which line the nation's highways.

And, except for the prairie sun and sky, it could be in Bangor, Me., Anniston, Ala., Richmond, Ind., Vandalia, Ill., or almost anywhere.

For the attempt is there, across the country, to make sure that traveling America's millions will feel that they have never left home and that their vacations are never ending.

The same imitation-French, imitation-Italian, imitation-Spanish, imitation-English, and imitation-Colonial restaurants abound, plush in decor, dim with candlelight, their menus rampant with steaks and lobster tails. At the Glenwood Manor, it's Ye Olde Tudor Room:

> *We at Glenwood bid you*
> *a hearty greeting*
> *And welcome you to the*
> *room of fine eating.*
> *For an occasion you will*
> *long remember*
> *Enjoy the Tudor Room*
> *in all its splendor.*

Not many years ago, purebred Angus cattle grazed on Glen Dickinson's farm, a few miles from the spot where 19th-century travelers thronged in covered wagons for the trek west on the Santa Fe Trail.

But by 1960, the grazing land was being hemmed in by the new affluence of Overland Park, a sleepy village in northeastern Johnson County, which was being transformed by builders into the Westchester County of Metropolitan Kansas City.

In 1960, Overland Park, with a population of 28,000 persons, was incorporated as a city. The same year, the Dickinson family, which runs a chain of 36 theaters, built Glenwood Manor, with 75 rooms and one banquet room. Overland Park now has a population of 80,000 and Glenwood Manor has 275 rooms and 35 banquet rooms, the largest of which seats 850 persons.

Across from a string of automobile salesrooms and shopping centers on Route 69, a moderately well-traveled north-south highway, Glenwood Manor

Americans will drive hundreds of miles in search of new scenery and new experiences. But at night, they flock to motels, mini-cities that remind them of the comforts—and discomforts—of home.

NYT

still has the spacious farmland on which to expand and to provide the resort atmosphere for which it strives.

In addition to its pool and covered patio dining area (featuring a chuck wagon buffet), it offers on its 120 acres a Western museum; a 60-acre picnic ground with a 15-acre lake for swimming; boating and fishing; two softball diamonds; a volleyball court; a badminton court; a horseshoe pitch; an 18-hole putting green; a four-hole pitch-and-putt golf course; a children's playground; a sauna; a health club; and two championship tennis courts, where it stages a $10,000 invitational tournament each spring.

"What we've tried to do here," Joe F. Ross, the 33-year-old manager, explained recently, "is to create enough of a resort atmosphere during the summer months to encourage the traveler to stay an extra day or so to make it part of his vacation.

"We've even put in—now get this—a jogging track. We're the only hotel in America with a half-mile jogging track."

As he spoke, the Kansas sun was blistering the broad lawns with temperatures of more than 100 degrees. The tennis courts, the playground, the picnic area were silent, deserted in the prairie heat. Only the pool, its apron made bearable to tender feet by indoor-outdoor carpeting, was alive with guests.

The following day, when the heat had broken, Don Bowlby of Indianapolis, bearded and clad only in shorts, flipped a Frisbee indolently on the lawn near the pool with his teen-age son while waiting for his wife and two other children. Pausing for a few moments, he said wearily:

"We're finishing up a two-week jaunt to Spokane and Los Angeles and headed back to Indianapolis. We were just going to stay for one night, but we've been going so hard—I just put 7000 miles on my car—so we're going to take a little rest. This is the first chance we've had to slow down."

Then, brightening, he added: "But we're going to be back in Indianapolis tomorrow and then the next day we're going to take off for Standing Stone Park down in Tennessee. Every year we make a family thing of it. We get five or six cabins and my folks come and some of the rest of the family and we stay for a week and it's great."

Still, not all Americans are obsessed by the road. Or perhaps they are, and time or cash or both prevent extensive trips. In any event, the new motel-resorts, especially in the recreation-starved midlands, have found that local residents, yearning for the freedom of a home away from home, can provide a booming weekend business.

Take Duane Beet of Overland Park, lazing in the sun, sipping rum and Coke with his young wife, Diane, and John Milliken, a neighbor.

"This is the first time we've been out here," he said. "We've got a new addition in the family—a little boy, about eight weeks ago. I only had three days off so we decided to come over here and cool it.

"They've got a lake over here. We planned to take a charcoal grill over there last night, but after four hours in the sun with gin and tonic, we went to bed early."

"With a headache," his wife added.

Or take the group of seven couples from Overland Park and Prairie Village, who with their score of children have spent every summer holiday weekend for years at Glenwood Manor.

"We rent two rooms for the weekend and we drive 15 minutes to be here," Herb Taubin said as one of Steve Pack's youngsters poured water from the pool over his father's head, "and we could be in Florida or any resort in the whole country."

A new bridge in Tennessee will
end a village's century of isolation

GEORGE VECSEY

Big Springs, Tenn.
December 1, 1971

The noisiest thing in Big Springs is usually the recess hour at the one-room schoolhouse. The second noisiest thing is the chickens picking in Parralee Hurd's front yard. And when it gets real quiet, you can hear the Clinch River flowing by.

But Big Springs (population 163) has been unusually noisy this month with the big cement mixers chugging down the dirt road and the crane grinding away. Pretty soon there will be the occasional rumble of a car crossing the new bridge—and then Big Springs will be joining the rest of Tennessee after a century of isolation.

"I think everybody wanted the bridge," said Miss Hazel Begley, the warm-faced schoolteacher, who envisions both the school and her professional career coming to an end. "Now I think people are afraid that Big Springs will lose its charm."

Named after the clear, cool spring that bubbles to the surface across the road from Mrs. Hurd's house, Big Springs has been just about as isolated as any community can get, even in Appalachia. With no stores and no telephones, Big Springs is 12 miles down the dirt road from the nearest paved highway and the nearest store and gas station, on the way to Clinchport, Va.

To get to Sneedville, the seat of Hancock County, Tenn., the farmers of Big Springs still have to drive the corresponding 12 miles back along the

230

Progress, in the form of a new bridge linking Big Springs to the rest of Tennessee, will replace this old bridge and may, some believe, mark the end of the one-room schoolhouse.

NYT/KENNETH MURRAY

other side of the slow greenish Clinch River, then continue on for 18 more miles. Thus, the new bridge will save them 24 miles, almost an hour of driving on the twisting, rutted cow-trail road. But what else will it mean?

"It will mean they can take their burley tobacco to market in Tennessee instead of Virginia," said Representative James H. Quillen, a Republican from Kingsport, who led the drive for the new bridge. "It means they can do business in their own county seat."

Standing in the doorway of the schoolhouse, Miss Begley predicted that the new bridge would help close down one of the last of Tennessee's one-room schoolhouses.

The grade-school children have always remained in Big Springs because nobody wanted them crossing the 50-yard-wide river in the small flat-bottomed boats used by adults or on the swinging footbridge downstream.

Swinging bridges are common all over Appalachia, the only way across creeks for thousands of families. But while Big Springs teen-agers have crossed the bridge to take a bus to high school in Sneedville, nobody wanted the little ones crossing the swinging bridge in the morning haze or the evening darkness.

However, in another month or two, the new bridge will take cars easily to Kyles Ford, 10 miles down the road, where there is a more modern elementary school.

"They've got a big brick building down there," said Miss Begley, "with a new cafeteria for hot lunches."

Miss Begley expects her school to remain open until next June, but then she expects the 15 to 20 children to be transferred to Kyles Ford the following fall.

"I don't know what will happen to me," she said. "I only got one year of college by grubbin' and catchin' where I could. But my mother and daddy were both sick and I helped around the house and that's all the time I could go to school. I don't regret it. We only have one mother and daddy."

The teacher conceded that a bigger school would probably benefit her charges, whose ages range from 5 to around 13 or 14, and who have had to rely on an occasional visit from state education officials for special instruction in art, music, and drama.

The people of Big Springs have been trying to get their bridge for six years since they talked with Mr. Quillen at one of his "open house" meetings in Sneedville.

"I talked to the state, with no results," he said. "The county didn't have any money—it's the seventh poorest county in the entire United States. Finally, I went to the Appalachian Regional Commission and they broke the logjam."

The commission, whose characteristic approach to the region's problems has been to build roads and bridges, came up with $35,000 for Big Springs. Then came a "domino effect" of aid—the county road commission supplied some labor and equipment; Operation Mainstream provided 17 trained workers; the Tennessee Valley Authority drew up plans and provided a skilled supervisor, John Morris; and the state provided a bulldozer and crane and operators. The extra cost has been estimated at $20,000.

The farmers of Big Springs themselves will cut the wooden planks that will be used on the steel bridge.

When the bridge is completed, what else can Big Springs expect?

"I don't know," said James Hurd, squatting in mountaineer fashion by the side of the river, whittling with a sharp knife into a soft branch as he watched cement being poured into the circular steel piling forms.

Mr. Hurd occasionally travels to Morrisontown to work as an upholsterer. Most of the men in Big Springs still work the land for table crops and burley tobacco and raise a few hogs and cattle and chickens. Mr. Hurd didn't think the bridge would change any of that.

"Be quicker to get your license plate," Mr. Hurd volunteered. "That's about it, I reckon. We'll just wait and see."

Ill winds buffet Children of God

JAMES T. WOOTEN

Mingus, Tex.
November 24, 1971

Although the boy who calls himself Adonikum was born but 20 years ago, there is a loneliness in his eyes that is older than human history, and when he speaks, his soft words echo the accumulated desperation of the species.

"It is easy to know when you are not wanted," he said rather sadly here yesterday as the first serious winds of the winter sliced across the barren prairie around him. "What is not so easy is to leave."

But however difficult it is, leaving is an experience for him and the hundreds of other members of the Children of God, a youthful, rigidly Fundamentalist group of Christians who believe the universe is on its last legs and and who have left family, friends, and society behind in their retreat to isolated communes scattered from this West Texas hamlet to Canada, Mexico, and Europe.

Recently some new dimensions of alienation were added to the lives of many of the group. Parents in Texas and in California, angered by their children's departure to the sect, have set out on a course of energetic opposition. The group's principal benefactor has evicted members from communes here and in California.

Finally, this week the organization announced that despite its belief in the New Testament counsel that anyone who does not hate his parents cannot be a disciple of Jesus, many Children of God will be going home for the holiday season.

The sect had its origins among a small group of conservatives within the Jesus Movement, a nationwide Fundamentalist movement among youth, and served only as a reactionary facet of that group until early 1970, when it mushroomed into a full-fledged sect.

Louis Ingersoll, who edits the Children of God newsletter, says the group now has 2000 members in 39 communes in seven countries. Until late last summer, the bulk of the American membership was in Texas and southern California, but there now appears to be a general migration to colonies and camps in the Northwest.

Some observers who have watched its evolution are now persuaded that the recent rash of problems has dealt a mortal blow to the group. Adonikum quietly disagrees.

"What is happening to us is nothing new for the Children of God," he said, shivering in the wind. "We know that by doing the will of Jesus we run the risk of rejection—He was despised and rejected, a man of sorrows and acquainted with grief—but we also know that His spirit is among us and will not leave us alone, and that is what is important."

"Amen," said a boy who calls himself Ecclesiastes.

"Amen, praise Jesus," intoned a boy who calls himself Hamath.

The three were part of a grimy rear guard of the 250 members who left a 350-acre ranch-commune near here over the last month. Some of them headed for new quarters in Dallas and Fort Worth, 100 miles away, but most of them went to a new encampment near Seattle, where they joined many others who had been similarly displaced from communes in southern California.

In their new sites, they hope to resume the ascetic, communal life-style they believe to be patterned after the earliest disciples of the Christian faith.

The Children of God eschew tobacco, liquor, and premarital or extramarital sex, devoting themselves within their nearly self-sustaining communes to chanted prayers, hymns sung ecstatically, an almost constant study of the Bible, meditation, and conversing in languages that they say come to them through prayer on the spur of the moment.

Like most of the devotees of the dozens of other youth cults that have arisen over the last decade, most of the Children of God are from white, middle-class families. Most are in their early 20s, and all are convinced that society is beyond repair and must be forsaken by the true believer in Jesus Christ.

Each of them adopts a Biblical name on his entrance into the sect. Although many members are married to other members of the sect, there are few children. Day in and day out, the mood of their communes is somber and grim, and laughter is a scarce commodity. Their support has been mainly from parents and individuals sympathetic to their pursuit.

Their problems began in August when group of adults in the San Diego area, chagrined by their children's membership in the sect, formed an organization called The Parents Committee to Free Our Sons and Daughters from the Children of God.

By mid-September, the committee had persuaded the Rev. J. Fred Jordan, a wealthy television evangelist in Los Angeles, who is the principal benefactor of the sect, to denounce it publicly and to ask its leaders to leave the communes he had provided near Coachella, Calif., a desert community not far from Palm Springs, and at the ranch he owns near here.

In protest, about 40 members at Coachella, 100 in a skid row house in Los Angeles, and 60 living at a dilapidated 32-acre dairy farm in the arid, brown sandy hills near San Diego, chose to leave along with their leaders. The same decision was reached in late October by the members of the commune here.

Mr. Jordan, a native of the desolate sprawling land through which the muddy Brazos River aimlessly meanders, said he had no quarrel with the members, just the leaders; and the parents on the new committee said they had no objection to the sect's literalistic beliefs, but rather to the control exercised by its leaders.

"These people are antigovernment, antireligion, and antischools," said William M. Rambur of Chula Vista, Calif., whose daughter, Kay, joined the Children of God last summer and refused to go home when he came here to get her.

Later, Mr. Rambur, a retired Navy officer, found that his 22-year-old daughter, who calls herself Comfort, had gone to Seattle with many of the others from the commune here, and he went there to try to persuade her again to go home.

"If I have to leave, I'll die," she screamed.

"I don't know what kind of hold they have on those kids," said Mr. Rambur. "I think it's some kind of mass hypnosis or witchcraft."

There are several similar stories of parents who tried to retrieve their children, but a barber in Seattle was apparently one of only a few who were successful.

The daughter of a Long Island couple joined a commune in Texas, where her mother visited her several times last summer. In August, the girl was transferred to the Los Angeles colony, where her father spirited her away in an automobile.

She escaped at Phoenix, and three weeks later the father received a postcard from Scottsdale, Ariz.

"Daddy," his daughter wrote, "you really shouldn't have tried to kidnap me. I'm still working for my Lord and my brothers and sisters. Please do not try to get in touch with me ever again."

Another committee leader is Ted Patrick, Gov. Ronald Reagan's minority affairs director in the San Diego area. Mr. Patrick, whose son is a member of the sect, believes all of the members were "hypnotized into joining" and charges that drugs are common in the group.

The leaders of the sect accuse Mr. Jordan, the television preacher, of using the Children of God for monetary gain. They say he asked them, and they consented, to appear on his television program, after which he made appeals for money.

"We never saw any of it," said one spokesman for the group.

The leaders also denied the parents' charges that members are taught or persuaded with drugs or hypnosis to detest their parents and forsake their families.

Perhaps in response to the parents' criticism, Mr. Ingersoll, speaking for the new Dallas colony of about 75 young people, said Monday that the "2000 members of the Children of God in 39 communes in seven countries will start for home this week."

"God led us to take this drastic step," said Mr. Ingersoll, who calls himself Abel. "It is a test of our discipleship and to prove once and for all that we are not the victims of hypnotism, brainwashing, drugs, kidnapping, or coercion."

Some members, he said, will remain home over the Christmas holidays, and some may stay at the communes.

"It will be their decision," he said.

The Dallas colony was formed by a few members of the commune that was closed here by Mr. Jordan.

The Dallas colony is headquartered in an unheated building in a rundown part of town, and its principal activity is to publish the sect's international newsletter. It is to these quarters that Adonikum, Ecclesiastes, Hamath, and the dozen or so other youngsters left behind here will eventually go.

But for now, the immediate task for them is to repair a variety of old vehicles parked on the property of Randy Bennett, a 30-year-old affable, wealthy rancher who befriended the group before its eviction because "as far as I could tell, they just wanted to be left alone, and that's sort of how I am too."

By midafternoon, the boys' hands were black with the dirt and oil from the various motors on which they had been working throughout the day. The wind had increased substantially, and it was now sweeping unchallenged over the rolling hills, stirring the mesquite and the sagebrush, cutting like a scalpel through the boys' clothing.

Adonikum embraced himself and rubbed his hands before pronouncing what was for him a benediction to the day.

"Out there, I found everything that I wanted except love, which is really what I wanted," he said. "With the Children of God, I found love, and so can anyone else who wants it. Out there I felt that love did not exist. Here, it is all around me."

Are you going home for the holidays? he was asked.

"If my parents send the money," he said as he walked toward a great blue bus that rested stolidly on its axles, tumbleweeds bouncing off its flattened tires.

On farm in Dakota, missile is something to plow around

ANTHONY RIPLEY

Grand Forks, N.D.
March 19, 1969

A part of the massive nuclear retaliatory capacity of the United States is buried out on Merlin Fingarson's farm, 60 miles northeast of here.

The pancake-flat valley country of the Red River of the North gives way to gently rolling land near Edinburgh, N.D., and Mr. Fingarson's farm is nearby.

A half mile down the road from his house, a 70-foot Minuteman missile is buried in a steel and concrete silo. It is on a half-acre plot, surrounded by a 10-foot chain-link fence topped with barbed wire.

There is some talk in Edinburgh that Mr. Fingarson has become "a little uppity" since he got his missile, but he is warm and cordial to visitors and says he sleeps well at night with his nuclear neighbor.

Like most of the scattered farmers in North Dakota, he knows there are more missiles coming—the antiballistic missile system to guard the Minuteman. But unlike suburbanites around America's major cities who raised angry protests over the possible location of missiles near their homes, Mr. Fingarson is not worried.

His Minuteman has become just another part of the landscape.

There is little to be seen inside the chained and padlocked enclosure numbered C-21.

There are two hospital-green square ventilator hoods, four gray electronic

238

sensors looking like a ship's ventilator stacks, staring blankly at each other across a snow-swept, 80-ton concrete lid.

Four telephone poles, topped with lights and a yellow concrete cylinder that Mr. Fingarson thinks is an aiming post, are also there.

A sign outside the enclosure warns, "Keep Away from Underground Antenna."

Mr. Fingarson, thin and 49 years old, has three sons and a daughter. He farms 560 acres, mostly in wheat, and has 14 head of beef cattle. His net income last year was $2,500, and his wife works part time as a nurse.

Standing in his linoleum-floored kitchen with a pipe, bib overalls, a plaid flannel shirt, and high-top workshoes, Mr. Fingarson said he gave little thought to the awesome weapon down the road.

Nor has he thought much, he said, about the new antiballistics missile system that President Nixon announced would be built near here to guard his missile and 149 others like it in the Grand Forks area.

"We hardly even mention it," he said. "You hardly even know there's a missile on your land."

He just plows around the 10-acre site the Government bought in 1963 for $300 an acre.

Occasionally, he said, he pauses near the fence and looks inside.

"It's amazing how complex it is," he said.

He sometimes thinks, he said, "how much money is sunk down there—it probably cost the Government $1 million."

"There's been some talk about Minuteman won't leave the ground. I think it will work."

He was referring to three failures to fire Minuteman on seven-second test runs from silos near Michigan, N.D.

Following a successful test firing from a silo near Rapid City, S.D., in 1965, the Air Force scheduled another test shot called Operation Long Life 2 for Oct. 12, 1966, near Michigan.

Four days before the test, a malfunction was discovered, and the firing was put off until Oct. 19. That day it failed to operate because of a substandard resistor in the launching power supply, which, the Air Force said, could have been bypassed by a second system under wartime conditions.

The shot was rescheduled for Oct. 28 and failed again, this time because of a failure of a miniature capacitor in the guidance and control mechanism.

Last Aug. 14, the test, renamed Operation Giant Boost, failed again before an audience of high-ranking officers of the Strategic Air Command, Pentagon officials, and members of the North Dakota Congressional delegation. A faulty pin in one of the umbilical connectors was at fault.

Acting Air Force Secretary Alexander H. Flax, in a letter March 12 to Senator Milton R. Young of North Dakota, said that further tests would be held later this year.

The failures have led to cynicism on the part of some.

"They always have a wet fuse or something," said James Wallace, a restaurant equipment salesman from Fargo, 74 miles south of Grand Forks.

Mayor Herschel Lashkowitz of Fargo, an opponent of the antiballistic missile system, said he felt neither qualified nor willing to "sit in judgment of the President of the United States." But he added his personal thoughts:

"There is no probable certainty that the Minuteman missiles themselves have a capability worthy of being guarded.

"One of the tragic-comic events is the repeated failure of the Minuteman missile in the face of glittering promises and expectations.

"Furthermore, I've heard a great deal of concern expressed that the Sentinel system means a possible neglect of the priorities of the American cities."

The Air Force, thought to be privately embarrassed over the misfirings, points to several hundred successful tests at Vandenberg Air Force Base in California.

Though there were demonstrations in Fargo and Grand Forks last weekend against the ABM, they involved college students primarily. Residents there seemed more interested in the predicted heavy flooding of the Red River, which flows north past the city into Canada.

In rural areas, the worry was more over the low price of wheat—$1.40 a bushel.

In Concrete, N.D., 18 miles north of Mr. Fingarson's farm, few questions are raised about either the Minuteman or the Sentinel system. Both are regarded as a boon to the local economy.

Since a cement plant closed in Concrete more than 40 years ago, the town has been dwindling. Sixteen people live there and lately Army Corps of Engineers trucks have been seen, taking test borings of the soil for a possible ABM site.

Mrs. Melvin Herzog runs the post office in an old bank building that also serves as a general store. She feels it is likely that Concrete could be chosen as a Sentinel site. The Army digging has been going on since last summer.

Mrs. Herzog was upset with an article in *The Grand Forks Herald,* which said Concrete was a "ghost town."

If the missiles come, her husband is thinking of opening a trailer park.

"We all think it will create a lot of excitement," she said.

Lawrence Lawson, whose farm is near Concrete, will not be tilling his two quarter sections this year. He rented the land out, he said, and plans to "get a job in the missile."

Asked his reaction to the demonstrations against the ABM, he said, "A bunch of kids in Grand Forks are doing all the protesting. What the hell do they know? They're 100 miles away."

Arnis Johanneson, a farmer interviewed in a general store in Mountain, N.D., said he had no worry over the missiles. He is struggling to make a living on a 320-acre farm.

"If I could get $2 a bushel for wheat, I wouldn't have no worry," he said.

Through the countryside, cables linking the Minuteman missile silos can be traced by posts topped with a dayglow orange stripe.

In an Air Force press release printed in the "Farm and Home" tabloid insert of *The Grand Forks Herald* last June 8, farmers were asked not to tamper with the sometimes inconvenient posts. The release stated:

"Your cooperation as a modern Minuteman assisting the Air Force in the defense of the United States will be greatly appreciated by the Air Force and will give you that old warm feeling deep down inside for doing your part as an American."

In Small Town, U.S.A., women's liberation is either a joke or a bore

JUDY KLEMESRUD

Hope, Ind.
March 22, 1972

Hardly anyone in this central Indiana farming town of 1500 has heard of Betty Friedan. Gloria Steinem is as foreign to the white Protestant natives as a breakfast of bagels and lox. The term "consciousness-raising" is likely to elicit a furrowed brow and a "Huh?" while a male chauvinist pig would probably be identified as just another breed to haul to next summer's Bartholomew County Fair.

No, women's liberation has not reached Small Town, U.S.A.

At least it hasn't reached Hope, which seems fairly typical of the thousands of small towns scattered throughout the country, towns where traffic lights are nonexistent because traffic is almost nonexistent. And the first (and last) picture show has closed down because of lack of business. And strangers are greeted with smiles and "Hi's" on the town square. And hardly anyone has been to college. And bored teen-agers guzzle Cokes at a hangout on the outskirts called Judy's Drive-In.

It has been called a major weakness of the women's movement, this failure to reach the boondocks. It is not that the people haven't heard of women's lib. They hear about it regularly from their beloved Johnny Carson and read about it in their favorite magazines, *Life, Redbook,* and *Good Housekeeping.* It's just that they don't care enough about it, or don't understand it, to want to know more of the specifics.

242

Mrs. Taylor in the hardware store which she owns and operates in Hope, Indiana.
NYT/BILL KRIDER

"What you have here are a lot of happy women," explained Mrs. Katherine Stafford, the 56-year-old college-educated Hope librarian, who so far has not added any of the various women's lib books to the town stacks. "Maybe if they weren't so happy, there might be more interest in women's liberation. As it is, we talk about it only very jokingly—if at all."

So far, none of the town's major women's organizations—the Royal Neighbors of America, Eastern Star, Kappa Kappa Sigma, and the Woman's Christian Temperance Union—has discussed the women's movement at their meetings. But last summer, a woman described as "a radical schoolteacher" from nearby Columbus, Ind., came to speak about women's liberation to members of the all-male Lions Club.

"The men were fighting-mad afterwards," recalled Mrs. Betty Taylor, 39, who runs the town's only hardware store while her husband works at the Cummins Engine Company in Columbus, employer of many Hope men. "She told them that people shouldn't be judged by what's between their legs, and ever since, people around here just haven't been too serious about women's lib."

The gray-haired Mrs. Taylor is probably one of the more liberated women of Hope, but she doesn't think of herself that way. She does all of the things in her work that a man would do, including cutting pipe. Her back room doubles as a day-care center for female employes who want to bring their babies with them to work. She believes she started the fad among Hope women of wearing pants to work. Her husband, Kenneth, helps with the housework.

Like most Hope women, she is vociferously in favor of equal pay for equal work. But the first words that come out of her mouth when asked about women's lib are: "What does burning bras have to do with making things equal?"

And the so-called radicals in the movement bother her. "Some of them are just like the radicals of the colored race," she said. "They do more harm than good."

Still, change has come creeping into Hope, not all of it the kind Hope residents like. People are still talking about the woman who ran out on her husband and children a few years ago and hasn't been seen since. She is referred to as "that runaway mother."

Four housefuls of alleged drug peddlers were recently run out of town after irate residents held a "town meeting" at Hauser High School, named after the town's Moravian founder, Martin Hauser. The high-school pregnancy rate is up, and so is the town's divorce rate. In fact, some squabbling couples have taken the somewhat radical step of bypassing their local clergymen and taking their troubles to a family counseling service in Columbus.

"Are those city women really feeling oppressed?" asked Mrs. Judy Douglas, 26, with a grin. "Why do they get married then? Why make innocent kids stay home with a baby-sitter?"

Mrs. Douglas has two sons, age 8 and 7, and after school lets out, they come to the jewelry store she runs on the town square, and they sit in a back room and watch television until closing time. Someday, when Mrs. Douglas' husband takes over the store (he is now attending a watchmaker's school in Seymour, Ind.), Mrs. Douglas and her sons will both be at home after shool.

"I for one don't want equal rights with men," she said vigorously. "I just want to be a woman. I believe a man should be the head of the house. I want to can, freeze, baby-sit, all those things that bore most women."

Several women said they thought that the lack of interest in the women's movement was because so many Hope women were born and raised on farms.

"The women on the farm have always been working hand in hand with their men," said Mrs. Marie Harker, 59, whose husband farms 80 acres northeast of Hope. "I don't think we feel this pressure [for equality] that some women do. But then I'm not so sure that women are held down as much as they pretend to be, either."

What do Hope women do for entertainment? Almost every woman seems to belong to a bridge club, where she exchanges town gossip with friends and talks about how she plans to vote for President Nixon again. Sometimes couples go bowling or to the movies in Columbus, or for a big night out, they might drive the 50 miles northwest to "Indy." And almost everybody is an avid fan of the athletic teams at Hauser High School.

Most of the women who were interviewed seemed strongly opposed to legalized abortion and felt that they could never bring themselves to mark an X beside the name of a woman Presidential candidate.

"I think if someone has an abortion, they ought to take 'em out and hang 'em," said Mrs. Wavelene Embs, 32, a self-styled "grease monkey" at her husband Herbie's Sunoco service station. "If it wasn't God's will, they wouldn't have gotten pregnant in the first place."

Mrs. Embs, a Baptist who was married at the age of 14 and now has four children, slapped her hand against a stack of tires and howled when asked if she would vote for a woman for President.

"Hell, no!" she replied. "They're so weak, they'd have headaches and wouldn't be able to run the country. They'd be sick in bed all the time."

Mrs. Shirley Mills, whose pharmacist husband pays her $75 every Friday for doing the bookkeeping at their drugstore, was one of the few women who could identify a women's liberation leader.

"I read Germaine Greer's article in *Playboy*," said Mrs. Mills, who like many of her friends has a puffy bouffant hairdo and rhinestone-trimmed eyeglasses, "and I saw her on Johnny Carson. I think she's very gross. Being in the drugstore, I hear a lot of off-color talk, but Germaine Greer's talk is just outlandish!"

One of the few—and perhaps the only—women in Hope who is openly sympathetic to the women's movement is Mrs. Kathie Johnson, 23, a former Purdue coed who has returned home "to get my ship together" while going through a divorce. She has a 4-year-old son, Scott.

"I especially like this Ms. thing they talk about," she said, while sitting on a bicycle stand in front of her father's Clouse's Regal Market ("Super Foods"), the town's largest business. "It's been pointed out to me now that I'm going to be divorced that I'll still be called Mrs. I don't like that. I'm nobody's wife now."

Out at the modernistic $1.5 million Hauser High School, on the south edge of town, women's lib has seemed to have made a slight dent. Mrs. Betty Burney, who has been the home economics teacher for 16 years, tells her girl students as well as the boys in her health class that "there is no such thing as women's work" and that a married couple should share the housework if the wife has a job.

"I get quite a bit of static from the boys," the soft-spoken teacher said, "and some of the girls think it's degrading for a man to do housework or the dishes. But the fact is that it's impossible for a woman who works to take care of the children and the housework and her job, too. That really takes a superwoman."

Otherwise, things at Hauser High seem pretty much the way they always were. Cheerleading is still the most prestigious activity for girls. One of the smartest students in the senior class, Susan Boyle, 18, yearns for the day when she will walk down the aisle in a long white wedding gown and then go on to have five children. Debbie Smith, 16, a former homecoming queen and a majorette, said she had heard of the term "sex object" but didn't think there was anything wrong with a girl trying to look as pretty as she could for the opposite sex. She would never, she said, think of going without make-up—or a bra.

Back in Hope, Mrs. Patsy Harris, 30, who described herself as "a wife [of a schoolteacher], mother, and homemaker, in that order," sat watching color television with her hair still in rollers. A colored picture of Jesus Christ hung over the set.

"I just don't want a job," she insisted, as two of her four children, Tracy, 6, and Jennifer, 4, squirmed on her lap. "I love staying home. I cannot imagine in my wildest dreams getting up in the morning, dragging the kids to a baby-sitter, and going to work. I like to be able to sit down and read a book. I feel like my time is my own. I mean, how could a woman be any happier than that?"

July 4 on the road:
A stop at Howard Johnson's

JAMES T. WOOTEN

Valley Forge, Pa.
July 4, 1971

Laniel Hopkins Lawson III had flipped his fourth french-fried potato at his sister, using his fork as a catapult, and was preparing another launch when his mother's patience expired.

"That's enough," she snapped at the 4-year-old boy, her voice rising above the clatter of dishes and silverware and the hum of conversation in the crowded Howard Johnson restaurant just off the busy Pennsylvania Turnpike—and all over the dining room, heads turned toward the Lawsons' table.

"One more time, Buster, and you're going to get it," she continued, unruffled by the attention. She glanced at her husband for some sign of assent, but Laniel Hopkins Lawson Jr., an airline mechanic in Cleveland, was biting into a mammoth hamburger, oblivious to the impending family crisis.

"Can't you help?" she whispered raspingly to him as the sixth potato strip whizzed across the table and splattered against the dress of the little girl. Mrs. Lawson wiped the catchup smears away, placed her hands in her lap, and sighed. "Never again," she said quietly to no one in particular. "I will never again agree to another trip on another holiday—not next Fourth of July, not the next one, and not ever, ever again."

Although her vow was no doubt sincere, the odds are that come next Independence Day, the Lawsons will once again join that mass of Americans for whom a summer holiday means a motor trip to somewhere—to the

247

Joanne Anthony, 17, a Howard Johnson restaurant waitress, and her holiday customers just off the Pennsylvania Turnpike.
NYT/MICHAEL EVANS

mountains, the shore, the lake, the park, Grandma's house, or any place that strikes their fancy—and an inevitable stop at one of the thousands of road-side inns that have become a national institution.

Yesterday and today, for instance, more than 3000 of these weekend gypsies wheeled out of the eastbound lane of the Pennsylvania Turnpike and into the parking lots of the Howard Johnson restaurant near this historic village.

They were old and young and black and white, and they came in various shapes and sizes and costumes—in shorts and sneakers, jeans and sandals, bare midriffs and business suits, swimsuits and pants suits, sunsuits and T shirts, polo shirts and dashikis and diapers.

They arrived and left in cars with license plates from Iowa, Illinois and Indiana, and a score of other states—and in between, they consumed more than 2500 hamburgers, 7000 cups of coffee, 100 gallons of ice cream, 250 gallons of cola, 80 dozen eggs, and more than 1500 pancakes.

"We just try to make them happy and comfortable while they're here," Ralph L. Kleintop, the restaurant's manager, explained. "We don't always succeed, but we keep trying."

One of those who tried is Joanne Anthony, a 17-year-old waitress who lives in nearby Wayne. Early this morning, an elderly man sat down at one of the stools in her section and asked for an order of pancakes.

"And make them well done," he growled.

When she returned from the kitchen, he called her to him again. "You didn't tell them, did you?" he said.

"All of our pancakes are well done," she replied.

"But you didn't tell them, did you?" he repeated.

"No, I forgot," she admitted.

"Well, go tell them," he insisted, and she did so a bit sheepishly because the cooks in the kitchen had never heard of "well-done" pancakes.

"But most of our customers are really very nice," Miss Anthony said later.

The little boy's mother was staring out the window, when, in a gracious mood, he extended an ice-cream cone toward her with the invitation to share it.

"Have some, Mommy," he squealed. "Have some."

As she turned, the boy's chocolate ice cream inserted itself precisely in her left eye.

"Is it good, Mommy?" the boy inquired.

At noon today, the red-carpeted restaurant was filled with customers, most of them in family groups. In the gift shops in the lobby, other travelers were browsing and buying from an assortment of knickknacks and souvenirs.

In one booth, Mr. and Mrs. George R. Smith of Reading, Pa., and their three children watched as Jennifer Rolland, their 8-month-old granddaughter, methodically transferred large chunks of food from her tray to the floor.

As a middle-aged matron in another booth turned over a glass of iced tea, Mr. Kleintop, the manager, rushed by with a broom handle to be used as a cane by William L. Delligatti who had turned his ankle earlier in the day at his home in Uniontown, Pa.

As Mr. Delligatti and his wife left, a busboy and a waitress collided, a burly man in a white shirt banged on the cigarette machine, a lanky teen-age boy continued to suck on the straw in his glass after its contents were gone, and a mother wearing curlers slapped the hand of her little boy as it reached for her coffee.

"The thing I try to remember is that nothing is forever," sighed Rodie Alvare, the 20-year-old hostess who had spent her holiday seating the customers.

"The thing I remember," said Mr. Kleintop, checking the cash register, "is that there'll be another 2000 tomorrow."

"The thing I remember," Miss Anthony injected, "is that on Tuesday I'm off."

Ex-P.O.W. finds
"We're a whole family again"

STEVEN V. ROBERTS

Coronado, Calif.
February 24, 1973

Kirk Jenkins weeds gardens to make extra spending money and he has been saving up for something special.

This week, his father, Capt. Harry T. Jenkins Jr., came home after almost eight years in a North Vietnamese prison camp. Without telling anybody, the 13-year-old boy went out and bought a big chocolate cake to celebrate. The inscription on it read: "Welcome Home. Now We're a Whole Family Again."

In recent days, the 143 men in the first group of returning war prisoners have been meeting their families and slowly readjusting to American life. Most are undergoing exhaustive physical examinations at one of 31 military hospitals, but they are usually free to come and go and to spend a night at home.

When Captain Jenkins arrived here from the Philippines, his wife, Marjorie, met his plane and sent her three children—Chris, 21, Karen, 15, and Kirk—to wait at the hospital. "I told them," she said with a laugh, "that after eight years I was going to have a few minutes alone with him."

Like many wives, Mrs. Jenkins was surprised by her husband's apparent good health.

"He looked exactly as he did eight years ago, only a little thinner," she said in an interview at her home here. "He still had dark brown hair, it wasn't a bit gray. I thought he would lose it all from malnutrition. He told me they

251

exercised every morning. They wanted to walk out of that camp, but they didn't want to be carried out on litters."

When the Jenkinses arrived at the hospital, the children were nervous. Karen had earlier moaned to her mother, "What am I going to say to him?"

"It was not as stiff as the kids thought it would be; Harry took over the whole conversation," Mrs. Jenkins said. "I'm surprised he's done as much talking as he's done. Whenever the conversation would lag, he'd always say, 'That reminds me of a joke.' They must have had thousands of jokes in the camps."

Captain Jenkins was stunned by the warm welcome the men received.

"They had been led to believe that they would be shunned when they got to America, that people wouldn't even like them," said Mrs. Jenkins, a vivacious woman of 42 dressed in a black pants suit. "They always heard about the riots and demonstrations over here."

Mrs. Jenkins was stunned, in turn, by her husband's eagerness to get back to work. Even though he is 44 and eligible for retirement, he called a friend in Washington and asked about his chances of commanding an aircraft carrier.

"When I heard him talking, I said, 'You haven't been home for a day, and you're talking about a carrier. This is unreal!' So he said into the phone, 'Bob, I'll talk to you later, when Marj isn't around.' "

"None of the wives expected this," she added. "We thought they'd be ready to relax and lie in the sun and do nothing for a while, but they're not. It might be a feeling that they're making up for lost time."

The children were also a surprise. When Captain Jenkins last saw him, Chris was 13. Now he is about to get married and graduate from college.

"Harry expected them to be bigger," said his wife, "but he was kind of startled to find that they were all grown up."

Beneath the joy and the jokes, the harsh reality of the last eight years occasionally poked through.

"He told me that he had made three vows in prison—that he would never be cold again, that he would never be hungry again, and that he would never wear unpressed clothes," Mrs. Jenkins said. "So I said, 'You never wore unpressed clothes before you left,' and he said, 'I know, but I have for the last eight years, and I won't ever again.' "

About a year and a half ago, Mrs. Jenkins moved the family to Coronado and bought a new house, and her biggest worry was that her husband might not like it.

"I had put so much money into it and decorated it myself, without any opinions of his at all," she said. "We always had thought alike, but I didn't know if we still did, and we don't—at least not about that carrier!"

Much to their mother's surprise, the children cleaned up the house without being asked and hung a sign out front that said, "Happiness is an X-P.O.W."

When Captain Jenkins saw the house, he seemed delighted with every-

Captain Harry T. Jenkins, Jr., after almost eight years in a North Vietnamese prison camp, with his wife, Marjorie, and son, Kirk, 13, shortly after he returned home to Coronado, California.
NYT/D. GORTON

thing—from the self-cleaning oven to the king-sized bed. He turned to his wife with a smile and said. "It does cost much more to go first class."

After dinner and Kirk's cake, Captain Jenkins went upstairs to help his son with his math homework. "Kirk said he hadn't studied so much in years," laughed his mother.

When the Jenkinses finally got to bed, a tiny Yorkshire terrier named Babe was perched on a pillow. Captain Jenkins suggested that the dog sleep on the floor, and Mrs. Jenkins recalled the scene:

"So I said, 'That would be impossible; he's slept in the bed ever since I got him. I thought you'd be thrilled that I'd chosen a dog instead of a man.' How could he argue with that?"

The next day, Captain Jenkins went back to the hospital for more tests, and Kirk went to school to show his classmates a dirty, cracked porcelian cup—the only dish that his father had used for the last eight years.

The outer City:
No firm stereotype

DOUGLAS E. KNEELAND

Pasadena, Tex.
May 31, 1971

After World War II, when the trickle to the outer cities became a tide, a myth was built. It was called suburbia.

The myth—the easy stereotype—was nourished by television and the movies, by newspapers and magazines and novelists, even by Dick and Jane and Alice and Jerry, those monosyllabic suburban tots who ran, jumped, looked, saw from the pages of most of the nation's first-grade readers.

Somehow the suburbs, despite their diversity, became one, frozen in the American mind as solidly as the Main Street of Sinclair Lewis—all green velvet lawns and swimming pools and two-car garages viewed through picture windows by practicing Republicans.

Main Streets there were and are, hundreds, perhaps thousands, almost interchangeable. But the myth is unreal. The homogenized, split-level dream is only a fragment of the new America of 76 million people that has taken root around the nation's inner cities.

Visits in the outer urban areas around five major cities across the country produced ample evidence of problems and life-styles as diverse as those found in the New York area's Bayonne and Levittown and Scarsdale.

"Campaigning in the new suburbia drives you crazy," complained a politician from De Kalb County, which takes in a corner of Atlanta and grew

255

more than 150,000 to 416,000 in the decade of the '60s. "It's different from one neighborhood to the next."

And that is the pitfall for politicians or planners or economists or sociologists who view the new America of the outer cities as monolithic, predictable, and singleminded.

Pasadena, just south of Houston, is a clutch of what once was suburbia. It is pushing 100,000 population and is plagued by pollution and the reluctance of its people to let loose of small-town concepts.

Lakewood, Ohio, on Cleveland's west side, did its growing in the early part of the century. Despite a scattering of new luxury apartments along the shore of Lake Erie, its population is relatively stable at 71,000. Lakewood worries most about preserving its property values, its sense of quality. It has adopted strict building codes and last year conducted a door-to-door campaign to check on enforcement.

Newport Beach in Southern California's Orange County is a wealthy playground turned bedroom, where sailboats are as ubiquitous as automobiles. And while its residents fight high-rise apartments and small-home developments, a tract of 6500 homes in the $250,000 class is being built.

Decatur, Ga., a small and gracious, but aging, island, one-third black, is awash in the surge of migration into metropolitan Atlanta's De Kalb County. As one of the few refuges for blacks in the county, it is shunned by whites and fears the fate of such overwhelmingly black suburbs as East Cleveland, Ohio, and Compton, Calif.

Turner's Station in Maryland's Baltimore County, crowded onto a bleak point on the outskirts of the steelworkers' town of Dundalk, has never had that worry. It was built for blacks and suffers from most of the problems of the inner-city ghettos.

And so it goes, across the land. Suburbs all. Or what were suburbs. Now caught like hundreds of others in the web of the new outer cities—with problems as varied as their landscapes.

The Nixon Administration has been pressing hard for decentralization and local solutions to the nation's troubles. But from Baltimore County to Cleveland's inner and outer cities, from Orange County to Houston and the Atlanta suburbs, mayors, county officials, planners, poverty workers, and urbanologists all sounded the same note:

Without strong Federal leadership and financial assistance, no dent can be made in a multitude of problems, ranging from poverty, housing, and integration to sewers, pollution control, and population dispersal.

In every case, the pleaders were not talking about revenue sharing; they were asking for moral leadership and a national policy, as well as aid.

Even Santa Ana, the seat of conservative Orange County, is seeking help through a number of Federal programs to deal with its woes. "Until 4 years ago I was never permitted to take any Federal money, even for civil defense," City Manager Carl Thornton said.

And in nearby Anaheim, City Manager Keith Murdoch declared that, in all probability, only the Federal Government could deal with the problems of poverty. "It will take something with a much broader economic base than a single city, even maybe than a single state," he said.

Here in Pasadena, hard against the so-called navigation district along the Houston ship channel, where miles of petrochemical plants and other industries spew smoke and gases, Mayor Clyde Doyal was also looking for Federal help.

"Pollution is our biggest problem," said the Mayor, tall and tan, as he relaxed behind his desk. "Up to this point we've been unable to do anything. We're close to them, but we derive little revenue from there. And we can't go outside the city limits to enforce pollution laws."

Nothing that even if Pasadena had control, local laws might frighten away, rather than clean up, the industries on which its growth have been based, he added:

"I think it's going to cost a lot of money to clean up pollution. That's why I think the Federal Government should set the standards. If the Federal Government set national standards, it wouldn't cause any loss of jobs."

Under the shadow of a new freeway here that has yet to feel the rush of cars, the Vernon Collins Motel and truck stop and the old Wright Grain Company Store languish as grimy reminders of another Pasadena, another Texas.

The contrasts in Pasadena, with its half-vacated old downtown and the new steel-and-concrete center springing up around its modern City Hall, in some ways mirror the contrasts in the suddenly emerged outer cities. In Pasadena, $16,000 will still buy a three-bedroom house with air-conditioning, but there are growing neighborhoods of $60,000 homes.

While Mayor Doyal is concerned about pollution, he is not especially worried about the population growth troubling many of the outer cities.

With workers flocking to the area for jobs along the ship channel and whites fleeing a black southward push in Houston, Pasadena, which has "one or two black families," went from a population of 58,000 in 1960 to 89,000 in 1970. A recent annexation and continued in-migration, the Mayor said, have put the total at about 100,000. He believes it will reach 400,000.

This poses some difficulties for the Pasadena that grew up with the Vernon Collins Motel and the Wright Grain Store. For one thing, the city has had to stop serving free coffee in its municipal offices. Last year the bill was $4500. And there are other problems.

"You're starting like a new city and yet you had all these people already here, used to doing things the old way," Mayor Doyal said a little plaintively. "We had this small-town atmosphere. We went to one-way streets and that kicked up a hell of a furor. We went to paper sacks for garbage collection and that caused a flap. But they like it now."

The citizenry may be lagging, but Pasadena is catching up with itself. Already filling the open stretches around City Hall are a gleaming, 12-story bank, a low-built but luxuriantly landscaped post office, a department store, a new telephone building.

"And we've got another little development coming," Mayor Doyal said casually, gesturing toward a big field on the north side of the building, "out there behind City Hall. It ought to run, oh, about $100 million."

With that, he pulled out a brochure for the planned 40-acre Triton Center, a complex including a hotel, office high-rises, shopping and parking structures, and a labor-sponsored Robert F. Kennedy Memorial Hospital.

That is the Pasadena, Tex., of the twentieth century—part of the new America, the outer city.

Can it be stereotyped with Santa Ana, Calif., an aging city caught up in Orange County's voracious growth?

Twenty years ago, when Carl Thornton went to Santa Ana as city manager, it had 42,000 people. Now it has about 160,000 and harbors 66 percent of Orange County's 10,000 blacks and many of its Mexican-Americans. Ghettos and barrios, some shabby and forlorn, some middle-class and well-kept, freckle the city.

While Pasadena, Tex., dreams of 400,000 citizens, Carl Thornton shudders at what would happen if unchecked apartment construction, which is threatening as banks make more money available for that than for single-family homes, should drop 50,000 more people into some sections of his city.

He also fears the pull of the new city of Irvine that is planned on the outskirts of Santa Ana—a city that some day would have 430,000 people. If whites should abandon Santa Ana for Irvine, he said, his city could follow the path of Pomona in Los Angeles County.

"Pomona has racial problems till hell wouldn't have it," Mr. Thornton said, his wrinkled brow tightening. "What has happened is welfare cases have moved in. As the housing developed, the new towns, their people moved, some of them in flight, some to upgrade. Vacancies became available. Welfare didn't put them in, but the vacancies were there. This could happen to my town—over my dead body. I'm going to fight."

But while he's battling to force Irvine to include enough low-income housing in its new city to ease some of the flow of poor and blacks and Mexican-Americans into Santa Ana, he can already see the signs of blight that cause him to characterize the western part of Orange County as much like an old inner city.

"You have a tendency to get old fast under such circumstances," he said, shaking his head wearily. "This is a pressure cooker."

Or can you equate Turner's Station, Md., a black enclave of dreary garden apartments across an estuary from the red smoke and flame of Bethlehem Steel's Sparrow Point Works, with Newport Beach, a paradise of yachts and sailboats and sandy beaches where narrow but elegant waterfront homes command $100,000 to $250,000? They are both on the waterfront. They are both by definition suburbs.

At Turner's Station, where the shabby brick apartments were built primarily for black workers at the steel mill, a small beach on the muddy water is littered with cans and glistening shards of glass.

A power line right-of-way, grown to weeds under the humming wires, slices through the community. The streets are potholed, and only a few struggling flowers brighten the yards outside the buildings. Most of the small frame stores have been boarded up.

Standing on her plot of grass behind a wire fence, an elderly black woman, who refused to give her name, summed up life at Turner's Station.

"It's terrible," she said, "but it's better than Cherry Hill."

Cherry Hill is a festering ghetto in the city of Baltimore. She lives in the suburbs, too.

Town in Kansas is willing to live with atom dump

B. DRUMMOND AYRES JR.

Lyons, Kan.
March 9, 1971

Sometimes the twentieth century brushes only lightly against a part of America.

Lyons is one of those places.

There is a clean, well-lighted little hotel here, called the Ly-Kan, with a room clerk who asks: "Will that be with or without bath, sir?" In the lobby, matrons in wool suits and flowery hats sell tickets to a Guy Lombardo community concert.

Down the street at the Imperial Cafe, a congenial rendezvous that smells of rich black coffee and home-fried potatoes, a gossip suddenly excuses himself and rushes out, saying: "Gotta go feed a nickel into one of our two dozen parking meters. Don't want to pay one of those 25-cent fines."

At the Town Hall, the clerk says municipal life is going so well that the Lyons treasury is overflowing with $150,000 in "temporarily idle funds," good last year for $10,000 in interest.

No wonder Guy Lombardo is coming here to play the sweetest music this side of heaven. The 4500 residents of Lyons have good reason to celebrate "Auld Lang Syne."

But what of the future? How much longer will the good times last?

Such questions arise because Lyons, squatting all alone out here on the

260

Great American Plains, recently was proposed as the country's newest nuclear "garbage" dump. The Atomic Energy Commission wants to use an abandoned salt mine that runs beneath the town as a burial vault for the fragmented, boiling hot, extraordinarily radioactive and entirely worthless atomic residue that falls out when nuclear generators produce electricity.

Since atomic power plants are popping up everywhere as the country searches desperately for more electric power, the heaps of waste are growing higher by the day. Within a decade, nuclear generators may be spinning off a railcar-load of residue every 24 hours.

The best way to handle atomic waste, the A.E.C. says, is to hide it below ground and let it "cook" for half a million years until its energy is dissipated. That's right—half a million years.

But why bury such potent stuff in Lyons? Why stash it away under this pleasant collection of jutting grain elevators and nodding oil pumps, Gothic office buildings and red brick general stores, fading frame houses lost behind big black oaks and wide streets that end abruptly in tilled sod? Why bring the frightening future to a place still happy with the comfortable past, where the good old ways still work, and well?

Primarily because salt is an extremely effective shield against radioactivity and because the salt under Lyons is a thousand feet down, 300 feet thick and as stable as any in the world. No flood or earthquake has hit these parts for more than 200 million years.

Is there any danger, then, in the A.E.C. plan?

Commission scientists insist that risks are negligible. They point to their safety record in recent experiments here and to their experience at other residue dumps in South Carolina, Tennessee, Idaho, and Washington.

The waste, they say, will be packed in heavily shielded cylinders, hauled in by custom-built trains, lowered into the mine with special machines, and covered with salt by remote control. They foresee no problem, and, in fact, are utterly confident that the people of Lyons will still be living the good life a half-million years from now.

Other scientists and some environmentalists, politicians, and concerned citizens are not so sure.

They doubt that the commission's scientists know enough about the long-term effects of atomic bombardment of salt and they think more tests should be run, or the waste should be buried somewhere else.

Surprisingly, only a few of the doubters live in Lyons. Most of the town's residents—perhaps 99 of every 100—are completely willing to go along with the A.E.C.

"I trust my Government," says William Chandler, a banker who sees atomic energy as "something that kept me from having to storm the beaches of Japan."

"Not only are those Government scientists trustworthy, but when they came here to run tests, they turned out to be good guys, good neighbors, and good church-going folks," says Ray Roeder, an insurance agent who thinks an atomic waste dump would bring dozens of new jobs and thousands of dollars into Lyons.

Mr. Chandler's and Mr. Roeder's trust—Lyons's trust—is an increasingly rare thing in America these days.

On the Eastern Seaboard, where the life-support system periodically malfunctions, the Federal Government sometimes is viewed with cynicism. In the South, it frequently is in conflict with state government. And in the Far West, it often seems remote.

But here in the country's unbuffeted middle ground, where the flag still flies from screened front porches, where lonely coyotes and lonely freights still wail at each other in the night, where a Sunday drive in Dad's pickup can still be a lot of fun, here in the heart of the Kansas wheat country, where William Holden and Kim Novak had their picnic, where a stranger is still innocent until proved guilty, where everybody still works half a day on Saturday, here, right here in Lyons, the Federal Government is still trusted and here, right here, is what "Auld Lang Syne" is all about.

John Sayler, who frequently sings of the good old days in his paper, The Lyons News, reports he has found only one resident who is "openly fearful" that the A.E.C. dump plan will ruin Lyons and its way of life.

"That's me," says Paul McKinnis, a rotund man whose business, fittingly enough, is waste matter. He adds:

"I've been dealing in scrap metal and worn-out things all my days and so I know what I'm talking about. The A.E.C. just hasn't run enough tests. Don't cry on my shoulder when someone starts glowing in the dark around here after they bury all that deadly pollution."

Mr. McKinnis paints a terrifying picture. But it fades rapidly.

Somehow, the phrase "deadly pollution" loses much of its odor and sting in a place like Lyons, where the air is as clear as Steuben glass and the water tastes like water and the only thing that kills trees is old age or an ax.

In New York and Chicago and Los Angeles, people may be talking about smog and algae and lingering pesticides, but out here, what counts is high-school football, church socials, new bird guns, a hot meal in the middle of the day, and last night's trip down to "Hutch"—Hutchinson, Kan.—to see a movie.

This is not to say that Lyons is concerned only with enjoying a way of life that perished long ago in many parts of America. It is not to say that Lyons does not worry about such twentieth-century horrors as pollution. It does worry. It does.

"Why, in the interest of combating pollution," says Walter Pile of the Lyons Chamber of Commerce, "we're willing to take all of the deadliest kind the country can produce."

*After seven years, a P.O.W. tries
to adjust to a changed world*

DOUGLAS E. KNEELAND

Dayton, Pa.
May 24, 1973

Wendell Alcorn has been gone a long time.

But kneeling in the dusty straw on the barn floor, his fingers, remembering things his mind should have long forgotten, are firm and sure as he tinkers with the rusting motor of the old grain augur.

Some things don't change.

Lieut. (j.g.) Wendell R. Alcorn was a 26-year-old Navy pilot when his A-4 Skyhawk, roaring in over Haiphong at 100 feet, was shot down Dec. 22, 1965, just 20 days and 28 missions after his first combat flight off the carrier *Enterprise*. For more than seven years, until last Feb. 12, he was locked up in a series of nine different North Vietnamese prison camps.

Now a 33-year-old lieutenant commander, his youthful face and smile still much like the younger pictures that adorn the spotless white farmhouse, he is back home like all the other war prisoners, trying to weave into the present those threads of absent years.

In some ways, for Wendell Alcorn, those missing years might never have been. He looks more country boy than naval officer as he putters around in denims and scuffed boots in the red barn, remembering.

Glancing up at the cobwebbed elevator that over the years has sent thousands of bales of hay tumbling onto the loft above, he pointed at the chain and gears near the top.

263

"My dad cut his finger off in that thing—in that chain up there," he said, his eyes clouding at the memory.

But some things do change.

His father, John Alcorn, committed suicide in 1968, apparently overwhelmed by the ceaseless work of the 116-acre dairy farm that has been in the family for generations and perhaps by thoughts of the son who had already languished three years in the prison camps.

Picking at the rotting roof of a small shed beside the barn, that son, returned, says sadly:

"If someone isn't here to fix things every day, it just all falls apart."

With his father dead and his brother, Donald, and sister, Nelda, both married and living out of the state, his mother, Mrs. Ruth Alcorn, has lived alone on the once-prosperous farm at the end of a winding dirt road about seven miles west of Dayton.

A neighbor, Ray White, has rented the land to raise barley, corn and oats for his own livestock, but there has been no one to tend to the daily hammer-and-nails upkeep that it takes to stay ahead of the wind and weather.

And for Ray Alcorn (Ray is a Navy nickname that has clung incongruously since everyone misguessed his middle name, Reed, in a game back in preflight days) the changes he has noticed most after being shut off from his world for seven years have been in small things, close to home.

Politics, philosophies, national goals, styles and sexual mores may have shifted drastically across the nation, but most things come slowly to Dayton, a drowsy village of about 700 persons, set amid the disappearing farms and played-out coal mines in the greening hills of western Pennsylvania, some 60 miles northeast of Pittsburgh.

Standing in the milking shed and gazing at the empty stalls where 30 cows once stood, Ray Alcorn shook his head.

"It was quite a shock," he said, "the first time I walked down here and there were no animals around."

A Pennsylvania State University graduate in forestry, he joined the Navy in the fall of 1961 when he was unable to find a job in his chosen field. He had worked on the farm all his life, including summers while he was going to college, and had no desire to stay with it.

"You know, the first thing I noticed when I got back was that there were no fences around here," he said, appreciatively, looking off into the distance across the wooded hills and valleys. Then, he added, "I've thought about it sometimes, but I don't suppose I'll ever come back here."

So he is checking out all the equipment that has lain idle since his father's death, trying to get it into shape for sale at an auction soon.

He plans to stay in the Navy when his convalescent leave is up in July unless he can get a job as an airplane pilot. Either way, his mother will once again be alone on the farm.

Climbing on the old orange Allis-Chalmers tractor to give the working parts of a hay rake a test run up across a field above the house, he mused:

"You know, even the lay of the land somehow seems different to me. This hill up here used to seem a lot steeper. But I walked up there the other day and it seemed to have flattened out."

Stopping at the top of the hill, near a row of fruit trees, he waved his arm across the landscape.

"No one's hardly farming around here any more," he said. "There used to be an old guy over there and he's dead and the people over there and up the road are gone."

It's not that Ray Alcorn hasn't noticed other changes, besides the homely ones, since he returned to the United States. He has.

Sitting over a root-beer milk shake and a cheeseburger in Dinger's restaurant, which used to be in a green shingled frame building on Dayton's unpretentious Main Street and has since moved to one next door with pink shingles, he pondered some of them.

"I suppose one of the biggest changes I've seen is the long hair on men," he said. "When I went away it was pretty well accepted that any man with long hair was a hippie type. Since I've gotten back, I've found that it doesn't mean anything—that guys with long hair are just like anybody else.

"Then there are a few new expressions. The one that struck me most was 'up tight.' I'd never heard that before—and this expression 'doing your own thing.'

"I've really noticed the changes in movies. I've only seen three, I guess. *Deliverance, The Godfather,* and *Godspell,* but I wasn't very much impressed. The use of foul language, the extreme amount of violence I just never imagined they would have on the screen—those mainly were the things that turned me off."

As for the nudity in some of the popular magazines, he said that it "amazed me that they had that type of thing right out in the open."

But the change that surprised him most, as a young bachelor who has been dating heroically in an attempt to make up for seven lost years, is "all these young girls who tell you they're on the pill."

Not that Dayton has been much less shocked by many of the latest trends than Ray Alcorn. In these conservative hills he has found few signs of attitudinal changes, even toward the war in Vietnam.

A strong supporter of President Nixon's Vietnam policies, like many fellow prisoners he has encountered nothing but reassurance in his reception by the home folks.

"I certainly haven't seen any dissent or apathy toward the war," he said. "As far as I can tell, everyone's been 100 percent behind the Government."

There have, of course, been some changes in Dayton since Ray Alcorn's been gone. He had never seen the new, modern one-story elementary school that replaced the aging two-story brick one, which is now being used for storage by one of the town's two grocers. Some new buildings and black-top roads have been built at the fairgrounds where each August the Dayton Fair, the village's biggest annual event, is held.

Wendell R. Alcorn, a former Navy pilot and prisoner of war, runs a tractor on the family farm near Dayton, Pennsylvania.

Along Main Street, the Keystone National Bank has put up a compact brick building, knocking down the sprawling old one and leaving space for the town's first parking lot. Clark's Variety has taken over where the Faust Drug Store used to be. Reed Hoffman's Ford agency, the only car dealership in Dayton, is gone. And Preston Bittinger, the barber, was forced to move when the bank building was razed. Now, he's across the street in what was once the town's hotel, but he's getting on in years and is only open three days a week.

Still, not everything is different. Frank Bly's Funeral Home is still there. Raymond Barrett's lumberyard remains probably the biggest business in town. And Bill Hallman and his son, Jerry, are still operating the Dayton Feed Mill in a weathered store that's almost 100 years old. The Grange has torn down its sagging hall, but unlike the Odd Fellows, who have given up the ghost, they're still meeting—now in the headquarters of Dayton Memorial Post 995 of the American Legion.

Chatting over coffee at Dinger's, Mayor Clifton J. King, who had been Ray Alcorn's high school agriculture teacher, but who retired a couple of years ago after a series of heart attacks, thought for a bit about what shifts had taken place in the attitudes of Dayton residents in the last six or seven years.

"I would say probably there's been some progressing," he said. "I would say most of it's been for the good. I'd say more of them realize that communities have to get together, that what's good for Kittanning (20 miles to the southwest) is good for us and what's good for us is good for Kittanning.

"Oh, there's been some streets that's been paved that weren't paved. And we've got ourselves a borough garage—and we went down to Butler and bought a used grader I think will do us some good. And we bought a new truck to keep our street superintendent from getting killed and a new tanker for the fire department.

"We have done away with the old Board of Trade and we do have a new Chamber of Commerce. Now, if we could just get a small industry in, it would do so much."

Pausing again, he concluded:

"I can't think of anything else. We don't do anything very earth-shaking, I guess."

At the high school, "Welcome Wendell" was spelled out in large letters in the front windows of one wing, a reminder of Dayton's recent Wendell Alcorn Day. In his office, Leonard L. Holt, the principal, who had been there in the days when the former prisoner of war was on the school's basketball team and played the saxophone in the band and orchestra, also stopped to consider the question of change.

"Change comes a little bit slower in a rural area such as this," said Mr. Holt, dapper in a gold jacket, gold shirt, striped tie and brown pants. "However, we have noticed some changes taking place. The high school student is becoming a little more sophisticated and a little more free in his thinking and his action.

"But we have no more problems than we did when Wendell was going to school. Wendell and the group he went to school with were not bad. They were lively, and they kept me hopping sometimes."

Then as his former student smiled, he asked:

"Do you remember, Wendell, the day you dropped your trousers when you went off the stage on Senior Day and exposed your polka-dot shorts?"

Seven years is a long time, but Wendell Alcorn is home, where the folks all greet him happily, where nobody calls him Ray—and where nothing changes a whole lot.

Two men and a lion:
A wildlife dilemma

ANTHONY RIPLEY

Westcliffe, Colo.
May 8, 1971

Donald P. Tesitor and Bob J. Peters, both licensed hunting guides, are men who lead others to the kill, and many times in the last 10 years they have shared the brotherhood of the hunt.

Now they have parted ways. When the breakup came it was over a question of whether a mountain lion should live or die. The lion died.

It was just a personal quarrel, in a sense, but it also said something about the growing concern in the West over the decline of big game. And it gave an indication of the difficulty, human nature being what it is, of bridging the gap between those who would save wildlife to hunt it and those who would save it and then let it alone.

Mr. Tesitor, a restless, creative man, reasoned that both defenders and hunters of America's wildlife will have nothing left either to hunt or to defend by the year 2000 if they cannot work together to save game ranges from civilization, which frightens away wild herds.

So he formed an organization to bring the two groups together. Then he got caught in the middle.

His one-time friend, Mr. Peters, is a full-time, professional, big-game hunting guide, a mountain man as lean and tough and determined as the hounds he uses to hunt lions and bear in southern Colorado.

In 1961, Mr. Peters, now 40 years old, took Mr. Tesitor, now 33, under his wing and taught him the subtle signs left by mountain lions: the soft paw prints, the scratch marks, the signs where the solitary animals had rested.

He taught him the craft of a big-game hunting guide. Mr. Tesitor became a licensed guide and outfitter himself, adding it to his degree as a chemical engineer, his work toward a law degree, and his trophies as one of Colorado's top tennis players.

He is a senior field representative in Denver for Aerojet-General Corporation.

An adult mountain lion kills 40 or 50 deer each year, and the two men agreed that the lion's food source was plainly declining under the pressure of civilization's roads, mountain subdivisions, motorcyle and four-wheel-drive vehicle trails, oil rigs, mines, United States Forest Service roads, and ski resorts.

They worked successfully to ease the hunting pressure on deer, to end the $50 bounty on mountain lions, and to restrict lion hunting to a males-only season in March and April.

So when Mr. Tesitor formed a nonprofit conservation group called Wildlife 2000 last November, he put Mr. Peters, the professional hunter, on the board of directors along with a theoretical physicist, a wildlife biologist, a hunting lodge owner, a woman lawyer, and a biochemist.

For many protectors of wildlife, the hunter is an enemy absolute. Some feel that killing a big-game animal for no other use than mounting his head or pelt for display in a living room is an act close to being obscene.

The mountain lion once had the greatest range of any American animal, and made its home from the State of Washington east to the Atlantic shore of Canada, and south into Florida and South America.

Although not yet on the endangered species list of the Department of the Interior, the mountain lion has been almost completely wiped out by hunting in most of the Midwestern states and in every state east of the Mississippi. Only 8000 to 12,000 of the animals still exist in the Western states.

Mr. Tesitor came to Westcliffe recently to show one of his board members, Dr. H. Peter Metzger of the Colorado Committee for Environmental Information, and members of the press how a lion could be captured alive, studied and tagged for an accurate appraisal of his habits. Mr. Peters was to lead the hunt.

Westcliffe is a town of 306 people in the 8000-foot mountain valley between the 14,000-foot peaks of the Sangre de Cristo Mountains and the Wet Mountains.

The town is alive with real estate speculators.

Mr. Tesitor, who grew up in Westcliffe, shouted to one of the salesmen for Livingston & Associates of Denver, "What are the lions going to do when you sell all the range for deer that they live on?"

"Beats me, chief," the man answered, "I've got seven lions at home to feed."

Mr. Peters, too, had financial considerations.

Hunting guides get $500 to $600 for leading a mountain lion hunt and, although Mr. Peters knew it was to be a demonstration with the animal captured alive and then released, he took along a bow and arrow hunter who planned to kill the animal instead.

"I've got to make a living and I didn't figure it would make any difference," he said.

Mr. Tesitor thought it did make a difference, and the matter simmered during the hunt.

Six hounds—two of them Mr. Tesitor's—came across a lion's footprints and scent in a sandy gully on Badito Cone in the Wet Mountain range, about 40 miles soutwest of Pueblo, Colo. Mr. Peters figured the prints were 15 hours old, and the baying dogs set off.

During the next four hours, in which the dogs followed the lion's scent, the hot, sunny day suddenly turned to 15-degree weather and five inches of snow fell quickly.

It was an exhausting, 14-mile chase on foot, through underbrush, over rocks, down gullies, up mountainsides, and the hunting party became separated.

Despite the weather, which was beginning to mask the lion's footprints and scent, the dogs found him, and the 155-pound tom took refuge in a Ponderosa pine tree.

In the case of the mountain lion, the chase is tough but the killing is easy. The animal has the suicidal habit of climbing a tree when in danger.

The hunter was there, J. D. Dodge, a gregarious cement contractor from Oklahoma City, and he settled the issue of the lion's life with a single metal-shafted arrow.

Mr. Tesitor was with the party that was separated in the hills and didn't see the kill. He was just as glad.

The two friends quarreled privately over whether it was more important to kill a lion for pay or to show how lions might be preserved for future generations.

Mr. Peters quit the board of directors.

Later, Mr. Tesitor reflected on his basic assumption that defenders and hunters of wildlife can work together in a common cause:

"I've had several people tell me it's an untenable position. I still don't believe it."

Indiana campers' farm: Quiet haven for the restless

DOUGLAS E. KNEELAND

Richmond, Ind.
June 30, 1970

State Route 227 is a slender ribbon of blacktop meandering through the fields of soybeans, oats, and knee-high corn north of this city of 44,000.

But late almost every afternoon from mid-May to mid-September its solitude is broken by dozens of cars pulling trailers or campers, by made-over school buses, by Volkswagen minibuses—an irregular fleet from east and west fleeing the inhospitable thrust of Interstate 70 a few miles from the Ohio line.

The people seeking a haven for the night in this quiet corner of the Middle West are only a few of the millions of new gypsylike Americans, driven by sun and summer and by the notion that time off earned is time off to be spent answering the call of the road.

About a mile north of the simmering interstate, they turn off the narrow blacktop into a shady 10-acre grove of sycamores, beeches, and walnut trees in a bend of the shallow Whitewater River. This is Grandpa's Farm, a campground of high repute among the more than 18,000, public and private, across the nation.

Here for $2 a night for four persons (25 cents more for each extra one and 50 cents to hook into the electric lines) they can park their trailers or pitch their tents on a grassy plot beneath a tree.

272

They can cook in the fireplaces, eat off the picnic tables, use the rest rooms, and take hot showers. Their children can take a dip in the muddy Whitewater, search for the top 40 tunes on the jukebox under the corrugated tin-roofed shelter adjoining the office, play ping-pong, pool, or pinball, or feed their coins into a machine that will test their driving skills against the day when they, too, will hunch relentless over a wheel on the endless interstate.

William Sheard is a tall, thin, dark-haired Hoosier with light-blue eyes who works most of the year as a truck driver for I.R.C.&D. Motor Freight, Inc., a local company.

But from May 15 to Sept. 15, he and his wife, Tonie, a friendly, grayhaired woman, and their four sons, Jim, 19 years old; Tom, 16; John, 15; and Mark, 11, leave their home in nearby Fountain City to live in a trailer and operate the 75-site campground at Grandpa's Farm.

"We used to ask the kids where they wanted to go camping," Mrs. Sheard said with a slow smile, "and they'd always say 'Grandpa's Farm.' So when we opened this 7 years ago and were looking for a name, my husband said, 'Why change it?' "

"We call it Grandpa's Farm," Mr. Sheard added, "because it is my dad's farm."

Grandpa, George Sheard, still farms 192 acres of it, planting corn, soybeans, and oats, like his neighbors, and raising more than 100 head of cattle, mostly Herefords, who browse nosily through the underbrush about 25 feet across the Whitewater from the campground's small beach, which was made with trucked-in sand.

But Grandpa doesn't have any horses, so grandson Jim uses a tractor to provide the 35-cent Saturday night hayrides.

About 5000 campers (of the nation's more than 29 million) come and go each summer at Grandpa's Farm amid a bustle of nighttime unpackings and a scurry of morning repackings. Mr. Sheard, himself a camper before he became a campground owner, is continually fascinated by the coincidences and near-coincidences upon which the fraternity feeds.

"You know," he said, shaking his head, "a lot of interesting things happen here. One time a fellow came from some place in Maryland and we had a site reserved for him and there happened to be another fellow here from the same town. He asked me who he was and then he said, 'Gee whiz, that's my neighbor.' And I said, 'Well, there's his outfit right over there and just happens the site we had reserved for you is right next to him, so you can be neighbors here.' And he said, 'It's a small world.' "

Along with overnight travelers, Grandpa's Farm draws weekend campers from around the area and there are 17 campsites rented for the summer to people who come for their vacations or to spend their weekends in the grove.

Among these is Malcolm Fulton, who said with a scowl from the folding chair outside his new trailer:

"I come because there's no telephone down here."

"He's the fire chief in Fountain City," Mr. Sheard explained.

Hal Gray of Huntington Beach, Calif., leaned moodily on the picnic table outside his green umbrella tent the other morning as his wife and seven children finished up their dishes of cold cereal. He was headed back to California after a trip to Akron to visit his in-laws.

"Those mosquitoes in Texas almost ate me alive," he said sourly, pointing to his spotted and swollen face. "I guess I must be allergic to them. We haven't figured how we're going back yet."

"The fastest way," his wife interjected with finality.

Not far away, Les Fowler of Fort Wayne, still unshaven, sat outside the Volkswagen bus outfitted as a camper while his wife, still in her housecoat, tried to tidy up the cramped quarters. They were on their way with their four children to Philadelphia, Niagara Falls, Detroit, and then back home.

"Actually, we're coming from the guppy show in Indianapolis," he said. "Three guys had sent fish out to me for the show—we do that all the time—and I'm taking them back to them. You know, it seems funny—I've got these fish and I've never met the guys."

Did his wife enjoy camping?

"Enjoy it?" she answered. "For a week."

"If it doesn't rain," he added, looking thankfully at the sunny skies.

John Willett, a powerhouse operator from Nanjemoy, Md., was returning with his wife and five children and their babysitter in his converted 1955 International school bus from the Junior Chamber of Commerce convention in St. Louis.

Leaning back in a lawn chair sipping a beer, his red hair set off by a fuchsia shirt and pastel plaid pants, he discussed campers and camping.

"People are extremely congenial," he said, "extremely helpful and friendly. Regardless of their financial status, they are extremely helpful—to the point of forcing their ideas on you."

"By the way," he asked, dropping his voice although his nearest neighbors were more than 100 feet away, "have you had the mumps? One of the kids has them. She's in the bus. We don't want to spread the word around and panic the camp grounds, but she has them and we've kept her inside."